P9-AFX-543

Grammatical Theory

Grammatical
Theory Its Limits
and Its
Possibilities

Frederick J. Newmeyer

THE UNIVERSITY OF CHICAGO PRESS

Chicago and London

The University of Chicago Press, Chicago 60637
The University of Chicago Press, Ltd., London

© 1983 by The University of Chicago
All rights reserved. Published 1983
Printed in the United States of America
90 89 88 87 86 85 84 83   5 4 3 2 1

Library of Congress Cataloging in Publication Data

Newmeyer, Frederick J.
  Grammatical theory, its limits and its possibilities.

  Bibliography: p.
  Includes indexes.
  1. Grammar, Comparative and general. 2. Generative
grammar. 3. Language and languages—Variation.
4. Applied Linguistics. I. Title
P151.N44 1983   415   83-3549
ISBN 0-226-57717-1

  Frederick J. Newmeyer is professor of linguistics at
the University of Washington, Seattle. He is the
author of *Linguistic Theory in America: The First
Quarter-Century of Transformational Generative
Grammar* and *English Aspectual Verbs*.

P 151
N44
1983

To My Mother and My Brother

Contents

Preface

This book is for anyone who feels frustrated after his or her first exposure to generative grammar. Even many people who have succeeded in mastering the difficult formalism and unfamiliar style of argumentation are apt to leave their introductory course with the feeling that they have learned little more than a novel way of "playing with symbols" (to use an often-heard expression) and have achieved little insight into how language "really works." My goal here is to put forward the best case I can that any explanatory account of the workings of language must include, as a central component, a formal grammar. I have a two-part strategy for achieving this goal. The first is to document the ways the basic notions of generativist theory receive independent support from research outside the domain of grammar proper. The second is to show that generativist theory, in turn, has helped contribute to the explanation of a number of phenomena that most people would not regard as strictly grammatical.

I hope that even established generative grammarians will find useful material in this book. In this age of the "specialist," it is all too easy to lose sight of the broader questions raised by one's own investigations of some specific phenomenon. I have therefore attempted, whenever possible, to cite work that might, in ordinary circumstances, escape the grammarian's attention, yet that bears on the validity of some particular claim about the organization of the grammatical model.

I feel very fortunate to have received input from many of my colleagues while I was preparing this book. The following linguists read and commented on the entire manuscript or on a significant portion of it before publication: Geoffrey Pullum, Joseph Emonds, James McCawley, Judith Klavans, Sol Saporta, Carolyn Jenkins, Jerrold Sadock, Arnold Zwicky, Guy Carden, Barbara Lust, Derek Bickerton, Ellen Kaisse, Noam Chomsky, Michael Tanenhaus, Laurence Horn, Dwight Bolinger, Mary-

Louise Kean, Wolfgang Dressler, Philip Dale, Heles Contreras, G. N. Clements, Karen Zagona, Georgette Ioup, Annie Zaenen, Dee Worman, James Noblitt, and Diana Van Lancker. Their assistance is appreciatively acknowledged; the book would be vastly inferior without it. None of these individuals should receive any blame for the shortcomings that remain. I have a feeling I may soon wish I had followed more of their recommendations.

I would also like to thank Anita Tabares for typing the manuscript.

1 | The Generativist Approach to Linguistic Analysis

1.1 Introduction

The subject of this book is the linguistic theory commonly known as "transformational generative grammar." That is, it deals with the general theoretical and methodological principles that were expounded in Noam Chomsky's *Syntactic Structures* and *Aspects of the Theory of Syntax* and that have guided work in the various frameworks for linguistic description based on those principles. However, what follows differs from the standard introductions to "transformational generative grammar" in that it contains very little about what are commonly regarded as strictly "grammatical" facts. I will assume that the reader has ample opportunity to explore and evaluate the extensive literature of generative phonology and syntax. My goal is not to add to this literature. Rather, it is to examine some fairly *general* issues raised by the theory, among which are its view of the relation between formal grammar and language as a whole; the use made by its practitioners of introspectively collected data; its ability to help explain variation in language; and its potential application to "practical" language-related problems.

While the reader will (I hope) find the book nonpolemical in tone, it is nevertheless an advocatory piece of writing. I believe there is considerable evidence, much of it quite recent, that the theory's essential properties are correct. Naturally, then, a large portion of the book will be devoted to presenting such evidence. But I also believe that much of the skepticism about "transformational generative grammar" is due to a simple misunderstanding of its goals and methodology. Hence another significant portion of the book will be devoted to clarifying those points that seem to have engendered the greatest confusion.

The book's subtitle comes from my belief that only if the scope of grammatical theory is *limited* in a definite way, can its *possibilities* be realized. The remainder of this chapter discusses the principal limitation: rather than encompassing *all* regularity found in language, formal grammar has as its domain only those processes that are best formulated in a system embodying strictly grammatical primitives. This limitation is a desirable one, however. As we will see, the interaction of this grammatical system with other systems at work in language reveals the full explanatory potential of the generativist approach.

1.2   On the Autonomy of Grammar and the Modular Conception of Language

Despite its widespread use, the term "transformational generative grammar" is, unfortunately, a misnomer. In particular, transformational rules are neither necessary nor sufficient for a theory whose fundamental assumptions are consistent with *Syntactic Structures* and *Aspects of the Theory of Syntax*. A number of investigators (Brame 1978 and Gazdar 1981, for example) have recently questioned the need for transformational rules in grammar, yet they advance proposals very much in the theoretical spirit of models that do postulate such rules. And as those who have studied the history of modern linguistics are aware, transformational rules were not Chomsky's innovation. The structuralist model of Harris (1957) contained transformations yet was consistent with the empiricist approach to language that Chomsky rejected.

Nor is generativity a unique defining property of "transformational generative grammar." To say that a grammar is generative is to say no more than that it is explicit. Thus one can easily postulate a generative grammar without adopting what is essential to *Syntactic Structures* and *Aspects of the Theory of Syntax*. For example, Hockett (1955) incorporated a finite-state (and thus generative) grammar into his linguistic theory without advocating any of the basic assumptions that later characterized Chomsky's work.

There are two characteristics, however, that *do* distinguish "transformational generative grammar" from other current theories of language with which I am familiar. The first is its hypothesis that the grammar of a language is characterized by a formal *autonomous system*. That is, the phonology, syntax, and those aspects of meaning determined by syntactic configuration form a structural system whose primitive terms are not artifacts of a system that encompasses both human language and other human facilities or abilities.

The second distinguishing feature of "transformational generative grammar" is its *modular* approach to explaining complex linguistic phenomena—an approach based on the hypothesis that not just formal grammar, but *all* human systems (or at least all those at work in language) are autonomous "modules," each governed by its particular set of general principles.[1] In this view, the superficial complexity of language is a consequence of the *interaction* of such modules. Following the presentation in Anderson (1981, 494), one might represent the totality of "language" graphically as in (1), where each ellipse represents a module:

(1)

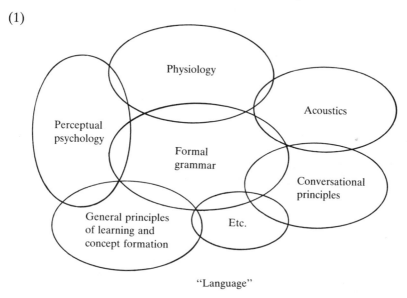

"Language"

I will henceforth refer to any explanation of a linguistic phenomenon that exploits the interaction of the formal grammar module with other modular systems as a "modular account" of that phenomenon.[2]

In recent years grammarians have more and more come to think of formal grammar itself as being modular in structure (see Chomsky 1981, chap. 1, for discussion). However, this book will have little to say about the internal structure of the grammar.

A particularly clear statement of the complementary hypotheses of

1. For an extensive discussion and defense of the modular conception of human cognitive functioning, see J. A. Fodor (1982). For specific proposals of autonomous mental facilities, see Anderson and Bower (1973) (long-term memory); Kosslyn and Schwartz (1977) (visual imagery); and Newell and Simon (1973) (problem solving).

2. General features of modular accounts of linguistic phenomena are discussed in Bever (1974, 1975), Hale, Jeanne, and Platero (1977), Chomsky (1980), Grosu (1981), Carroll (1981), and Green (1981, 1982), though not all use the term "modularity." "Interactionism," the term used by Bever, might strike one as more felicitous than "modularity." However, since the former term has been given a quite different interpretation in the work of Jean Piaget (see Piaget 1970), it seems best to stick with "modularity."

autonomous grammar and modular explanation has been given by David Caplan:

> One important discovery has been that, essentially without exception, the structures and operations which appear in modern theories of grammar do not find counterparts in theories of other cognitive capacities, either in humans or in other species . . . , a finding which has led to the view that a grammar is a species- and domain-specific cognitive structure which interacts with other such structures to yield normal intellectual function, including actual language use. (1981a, 60)

The opposition to "transformational generative grammar," diverse as it may be in other respects, stands nearly united in its rejection of the first of these hypotheses, that of the autonomy of formal grammar. Most opposing theories that allude to "grammar" at all do so with the explicit proviso that all (or most) grammatical constructs are but "convenient fictions" or a "shorthand abbreviation" for principles that are not specific to grammar. Thus we find proposals that most of what generativists would regard as properties of the autonomous grammar instead be considered reflections of the "utterance-response unit" as in tagmemics (Pike 1977, 156); their "conceptual base" as in conceptual dependency theory (Schank 1972, 553–54); the "exigencies of verbal social interaction" as in role and reference grammar (Van Valin and Foley 1980, 330); their "pragmatic purposes" as in functional grammar (Dik 1980, 46); "certain processing strategies" as in cognitive grammar (Lakoff and Thompson 1975, 295); or a variety of factors as in the approach of Givón (1979b, 3–4).

There also exists a tradition opposed to modular explanations of linguistic phenomena. The most extreme manifestation of such an approach is the radical behaviorist theory of Skinner (1957), in which all language is reduced in principle to reinforcement history. Not surprisingly, post-Bloomfieldian structuralists, who were heavily influenced by behaviorist psychology (see Hockett 1948a), rarely proposed modular explanations (though some less empiricist-minded linguists of that period, particularly Carl Voegelin, did do so—see Hale 1976a for discussion). Likewise, a number of generative semanticists in the mid-1970s seemed close to a nonmodular view of language, as they came to advocate a strictly grammatical treatment of most linguistic phenomena (see G. Lakoff 1974 and the discussion in Newmeyer 1980a,b).

It is important to emphasize that the autonomy hypothesis does not preclude the possibility that formal grammar is rooted in neurology; far from it: generative grammarians look with pleasure on the growing evidence that there are neurological structures specific to grammar (see section 1.3.3). In fact, what distinguishes the theory under discussion from its rivals is its *prediction* that such should be the case. Any theory that sees grammatical constructs as nothing more than diacritic devices for representing extragrammatical generalizations would presumably be forced to reject the idea of a neurological basis for grammar.

One might wonder why, if grammar does have a neurological basis, there is any point at all in writing grammars. Why not delay theorizing until the workings of the brain are fully understood? The answer is simple—at any given point one strives to attain the maximum degree of generalization. Given that autonomous formal grammars *do* express interesting generalizations about language, there is no reason for the linguist to wait for the neurologist. An analogy with other sciences might be helpful. Both atomic theory and genetic theory achieved considerable insights before anyone had the slightest idea what an atom or a gene looked like—or knew if they had any physical reality at all. The abstract systems proposed by early chemists and geneticists in fact helped to guide work devoted to ascertaining the material nature of the theoretical constructs. Along the same lines, the results of grammatical theory should prove useful to neurologists investigating the representation of language in the brain. After all, more than two millennia of grammatical research have, not surprisingly, given us a more detailed picture of the structure of language than a bare century of neurological research has of the structure of the brain.

The idea that grammatical studies should be delayed until the brain is better understood is reminiscent of a feeling among many chemists in the late nineteenth century that Mendeleev's periodic table should be rejected (or, more accurately, ignored) because Mendeleev provided no "physical" explanation for why the relationships it expressed should be true. Fortunately, there were chemists at the time who were delighted with the interesting generalizations expressed in the table and applied them creatively in predicting the properties of—and ultimately discovering—several new chemical elements.

In the remainder of this book I will refer to the theory of "transformational generative grammar" simply as "grammatical theory." Given that it seems to be the only nonreductionist approach to grammar, doing so does not strike me as an unfair rhetorical ploy. However, I will refer to advocates of this theory conveniently, if a bit misleadingly, as "generativists." No alternative designation comes to mind that has equal simplicity and greater accuracy.

1.3   Some Evidence for the Autonomy of Formal Grammar

1.3.1   Grammatical Evidence

The investigation of every level of linguistic structure reveals generalizations whose formulation requires that we postulate an autonomous grammar. For example, the 1970s saw numerous attempts to construct phonological theories whose primitive terms are all (or are largely) extragrammatical—theories such as Vennemann's (1973) and Hooper's (1976) "natural generative phonology" and Donegan and Stampe's (1979) "natural phonology." The goal of such theories is to provide "natural" explanations for phonological phenomena, that is, explanations rooted in systems whose properties are motivated externally to language itself. In the words of Donegan and Stampe:

> the living sound patterns of languages, in their development in each individual as well as in their evolution over the centuries, are governed by forces implicit in human vocalization and perception. . . . This is a *natural* theory . . . in that it presents language (specifically the phonological aspect of language) as a natural reflection of the needs, capacities, and world of its users. . . . It is a natural theory also in the sense that it is intended to *explain* its subject matter, to show that it follows naturally from the nature of things. (1979, 126–27; emphasis in original)

In recent years, however, there has been a clear shift back to a view of phonology more consistent with the generativist autonomy hypothesis, as evidence has mounted that many phonological processes are simply not "natural" in the sense used by Vennemann, Hooper, and Donegan and Stampe. Dinnsen (1980), Anderson (1981), and Dresher (1981) discuss some of the difficulties involved in attributing significant portions of phonology to extragrammatical factors. As an example, consider Anderson's discussion of the phenomenon of compensatory lengthening. This process, which is common in the world's languages, involves replacing a vowel plus consonant sequence with a single long vowel (XVCY→ X$\bar{V}$Y). Compensatory lengthening appears to have a likely external explanation based in phonetics—its function is plausibly that of "conservation of timing." If so, then the vowel is prolonged to preserve the overall temporal properties of the syllable. Anderson, however, argues that several peculiarities of compensatory lengthening pose difficulties for this sort of explanation. First, not all losses of a consonant trigger compensatory lengthening—the consonant must be *immediately* adjacent to the vowel that lengthens. Second, when a language has a rule deleting *any* consonant, such a deletion does not lead to compensatory lengthening. And third, compensatory lengthening does not arise unless a language already has distinctively long vowels and/or diphthongs. These facts suggest that if a language has an alternation, say, between / VC + V/ on the one hand and /$\bar{V}$ + C/ and /$\bar{V}$ #/ on the other, it is necessary to posit for that language a *phonological rule*, which might be stated as (2) below:

(2)   VC → $\bar{V}$/___$\left\{ \begin{matrix} +C \\ \# \end{matrix} \right\}$

An attempt to replace (2) by a principle rooted solely in a notion like "conservation of timing" leads to the incorrect prediction that compensatory lengthening should generalize to those environments in which it does not apply.

Anderson does not deny that a rule such as (2) might result *diachronically* as a consequence of one or more external factors, the need to "conserve timing" among them. Quite the contrary, he outlines the several historical stages of rule addition whose ultimate product is characteristically a compensatory lengthening rule like (2), and he shows that each individual rule added has a plausible external motivation. But the point is that (2) itself does not directly reflect these external factors. The reason is that (2) represents a "telescoping," so to speak, of the "natural" rules that underlay it historically, so that considered synchronically (2) cannot be replaced by a statement whose terms are purely phonetic. Thus the child language learner, who of course has no access to the history of the phonological system being acquired, must learn (2) on its own terms, as a rule whose form is not derivable from systems external to phonological theory.

Pursuing the question of "natural phonology," one wonders why a process should be considered more "natural" if it reflects, say, the human articulatory mechanism than if it reflects an internalized mental grammar. What is natural is, plainly and simply, what *is*. And the only way we can ascertain what "is" is through intensive empirical investigation. Since the facts lead to a phonological theory in which not all phonological rules are phonetically explainable, such a theory is therefore a natural one.

Turning to morphology, it seems inconceivable that the morphological complexities of language could be fully grounded extragrammatically. Take the grammatical gender systems of the Indo-European languages. What communicative function do they serve? What "cognitive strategy" do they facilitate? How do they reflect—directly or indirectly—human systems of belief? Or, more narrowly, what conceptual categories do they reflect? Not even the most confirmed Whorfian would dare attempt to relate the circumstance that in German 'sun' is feminine and 'moon' masculine, but the reverse is true in French, to any fact about German or French culture. And there are many well-known examples of gender assignment that, instead of following a readily available external principle, obey a purely formal language-internal criterion. So German *das Mädchen* 'the girl' is neuter because all nouns in that language ending in *-chen* belong to that gender class, even though German has a feminine gender class to which one might assume that *das Mädchen* would "naturally" belong.

While surface case inflection might *correlate* with semantic function in most languages, it almost never reflects it perfectly. Consider objective case in English (which, of course, is manifested overtly only in the pronominal system). One simple *structural* statement accounts for every instance of objective case within prepositional phrases:

(3) $[_{PP}$ P NP]
$\quad\quad\quad$ 1 2 $\quad \rightarrow \quad$ 1 $\quad\quad$ 2
$\quad\quad\quad\quad\quad\quad\quad\quad\quad\quad\quad\quad$ + OBJECTIVE

What are the possibilities of replacing (3) with a principle that avoids reference to constructs of an autonomous grammar such as syntactic category and constituency? They do not look promising. It appears that there are no semantic constraints at all on the pronoun. The pronoun can be an agent (*the inhabitants were killed by them*), a patient (*my dismissal of her*), an experiencer (*I showed the picture to him*), a comitative (*John and Bill left with us*), an instrument (*I made use of him to gain access to the king*), a locative (*I have no fleas on me*), and much more. Nor does the objective pronoun appear to play any consistent role in *discourse*. The discourse functions of the prepositional phrases (and the pronouns they contain) in the following sentences seem quite diverse:

(4)   a. With him went our last hopes for victory.
$\quad\quad$ b. With him, I'll never leave my money.
$\quad\quad$ c. I spoke with him about a number of problems.
$\quad\quad$ d. I spoke about a number of problems with him.
$\quad\quad$ e. I think that, with him, we won't have as many problems.
$\quad\quad$ f. We won't have very many problems, at least not with him.

In short, the semantic and discourse properties of a noun phrase seem irrelevant to the determination of its surface case (at least for objects of prepositions). Case assignment, then, poses a challenge to anyone who would advocate reducing grammatical facts to principles from outside grammar proper.

Number agreement poses the same sort of challenge to reductionist approaches as gender and case assignment. Consider, for example, a well-known fact about Classical Greek. In this language a verb typically agrees in number with the nominative subject that precedes it. But if the subject should happen to be a neuter plural, then the verb is singular. Hence we have *taûta egéneto* 'these things happened' and *tà oikḗmata épesen* 'the buildings fell'. Why should this be? An external explanation would have to involve, minimally, some principle from which a "natural" unity of singulars and neuter plurals can be derived. No such principle comes readily to mind.

It certainly seems plausible that gender, case, and number systems might have *originated* to serve a particular communicative (or other external) need. But as language has changed through time, a gap has grown between the structural properties of these systems and the need they arose to serve. The child language learner, who no more has access to the history of a morphological inflection than to that of a phonological rule, must learn these systems on their own terms, with their "function" (if any) providing at best only rough hints to their linguistic manifestation.

In chapter 4 I will discuss and criticize some specific proposals that attempt to show that the generativists' syntactic rules and constraints are nothing more than reflexes of the exigencies of discourse or reflections of principles facilitating perception. In this section I will review briefly some evidence against the view that syntactic categories and syntactic constituent structure can be reduced to *conceptual* primitives—a view that has led to the conclusion that "syntax is not a relevant object of study in its own right, but should be studied only as a tool for the understanding of meaning" (Schank 1972, 555). As a first example, consider the categorial distinction between adjectives and verbs in English. It is not difficult to demonstrate that on the basis of the meaning of a predicate it is not possible to assign a lexical item that embodies that predicate uniquely to one category or the other. Note that we find pairs of sentences, one containing an adjective, one a verb, that can be (close to) absolute paraphrases:

(5)   a. John [$_V$likes] Mary.
        b. John is [$_A$fond] of Mary.
(6)   a. I [$_V$know] that the house is around here somewhere.
        b. I am [$_A$sure] that the house is around here somewhere.
(7)   a. To please Bill [$_V$delights] me.
        b. To please Bill is [$_A$delightful] for me.

While no doubt differences in nuance can be found between the (a) and (b) sentences above, it hardly seems plausible that such differences predict the categorial difference. Yet a conceptually based syntax would be forced to make just such a prediction.

The categorial distinction between adjective and verb, nonsemantically based though it may be, nevertheless is crucial in predicting the range of possible syntactic constructions in English. For example, the active-passive relation cannot be regarded simply as a relation between sentences that share certain meaning properties, because, while sentence pairs containing verbs manifest it, sentence pairs containing synonymous adjectives do not. Hence (8a) is grammatical and (8b) is ungrammatical:

(8)   a. Mary is liked by John.
        b. *Mary is fonded (of) by John.

Along the same lines, verbs but not adjectives take infinitival complements with subjects unmarked by the prepositional complementizer *for*. Hence:

(9)   a.   I know the house to be around here somewhere.
        b.   *I am sure (of) the house to be around here somewhere.

Finally, adjectives but not verbs occur in the *"easy-to-please"* construction (see Chomsky 1964, 34). Hence we find (10b) but not (10a):

(10)   a.   *Bill delights for me to please.
        b.   Bill is delightful for me to please.

Examples of this sort could be brought forward from quite a few other category pairs. It seems to me that they strike at the heart of any attempt to dismiss formal grammar as artifactual. For if the *categories* are not artifacts, then how could the rules stated *in terms of* the categories be artifacts? The first step, therefore, for anyone whose goal is to overthrow formal grammar is to show that syntactic categories are direct reflections of some system whose primitives are nonlinguistic.

   Along the same lines, Grimshaw (1979) argues in detail that the co-occurrence properties of a lexical item are a function of *both* its semantic properties and its syntactic properties, the latter not being wholly predictable from the former. For example, consider the practically synonymous verbs *ask* and *inquire*. As we would predict simply from taking their meaning into account, both can take fully sentential embedded questions:

(11)   a.   I asked what the number of students in the class was.
        b.   I inquired what the number of students in the class was.

However, *ask*, but not *inquire*, can take a corresponding "concealed question" in which the *wh*-word *what* is suppressed:

(12)   a.   I asked the number of students in the class.
        b.   *I inquired the number of students in the class.

Why should this be? If co-occurrence were strictly semantic, we would predict the grammaticality of (12b) as well as (12a). Grimshaw reasons that since concealed questions syntactically are noun phrases, the contrast in (12) is a reflection of a *syntactic* difference between *ask* and *inquire*—*ask* subcategorizes for noun phrases, while *inquire* does not. Note:

(13)   a.   Mary asked (the guide) a question.
        b.   *Mary inquired (the guide) a question.

Semantics alone is not sufficient to explain the contrast in (12) and (13). Grimshaw concludes that "the distribution of concealed questions can be explained only as resulting from the interaction of two autonomous sets of co-occurrence restrictions [one syntactic and one semantic], each imposing its own conditions on well-formedness" (1979, 306).

By now there is widespread agreement on the reality of syntactic constituent structure. Even those who might originally have been disposed to dismiss the internal grammatical evidence for such structure have acknowledged that experimentation has borne out the grammarians' claims. The experimental evidence is summarized in Fodor, Bever, and Garrett (1974, 221–74) and Clark and Clark (1977, 50–85). In brief, it has been found that speakers' intuitive judgments about natural breaks in the sentence tend to coincide with linguistically defined constituents; these constituents act as natural aids for perception and memory; and clicks inserted at random intervals into recordings of sentences tend to be perceived at major constituent boundaries.

Now if syntactically defined constituents invariably reflected independently motivated semantic, cognitive, discourse-functional (or whatever) units, autonomous grammar would receive no special support from the reality of constituent structure. But there is no evidence that there is such an invariable reflection. Certainly the relationship between syntactic constituents and semantic units is not one-to-one. One need only think of the standard examples of sentences with discontinuous constituents or understood elements to illustrate this point. So, for example, in *whom did you give the book to, give the book to* is a (semantically nonintegral) syntactic constituent, while 'to whom' forms a (syntactically discontinuous) semantic unit. Likewise, in *was John working*, 'was working' functions as a semantic unit, even though syntactically the subject of the sentence intrudes. And in *John went to Boston and Mary to New York*, the two conjuncts are parallel semantically, despite the fact that the syntactic manifestations of the meaning common to each are quite different. While one might (reasonably) argue that in sentences like these the "fit" between syntax and semantics improves at some level of representation removed from surface structure, doing so represents a fundamental concession in the direction of autonomous grammar.

1.3.2   Evidence from Language Acquisition

Does grammatical theory receive any support from empirical studies of language acquisition? There is increasing evidence that it does. Many of the earliest studies of child language (Braine 1963; Menyuk 1963; Miller and Ervin-Tripp 1964; McNeill 1966, 1971) did not address this question squarely, since they simply *presupposed* that syntax was central to language development and viewed the main task as writing rules characterizing the grammar learned.[3] Later studies (Bloom 1970; Bowerman 1973a,b; Brown 1973; Schlesinger 1971, 1974) have concentrated on the

---

3. Though it must be pointed out that the rules proposed in most of these early papers could not be rules that describe the child's linguistic competence—they simply characterize the sentences the child *produces*.

child's acquisition of semantic structures, and more recently (Bruner 1974, 1975; Dore 1974; Bates 1976; Ochs and Schieffelin 1979) emphasis has been placed on the pragmatic function of language in its initial stages.

Nobody—and certainly no generativist—would question that a full theory of acquisition must account for semantic and pragmatic development. Once this point is acknowledged, we are still faced with the question whether language acquisition involves grammar acquisition. Some investigators (e.g., Edwards 1973) have said no on the basis of the belief that, since communication involves conveying messages and grammars (merely!) structure words, there is no need for a grammar. Such argumentation has a strong aprioristic flavor, since it presupposes that the principal purpose of language is communication and that the form of language reflects that purpose directly. But even if communication *is* the "principal purpose" of language (a matter I will take up in chap. 4), it does not thereby follow that the child does not acquire an autonomous grammar. As Waryas and Stremel-Campbell have observed:

> What are communicated in language are the semantic content and the pragmatic intent, but the vehicle for their transmission remains the lexicogrammatical structure of the utterance. Regardless of the mode of transmission—spoken language, written forms, manual signs or other symbolic systems—the ordering of elements in accord with structural principles . . . is an essential component in order for semantic and pragmatic content of an utterance to be expressed by a speaker and interpreted by a listener. (1978, 159)

The case for the autonomy of formal grammar has received support from the fact that (in extraordinary cases) linguistic abilities may be dissociated developmentally from other cognitive abilities. The most dramatic (and best-known) example of this phenomenon involves Genie, the girl who underwent extreme isolation and deprivation until she was thirteen and a half years old (for discussion, see Curtiss 1977, 1982). Genie, in effect, was faced with the task of first language acquisition as a teenager. Interestingly, her language development contrasts sharply with her power as a nonlinguistic communicator. While Genie's utterances were, even a decade after her release, largely made up of simple noun phrases, she had by then "well-developed use of gesture, facial expression, eye gaze, attention-getting devices, and turn-taking knowledge" (Curtiss 1982, 287). Furthermore, there was a marked disparity between her syntactic abilities and her semantic ones, since Genie's ability to convey meanings was advanced. Curtiss observes that "it is hard to imagine how a general intellectual deficit could account for such a linguistic deficit" (290). In fact, Genie

> has surely demonstrated sufficient intellectual ability to support a full linguistic system. That is, children with a comparable mental age have

language. It appears, then, that Genie's selective linguistic deficits cannot be attributed to lack of sufficient intelligence, and more importantly for the questions at hand, that the mechanisms by which Genie's general intelligence developed were not able to mediate the learning of certain aspects of language. (290–92)

Curtiss considers the possibility that Genie's failure to develop syntactic skills might be a result of her failure to develop certain *specific* cognitive abilities. For example, investigators have postulated that particular abilities are prerequisites to language, including means-end knowledge, drawing, symbolic play, knowledge that other people can serve as agents, attainment of object permanence, classificatory skills, and nesting ability and hierarchical construction ability. Curtiss reports, however, that Genie's skills in all of these areas were beyond those of the normal child language learner. In Curtiss's view, "This case, then, supports the hypothesis that there are language-specific learning mechanisms and suggests that these mechanisms may be responsible for the learning of syntax in particular" (292).

Just as the development of general communicative abilities may outpace that of specific linguistic abilities, the reverse may occur. Blank, Gessner, and Esposito (1979) report the case of a three-year-old who had an excellent mastery of linguistic form but virtually no ability to use language for interpersonal communication. He also failed to either understand or produce nonverbal communication (e.g., gestures). The authors suggest that "the structural and communicative aspects of language are based upon different sets of skills which particularly in cases of language disorder may function independently of one another" (1979, 329). Curtiss (1982) reports two similar cases. One involves a child, Antony, whose development was delayed in every aspect except language and short-term memory. While Antony's syntactic abilities were not significantly below those of other six-year-olds, "his play, drawing, copying, and general problem-solving behavior place him approximately in sensorimotor stage VI (20–24 months), possibly just beyond. . . . And like Genie's case, Antony's profile demonstrates that the mechanisms by which syntax is acquired are not general purpose learning mechanisms underlying the development of a general intelligence" (297–98).

In an important paper, Maratsos and Chalkley (1980) discuss the difficulties inherent in the (intuitively plausible) idea that the child's acquisition of syntax is a mere by-product of other development, in particular conceptual development. As they point out, such a view entails that certain types of *errors* should be common in child language. If the child learns concepts first, then learns to map these concepts onto syntactic categories and structures, we would predict that semantically atypical members of a syntactic category should be used erroneously as if they were members of a category that more directly reflects their meaning.

But errors of that sort, Maratsos and Chalkley report, are rare. For example, children rarely utter such sentences as *she naughtied or *he is nicing to them, despite the fact that naughty and nice are actionlike adjectives, and we rarely find such errors as *he is know it or *was he love her, though know and love are stative verbs. These facts seem to suggest that the child has specifically syntactic knowledge alongside semantic knowledge, and when the two conflict the latter does not automatically override the former.

Maratsos and Chalkley also discuss the problems involved in getting a theory of the acquisition of syntax grounded in "semantic prototypes" to work. In this approach, whose theoretical basis was laid by Rosch (1973) and which was applied to acquisition by De Villiers (1980), there does not need to be a perfect "fit" between syntax and semantics. Rather, children are said to be guided in their learning of classes of syntactic constructs by the semantically prototypical members of the class. Maratsos and Chalkley point out several problems with this somewhat weaker conceptually oriented theory of acquisition. First, prototype theory also makes the incorrect prediction that semantically atypical members of a syntactic class should be inflected erroneously. Second, it seems at odds with the fact that language offers ways for members of one syntactic category to be involved in constructions that mark some prototypical meanings characteristic of the best members of a different category. That is, it follows from prototype theory that constructions such as be careful and he is being noisy should pose special problems for the language learner, since the imperative and progressive constructions are properties of prototypical verbs, yet careful and noisy are adjectives. But such constructions do not pose difficulties. Finally, prototype theory demands that the most prototypical members of a category should be the ones that participate in all or most of the legitimate privileges of that category. So, for example, since only adjectives allow adverbs to be formed from them by adding -ly, prototype theory predicts that all (or most) prototypical adjectives should allow the suffix. But this is wrong: virtually all (atypical) process adjectives allow the suffix (noisy-noisily; obnoxious-obnoxiously), while a great many state adjectives do not (tall-*tally; red-*redly).

Several recent papers have presented evidence that the child is guided in language acquisition by highly abstract structural principles that do not seem reducible to extragrammatical ones. For example, Lust and Chien (1983) have made an interesting discovery about the acquisition of coordinate structures. In most languages, the principal direction of phrase-structure branching correlates with the order of the subject, object, and verb in the clause. English and Japanese are typical in that respect. In English the verb precedes the object, and the normal branching direction is to the right, as in (14):

(14)

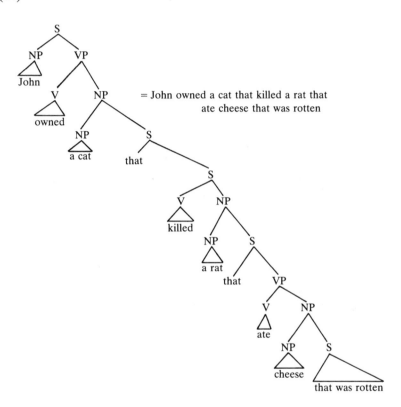

= John owned a cat that killed a rat that ate cheese that was rotten

In Japanese, on the other hand, the object precedes the verb, and syntactic structure branches to the left, as in (15) (the example is taken from Kuno 1973, 7):

(15)

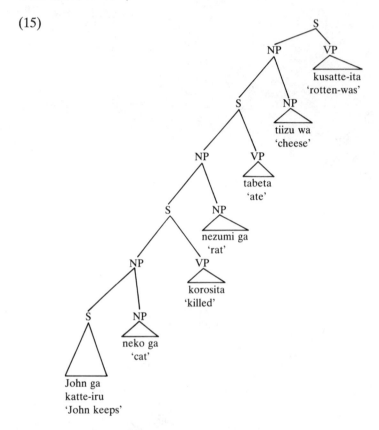

= the cheese was rotten that the rat that was killed by the cat
  that John keeps ate

There is a strong correlation, Lust and Chien found, between such properties and the types of coordinate structures that young children (two and three years old) find easiest. Children learning verb-object/right-branching languages prefer coordinate structures with *forward* reductions, as in (16):

(16)   the teddy bear walks and Ø sleeps

On the other hand, children learning object-verb/left-branching languages prefer coordinate structures with *backward* reductions, as in (17):

(17)   sumire-to Ø tanpopo-ga saku
        'violet   dandelion bloom'

A question arises about which type of coordinate structure will be preferred by children learning a language with an *atypical* correlation between the order of subject, verb, and object and the principal branching direction. Chinese is such a language. In Chinese the object typically follows the verb (as in English), while the principal branching direction is to the left (as in Japanese). Lust and Chien discovered that Chinese learners favor coordinate structures with backward reductions in predicative constructions. This seems to indicate that they are sensitive to the highly abstract, specifically *grammatical* concept of "principal branching direction"; it is this concept, not the more "accessible" properties of superficial word order, that constrains this aspect of the acquisition of Chinese.

Another structural principle that appears to influence first language acquisition is that of "c-command." To give a rough definition, one node c-commands another if the first branching node dominating the first also dominates the second (for fuller discussion and refinements, see Reinhart 1981 and Chomsky 1981). Hence in (18) below, F c-commands only G and H; C c-commands only B, D, and E; B c-commands only C, F, G, and H; and so forth:

(18)

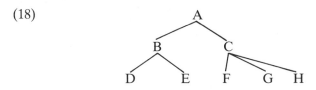

Reinhart (1981) has suggested that the c-command relation is relevant to the determination of possible pronoun-antecedent pairings. In particular, she has suggested that a pronoun may precede its antecedent ("backward pronominalization") in English only if it does not c-command it. Thus of (19a–h) below, only in (19f) and (19h) can the pronoun be interpreted as coreferential to *sheep*; in every other sentence the pronoun c-commands *sheep*:

(19)   a. He told the horse that the sheep would run around.
        b. The horse told him that the sheep would run around.
        c. He hit the horse in the sheep's yard.
        d. The horse hit him in the sheep's yard.
        e. He hit the horse after the sheep ran around.
        f. The horse hit him after the sheep ran around.
        g. He hit the horse after the sheep's run.
        h. The horse hit him after the sheep's run.

Solan (1981) devised an experiment to determine whether the c-command restriction on backward pronominalization is operative in children's grammars. He presented thirty-six children (twelve each of five-, six-, and seven-year-olds) with three tokens of each of the eight sentence types represented in (19a–h). The children were asked to act out the sentences using toy animals and a variety of props. In observing this activity, it became clear when they interpreted a preceding pronoun as coreferential to a following noun phrase. The children allowed backward pronominalization most frequently just where it is allowed in adult grammars—in those sentences in which the pronoun does not c-command the antecedent ([19f] and [19h]). This seems to indicate that c-command, a rather abstract structural principle not reducible in any obvious way to semantic, cognitive, or discourse-based principles, is part of the grammatical competence of even young children. Furthermore, since backward pronominalization even in *adult* speech is rare, it seems unlikely that the children's behavior was the result of memorizing a particular sentence type or was shaped by some inductive principle. Rather, it points to the idea that the child is equipped with knowledge of the c-command relation *before* the stage in which the language-specific details regarding pronoun-antecedent pairings are acquired.

Numerous modifications of the grammatical model have been proposed in recent years based in part on assumptions about the "learnability" of the grammatical construct in question. While interesting results have been attained through work along these lines (see especially the papers in Baker and McCarthy 1981), White (1981) and Menn (1982) have cautioned that extreme care must be taken when basing arguments about the nature of adult grammars on what it is believed might be "learnable" by the child (or, conversely, basing proposals for child grammars on results obtained from investigating the speech of adults). Each system must be evaluated on its own terms:

> Child grammars and adult grammars are possible grammars, as defined by grammatical theory, and the only relationship they have to each other is that of being members of the class of possible grammars. Consequently, data from acquisition can have no direct relevance for rules of adult grammars unless one knows that child and adult perceive the data alike (which is not to say that work on children's grammars may not have relevance to universal grammar). One cannot argue that because the child does such and such in acquisition, therefore the adult grammar *must* show the same properties. . . . [Much of the work on child language] gives one the impression of the child proceeding through a sequence of grammars toward the ultimate goal, the adult grammar, as if he is teleologically directed towards it, acquiring the adult grammar bit by bit. But the child can have no idea what the adult grammar is, so he can hardly aim towards it. Rather, the child's aim must be expressed in terms of the input; he seeks to deal with the data that he hears and to produce language of his own. He aims at a

grammar to deal with the facts; as his perception of those facts changes, so does his grammar. The fact that the child eventually attains an adult-like grammar is a consequence of perceiving the input language in an adult-like way. This is simply the logical consequence of viewing a grammar as a characterization of what somebody, child or adult, knows about his language. (White 1981, 255)

The relevance of White's remarks for the question of the autonomy of formal grammar is this: A number of researchers have advocated decreasing the "abstractness" of grammatical representations on the grounds that the less abstract the representation, the easier the learning task for the child. This view, when applied, for example, to phonology, has given psycholinguistic credibility to the conclusion that phonological processes are all (or are largely) "natural" ones (in the sense of "natural" discussed in the previous section, where it is taken to be roughly synonymous with "nonautonomous"). Recall that Donegan and Stampe intend their theory of "natural phonology" to embody a model of acquisition: "the living sound patterns of languages, *in their development in each individual* as well as in their evolution over the centuries, are governed by forces implicit in human vocalization and perception" (1979, 126; emphasis added).

Lise Menn, however, has argued that the facts obtained from studies of child language give no support to the idea that constraints on adult grammars can be deduced from an examination of child language. Menn (1979) discusses a variety of phonological processes that are found regularly in child language but are rare or nonexistent in adult language. To give one example, consonant-sequencing constraints occur commonly in children's grammars but have been attested in the grammar of only one (adult) language (Abkhaz). A typical constraint of that sort demands that two nonhomorganic stops in a word must occur in a fixed order (for example, labials must precede dentals). And Menn (1982) notes that the stage in which children overgeneralize the vowel change in *sing, sang, sung; ring, rang, rung*; to *bring, brang, brung* may point to their having imposed extrinsic ordering restrictions between rules (to account for this example, Menn suggests that the vowel-change tense-marking rule is ordered before the regular suffixation tense-marking rule). Menn is careful to caution that one cannot conclude from this that *therefore* there is extrinsic ordering on adult grammars. The point is simply that a priori ideas about what is "learnable" by the child do not necessarily lead to any insights into the nature of adult grammars.

For reasons I do not fully understand, many investigators seem to view the question of the autonomy of formal grammar as wholly subsidiary to the question of "innateness." Of course it is perfectly reasonable to ask which aspects of grammatical structure are innate and which are learned.

But the same question can—and should—be asked about *any* human faculty. There is no serious contender for a theory of language acquisition that does not posit a very rich set of innate mechanisms, though some theories claim that none of these mechanisms is strictly "linguistic." We have made great strides from the time—in the not so distant past—when it was considered a virtue of a particular model of acquisition that it postulated no mechanisms "not available to the albino rat" (Peizer and Olmsted 1969, 64) or, equivalently, from the view that it is correct to impose an "inductive requirement" on grammars that the child learn them "solely on the basis of data which is available to him" (Derwing 1973, 49).

The past fifteen years have seen a number of studies that point to the child's active contribution to the acquisition process (for general discussion, see Gleitman 1981). From the first day of the child's life, in which its movements synchronize with the articulated structure of adult speech (Condon and Sander 1974), to the last stage in the acquisition of the adult grammar, there are phenomena that can be explained only by a complex acquisition device. For example, McNeill (1966), Brown and Hanlon (1970), Braine (1971), and Slobin (1972) point out that correction seems to play a small role in shaping the child's speech. Ungrammatical sentences are not normally corrected, and correction seems to have little effect on output. This fact suggests that an internal language acquisition device plays at least as important a role in development as external factors. Along the same lines, the work of Brown and Hanlon (1970) suggests that there is no significant difference in how parents react when the child produces grammatical and ungrammatical sentences. And as Brown has shown: "Frequency and perceptual salience will be minor determinants of order of acquisition" (1973, 409).

The instinctual urge for symbolic communication is so great that even deaf children of hearing parents who have been denied access to a manual language will spontaneously create their own gestural language (see Feldman, Goldin-Meadow, and Gleitman 1978). Such gestural languages exhibit many of the properties of the communications of normally circumstanced language learners. While certain of these properties can be attributed to normal cognitive development, not all can:

> In contrast, the exploitation of sequence, the representation of content in terms of a hierarchically organized set of levels, and the adoption of regular principles for the selective omission of some material—all observed in the deaf subjects—seem to be specifically language-like, not variants of organization common to all higher-order mental functions. The emergence of these language-like formal means of representing thought by the deaf subjects without models suggests the existence of language organizing principles that account for the structure of their gesturing. (Feldman, Goldin-Meadow, and Gleitman 1978, 409)

At every stage of language acquisition there is a poor match between the child's input stimuli and the sentences the child produces. The stages in the acquisition of negatives and interrogatives are a case in point (Bellugi 1967, 1971). The child typically goes through a stage of uttering sentences such as "no go home" and "what me doing?" though such sentences are never heard in adult speech. Bellugi also noted that children initially produce verbal auxiliaries in their uncontracted forms, despite the fact that in their input corpus they are almost always contracted. Gleitman and Wanner (1982) discuss a number of cases that indicate that children are biased toward "canonical word order." For example, at first questions are marked in children's speech only by specially intoned subject-auxiliary-verb-(object) word order, even though the subject and the auxiliary are inverted in just about every question children hear. Russian children use a word-order strategy as well, omitting inflectional suffixes entirely at first, even though inflection rather than word order marks the semantically important relations in a Russian sentence (Slobin 1966a).

While the idea that language learning involves more than inductive generalization from the corpus is now well accepted, for some reason there is widespread bias against positing innate *syntactic* mechanisms. For example, Maratsos and Chalkley (1980) dismiss the hypothesis that syntactic categories are innate because it "is not disprovable" (132). Yet they are perfectly content to advocate a theory of acquisition with a rich nativist stock of *conceptual* primitives:

> Relation, relational entity, relational terms, and argument, are naturally very general primitives. They either subsume, presuppose, or must be supplanted by a number of other analytic primitives. In particular, we must assume the child has available whatever conceptual primitives are necessary for the analysis of semantic and pragmatic elements in utterances. (1980, 139)

One wonders what admits innate "relational entities," but not innate "nouns," into the realm of disprovability. In fact, neither is more or less "disprovable" than the other. Neither hypothesis can be confirmed or falsified through direct observation; both require sophisticated and highly abstract theories of human development and ability, and neither can be evaluated independently of myriad (not directly appraisable) assumptions and auxiliary hypotheses.

Models of language learning that attempt to downplay the role of syntactically based principles succeed as far as they do typically by adopting one of two strategies. The first is to assume that the child has innately or is able to construct semantic structures that are endowed with many of the crucial properties of syntactic structures (this point is stressed in Pinker 1979). The models proposed in Anderson (1976) and Moulton and Robinson (1981) are good examples. In both cases it is posited that the child, before syntax acquisition, has available semantic representations in which the structural relations do not differ significantly from the standard representations of syntactic structures in terms of constituent structure trees.

The second strategy is simply to *ignore* the complexities of syntax—in some cases entirely. Since the question of the nature of syntax does not arise, how could the question whether it has an innate basis? Work in the Piagetian tradition typifies this strategy (Beilin 1975 is a good example). Such work fails to demonstrate that language acquisition is explainable in terms of general cognitive growth because, among other reasons, it has an impoverished view of what the language is that the child has to acquire.

An important recent challenge to nativist views has come from studies of the verbal interaction between children and their adult caretakers. If baby talk[4] is a special register geared to "shaping" the child's language, then the nativist wins no points by referring to the complexity of normal adult speech. In fact, some investigators are convinced that parental speech is "finely tuned to the child's psycholinguistic capacity" and that therefore "there is less need for an elaborate innate component than there at first seemed to be" (Brown 1977, 20; see also Garnica 1977).

Wexler and Culicover (1980), in an extensive discussion of the topic, point out that there are three possible empirical results that might show that the nature of baby talk disconfirms the need for an "elaborate innate component":

1. Speech to children is simple, compared with speech to adults.
2. Speech to children becomes more complex as a child's (psycho) linguistic abilities increase (in a causal sense).
3. The more that a mother uses the special (simple) properties of [baby talk], the more will her child develop language. (1980, 72–73)

There is no evidence that any of these possibilities is true. Quite to the contrary, in an important article on baby talk, Newport, Gleitman, and Gleitman (1977) show that all three are false. First, there does not seem to be any way baby talk can be considered "simpler" than adult speech. The former contains a smaller proportion of subject-verb-object sentences than the latter, as well as a higher percentage of utterances involving optional movement or deletion transformations. Moreover, in baby talk, "there is a wider range of sentence types and more inconsistency to children than [when mothers talk] to the experimenter" (1977,

---

4. "Baby talk" means adult speech to children, not the speech *of* children. While the ambiguity of the term is unfortunate, the alternative term, "motherese," seems even less felicitous. Aside from its arguably sexist connotations, it has been found that fathers' speech to children does not differ significantly from that of mothers (see Wilkinson, Hiebert, and Rembold 1981). Interestingly, children have difficulty understanding their own "baby talk" when it is spoken back to them (see Shipley, Smith, and Gleitman 1969).

122). Second, the only clear positive correlations between changes in baby talk and child language growth are "with respect to language-specific structures (surface morphology and syntactic elements that vary over the languages of the world), and even then only through the filter of the child's selective attention to portions of the speech stream" (131). Importantly, "the child's growth in the use of complex sentences . . . is unaffected by the aspects of [baby talk] examined here. . . . These phenomena of language use seem to be dependent on cognitive and linguistic maturity. While they are functions of the child's age, they are not related to specifiable features of the maternal environment" (133). And, third, there is simply no convincing evidence that the more baby talk is used, the more the child will develop language. As Newport, Gleitman, and Gleitman point out:

> the finding that [baby talk] exists cannot by itself show that it influences language growth, or even that this special style is necessary to acquisition—despite frequent interpretations to this effect that have appeared in the literature. After all, [baby talk] is as likely an effect on the mother by the child as an effect on the child by the mother. (1977, 112)

Newport, Gleitman, and Gleitman conclude that "nativist assumptions are left intact by a close look at [baby talk]" (123). What is its function, then, if not to facilitate the learning of syntax? According to these authors: "We believe this language style arises primarily in response to the pressures of communicating with a cognitively and linguistically naive child in the here-and-now, not from the exigencies of the language classroom" (124).[5]

1.3.3 Neurological Evidence

From the earliest days, generativists have stressed the need for their theory of language structure to harmonize with the neurophysiologists' findings about brain mechanisms:

> First, since the psychologist and the mentalistic linguist are constructing theories of the same kind, i.e., theories with the same kind of relation to the neurophysiology of the human brain, it follows that the linguist's theory is subject to the requirement that it harmonize with the psychologist's theories dealing with other human abilities and that it be consistent with the neurophysiologist's theories concerning the type of existing brain mechanisms. (Katz 1964, 133)

---

5. Newport, Gleitman, and Gleitman (1977) is one of many papers in a volume on parents' speech to children edited by Catharine Snow and Charles Ferguson (1977). Despite the conviction of several of the authors that their findings undercut the arguments for a rich innate component to language acquisition, one reviewer of the volume concludes that the idea that adults "reduce their syntax in order to teach their children syntax in a sort-of language-teaching programme . . . is given very little support in the papers in this volume" (McTear 1978, 524).

Are the results of the two disciplines in harmony with each other? The evidence seems to be that they are. The first in-depth investigation of the biological foundations of language, Lenneberg (1967), confirmed at least indirectly that more than "learning" is involved in language acquisition. Since then, developments in the new field of neurolinguistics (see, e.g., Whitaker and Whitaker 1976–79) have strengthened the case for the properties of language being in part biologically determined.

Not surprisingly, the bulk of what we know about language and the brain comes from the study of aphasic patients. Much of the earliest research was devoted to investigating whether the competence/performance distinction could be *directly* evidenced from the nature of aphasic speech. For example, Weigl and Bierwisch (1970) and Lenneberg (1973) concluded, on the basis of the belief that Broca's aphasia severely affects production but (apparently) leaves comprehension intact, that this type of aphasia does not represent a loss of competence. Rather, they saw it simply as a disruption of the motor implementation of speech. I believe it is generally accepted today that such a view cannot be maintained. It seems implausible that the competence system could be so organically dissociated from the systems involved in speech production and other aspects of performance that one could be impaired without at least some effect on the other (see Kean 1981a for discussion of this point). It is not surprising then that recent investigation has shown that Broca's aphasia seems to have consequences for a wide variety of linguistic abilities (see Zurif and Caramazza 1976; Zurif and Blumstein 1978).

By the same token, since the grammar itself consists of a set of intricately interacting subcomponents, it is not surprising that deficits that affect *exclusively* one part of the grammar are very rare, if they exist at all. So, for example, Broca's aphasics, in addition to having what appears to be a striking syntactic deficit, also show moderate to severe phonetic deficits as well as some impairment in making judgments on the semantic relatedness of words. Likewise, Wernicke's aphasics, whose primary deficit appears to lie in the accessing of semantic information, also show a limitation in the syntactic routines they have available in speech production and a phonological deficit in speech production as well (for general discussion of these points, see Blumstein 1982).

Nevertheless, there is quite a bit of evidence from aphasic speech that points to the existence of an independently functioning grammatical system. For example, aphasics often show syntactic deficits with only minimal accompanying deficits in cognition or speech. Tissot, Lhermitte, and Ducarne (1963) and Zangwill (1964) discuss cases where language is impaired but cognitive functioning seems to be preserved. Along the same lines, Goodglass et al. (1972) and Gleason et al. (1975) give examples of syntactic loss that cannot have its roots in general cognitive loss, since patients are observed to use alternative strategies to produce sentences with equivalent meanings (see Blumstein 1981 for discussion). And Zurif (1980) shows that the syntactic control of the definite article by two Broca's aphasics cannot simply be a function of the concept of definiteness: loss of the former takes place without loss of the latter.

Interesting support for the independence of the language faculty from other mental faculties can be adduced from the results of two training programs carried out with aphasic patients who had almost no syntactic ability. Glass, Gazzaniga, and Premack (1973) succeeded in teaching their patients an artificial language system using cutout paper symbols for words. And Hughes (1975) taught her patients to communicate through the system of visual symbols originally devised by David Premack (1971) for use with chimpanzees. These results show the independence of specifically *grammatical* abilities from general cognitive abilities—even those cognitive abilities directly involved in communication. For, as Glass and her co-workers point out, these patients' conceptual systems and capacities for symbolization appear to have been only slightly impaired. If grammatical abilities were simply a function of conceptual and symbolic abilities, then we would be led to predict that the patients' competence in the former would be commensurate with their competence in the latter. But, in fact, even extensive training in the symbolic "languages" does not appear to have improved their grammatical abilities.

There is evidence that parts of the brain differ in their inherent ability to carry out the various functions associated with language. For example, Dennis and Kohn (1975) and Dennis and Whitaker (1976) have shown that language does not develop the same way in subjects whose right cerebral hemisphere is removed in infancy as in those whose left hemisphere is removed. While subjects with remaining left hemispheres develop all the syntactic skills possessed by normal speakers, those with only right hemispheres do not do so. Dennis (1980a) shows that even those syntactic tasks that the latter can carry out (say, processing positive passive sentences) involve operations different from those of normal subjects. While either hemisphere can acquire the sense and reference of common words, Dennis (1980b) demonstrates that only the left hemisphere can efficiently process those aspects of meaning determined by syntactic configuration (like discourse topic). The right hemisphere, on the other hand, seems better designed for the pragmatic aspects of language:

> The role of right hemisphere processing, however, seems to be quite different from that of the left. While the left hemisphere appears to be specialized for processing the linguistic grammar per se, that is the analytic and generative aspects of language production and reception, the right hemisphere contributes to the "pragmatics" of language use, on the one hand, and the integration of the linguistic grammar with

cognitive (nonverbal) processes, on the other. . . . Further, given sentences that can have a figurative or metaphoric interpretation, as well as a literal one (e.g., "he was wearing a loud tie"), right hemisphere patients interpret the sentences literally and concretely (Gardner and Denes 1973; Winner and Gardner 1977). Thus, again, they are performing at one level with a correct linguistic interpretation of the sentence, but at another level they are insensitive to the fine semantic-pragmatic structure of language communication. (Blumstein 1981, 250)

Along the same lines, Van Lancker (1980) has demonstrated that the strictly grammatical aspects of intonation (word-level tone, for example) are processed in the left hemisphere, and the more discourse-determined on the right.

While it appears that no grammatical component is ever affected *exclusively* by one type of aphasia, it is universally recognized that different types of aphasia tend to have different, yet consistent, effects (see Marin, Saffran, and Schwartz 1976 and Caplan 1981b for general discussion). This has been taken as support for the idea that aphasia can selectively affect individual components of the grammar and (as a logical consequence) as support for specific generativist models that incorporate such components. For example, Caplan concludes that the "agrammatism [of Broca's aphasia] supports the distinction between function and content word vocabularies, and between the semantic interpretation of syntactic structure and the semantic properties of individual words" (1981b, 6). And Kean has suggested that the syntactic deficit that Broca's aphasia appears to reflect might instead result from a deficit in the phonologically based stress system (1977) or from a disruption to a special lexical system for clitics (1981a).[6]

Research into the grammatical properties of aphasic speech has suggested the plausibility of certain central claims of linguistic theory. In Blumstein's view, "Performance of aphasic patients clearly shows that most of the linguistic primitives elaborated in current theories of grammar are instantiated in the grammar of aphasics" (1982, 208–9). For example, the notions "distinctive feature" and "markedness" receive support from the finding (see Blumstein 1973) that aphasic errors more frequently involve one distinctive feature than several, and more often a marked segment than an unmarked one. And Stark (1974) and Dressler (1979) argue for deriving German [ŋ] from an underlying /ng/ on the basis of aphasic speech. They found three ways patients treated [ŋ] as a

---

6. If Broca's aphasia is primarily a grammatical (i.e., competence) deficit as Caplan and Kean suggest, then it follows that the comprehension of those who suffer from it will be affected along the same lines as their production. This appears to be true. See Caramazza and Zurif (1976) and Bradley, Garrett, and Zurif (1980) for evidence that Broca's aphasics comprehend sentences agrammatically.

nasal-stop sequence. One was their mutual replacement of [ŋ] with [nd], parallel to their replacement of /mb/ with the same phonetic sequence. A second was their suppression of the rules that assimilate the alveolar nasal to the following velar stop and then delete the stop before a word boundary, so that *singender* was pronounced [singədə]. And a third was the deletion of the nasal in /ng/, so that *Wendungen* was pronounced [vendUgən].[7]

1.4 Some Modular Accounts of Linguistic Phenomena

In this section I discuss several linguistic phenomena whose explanation demands a modular approach to language; that is, an approach characterized by the interaction of autonomous systems, each system defined in terms of its own general principles. Before proceeding, let me note that quite a few attempts to refute grammatical theory have failed precisely because they have neglected the possibility of a modular explanation for the phenomenon under discussion. Typically the authors assume that a generativist would handle all the facts about a particular construction in terms of one specific rule. From the problems of getting such a rule to work they then conclude that the fundamentals of grammatical theory itself are to blame.

A good example of a paper that reasons that way is Gross (1979).[8] Gross demonstrates that the surface facts surrounding such constructions as passives, "subject-raised" sentences, relative clauses, and so forth, are extraordinarily complex. He then demonstrates for each construction the difficulty (if not impossibility) of building the account of all these com-

---

7. Some of the conclusions arrived at on the basis of the properties of the speech of aphasic patients about the correctness of alternative competing frameworks *within* grammatical theory, however, seem a bit premature. Whitaker (1971, 1972) and Schnitzer (1974) draw such conclusions, Schnitzer, for example, arguing that the aphasia-based evidence shows that the performative hypothesis (Ross 1970) is correct and that pronouns replace bound variables. Whitaker and Whitaker (1978) point out the difficulties with conclusions of that sort, given our present state of understanding, though it seems to me that they exaggerate the difficulty of forming *any* interesting hypotheses about grammatical theory based on aphasic speech.

8. Gross's paper is replete with misunderstandings about grammatical theory. For example, he asserts that "the justification for this passive relation is the fact that pairs of NP's . . . preserve the synonymy relation under fixed formal conditions." (863) But Chomsky (1957, chaps. 7 and 9) not only *denied* that actives and passives are synonymous, but rejected in principle the motivation of transformational rules by appeal to meaning relations (for discussion, see Newmeyer 1980a, 22–33). Or consider Gross's remark: "Chomsky appears to regard the exception to a linguistic rule as a physical scientist might regard an experimental result incompatible with his theory as being caused by some unperceived error in the experimental apparatus" (865). It is hard to imagine the source of such a peculiar idea.

plexities directly into the statement of one particular rule (Passive, Subject Raising, Relativization, etc.). His conclusion is that, since adequate rules seemingly cannot be written to account for the relevant data, grammatical theory must be abandoned.

But Gross's conclusion is a non sequitur. There is no reason to think that any ill-formed passive, for example, is necessarily ruled out grammatically by the Passive transformation by itself. Quite the contrary, many proposals show that the unacceptability of certain passive sentences is a result of the *interaction* of the Passive rule with other independently motivated principles, some grammatical and some extragrammatical. For example, consider ungrammatical sentence (20a) below, which is not a possible passive of (20b):

(20)   a.   *Rice was eaten by John and beans.
         b.   John ate rice and beans.

A nonmodular approach to syntax would be forced to build a restriction directly into the statement of Passive to block this sentence. But this is not necessary: its ungrammaticality follows from the interaction of the Passive with an independent constraint: the A-over-A Principle (see Chomsky 1964; Ross 1968). According to this principle, no element may be moved by *any* transformation if it is dominated by an element with the same category label as its own. Since in the structure underlying (20) the noun phrase *rice* is dominated by another noun phrase, *rice* may not be moved to become the passive subject. Example (21) illustrates the structure that disallows passivization of *rice*:

(21)

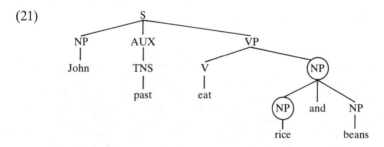

Or, to give a different example, it has been suggested that the ungrammaticality of (22) is, again, independent of any particular formulation of Passive; rather, its deviance is due to the interaction of Passive with a principle like (23) (see Chomsky 1973):

(22)   *The table was put the book on by John.

(23)   Each factor imposed by a transformation either is a morphological or a semantic unit or corresponds to a variable in the structural condition of the transformation.

Since, in the structure underlying (22), *put-the-book-on* is neither a morphological nor a semantic unit, passivization is impossible.

The explanation of the unacceptability of a surface passive in all likelihood involves factors outside formal grammar proper. For example, Robin Lakoff (1971) has observed that the contrast between (24a) and (24b) is a result of the fact that passives with *get* are most appropriate when the speaker wishes to convey a strong emotional attitude toward the subject matter:

(24)   a. The program has been prerecorded.
         b. The program has gotten prerecorded.

Since it is unlikely (though not inconceivable) that an announcer would feel (or at least betray) any strong emotional feeling toward the prerecording of a program, (24b) sounds rather peculiar.

While nobody would claim that we understand the structure of all the systems at work in determining the acceptability of passive sentences, the modular approach taken by generativists certainly undercuts attempted refutations of the sort Gross puts forward.

Sections 1.4.1–1.4.4 outline some ways other linguistic phenomena might admit of a modular explanation.

1.4.1   Multiply Center-Embedded Constructions

Chomsky and Miller (1963) noted that sentences with multiple center-embeddings are invariably unacceptable, as in example (25):

(25)   The rat [$_S$the cat [$_S$the dog chased] ate] died.

They demonstrated the implausibility of coming up with a strictly *grammatical* explanation for this. First of all, the unacceptability of (25) could hardly be due to its deep structure (or semantic) ill-formedness. Not only is (25) interpretable, but other sentences that are plausibly derived from the same deep structure are quite acceptable:

(26)   The rat died that was eaten by the cat that the dog chased.

Nor could the unacceptability be a consequence of the filtering function of the transformational rules—no (relevant) transformations apply in the derivation of (25) from its deep structure. And the only way to block (25) at the level of surface structure would be to incorporate into grammatical theory a device that would literally "count" the number and nature of embeddings in the surface string—a device unlike any ever proposed to govern grammatical processes.

But there *is* an obvious reason, Chomsky and Miller argued, for the unacceptability of (25), a reason that has nothing to do with grammar itself. The sentence is unacceptable because it is *confusing*. Without special aids (e.g., paper and pencil) it is difficult to figure out which subjects are paired with which verbs. Chomsky and Miller proposed to explain the confusing nature of sentences like (25) by a principle of sentence comprehension that states (essentially) that sentences are processed from "left to right" and that the processing mechanism cannot be interrupted more than once. Since the comprehension of (25) demands a *double* interruption of the process of subject-verb assignment, the sentence is therefore difficult to process.

In other words, sentence (25) is generated by the grammar, that is, is grammatical. Its unacceptability follows from the *interaction* of the grammatical principle of unlimited center-embedding with the perceptual principle stated above. Neither principle alone is sufficient to account for the unacceptability of (25) and the concomitant acceptability of (26).[9]

1.4.2 Tag Questions

While to the best of my knowledge tag questions in English have never been the subject of a really detailed generative grammatical description, most investigators have assumed a transformation of Tag Formation more or less as follows:

(27) $(not) - NP - VP$
$$1 \quad 2 \quad 3 \ =>$$
$$\emptyset, \quad 2, \quad 3, \text{ WH}, 1, \left[\begin{array}{c} 2 \\ + PRO \end{array} \right], 3$$

Rule (27), in interaction with other grammatical rules, predicts the following distribution of grammatical and ungrammatical sentences:[10]

(28)   a.   John has been there already, hasn't he?
        b.   John hasn't been there already, has he?
        c.   John has been there already, has he?
        d.   *John hasn't been there already, hasn't he?

The facts surrounding the formation of tag questions in English provide strong evidence for the necessity of formal grammar. It is hard to imagine what extralinguistic principle could account for the highly idiosyncratic properties of this construction. Indeed, English tags are unique. Even closely related languages form tag questions by entirely different principles.

---

9. Bever (1970) and Kimball (1973) propose perceptual principles to account for multiply center-embedded constructions that differ somewhat from Chomsky and Miller's. Both proposals, however, are as modular in their structure as Chomsky and Miller's.

10. I am assuming that rule (27) would be followed by the rules of Negative Placement, Subject-Auxiliary Inversion, and Verb Phrase Deletion. Hence sentences with tags containing more than one auxiliary verb, such as *won't he have*, are generated. As it is stated, (27) allows tags to be formed from nonmatrix clauses (see R. Lakoff 1969a for examples of such tags). For interesting remarks on tag sentences, see Arbini (1969), Huddleston (1970), Culicover (1973, 1976), and Armagost (1974).

Robin Lakoff (1969a) observed that some sentences predicted to be grammatical by (27) sound distinctly strange:

(29)   a. I'm worried, aren't I?
        b. I suppose the Yankees will win the pennant, don't I?
        c. I think we'll be there by five o'clock, don't I?

The question is how linguistic theory should deal with such sentences. A nonmodular approach would be forced to build some restriction blocking (29a–c) directly into the tag rule. But what would such a restriction be? Notice that (29d–f) are completely acceptable:

(29)   d. I'm strong, aren't I?
        e. I denied that the Yankees won the pennant, didn't I?
        f. You think we'll be there by five o'clock, don't you?

While some restriction could conceivably be formulated, a moment's reflection indicates that it would be a mistake to block (29a–c) by any grammatical principle. Why *do* they sound peculiar? Quite simply, because it is pragmatically bizarre to question one's own current internal state to a second person. That is, these sentences are unacceptable for the same reason as those of (30):

(30)   a. Do I have heartburn?
        b. Am I thinking about leaving?

Now the inadvisability of a grammatical treatment of (29a–c) should be completely obvious. Their unacceptability is a consequence of the *interaction* of the rule of Tag Formation with the commonsense observation about questioning one's internal state. Neither the rule alone nor this observation alone is sufficient to explain the distribution of acceptable and unacceptable tag questions in English.

Pragmatic principles differ from grammatical rules in an important respect. Since they are the principles of normal human cooperative interaction, their effects can be "canceled" by the speaker for particular communicative purposes (see Grice 1975). So (29a), for example, can be made to sound quite acceptable when it is embedded in a context in which the speaker is eager to call attention to his or her state of mind:

(31)   How can you tell me I'm cold and unfeeling? I'm as concerned as you are about the situation—you know that. I'm worried, aren't I?

Grammatical rules, on the other hand, being immune to alteration by the situational context, are much less likely to have their effects canceled by the speaker. Thus it is hard to imagine the following sentence (which is predicted to be ungrammatical by rule [27]) occurring in *any* discourse:

(32)   *John has been drinking a lot lately, hasn't been he?

1.4.3   Indirect Speech Acts

Another area in which we find an interaction between grammatical principles and pragmatic ones is indirect speech acts—utterances that, taken literally, have senses quite different from those they are intended to convey. For example, (33) is literally an inquiry about the hearer's ability to perform a certain action.

(33)   Could you pass the salt?

Sentence (33), of course, *might* be taken as just such an inquiry, but is in fact more likely to be taken as a request to pass the salt. We find indirect speech acts of a wide variety of types. For example, a statement of one's sincerity can convey an offer, as in (34a), or a request, as in (34b); and a statement of one's ability can convey a threat, as in (34c):

(34)   a. I'd like very much to help you.
         b. I'd like the door opened.
         c. I could tear you limb from limb.

Searle (1975) has shown that there is a fair amount of systematicity governing the use of indirect speech acts. For example, in many cases one can convey a speech act of a particular type by questioning one's own preparedness to carry out the act involved. Thus (35a) can convey a request, (35b) an offer, and (35c) an exclamation of desire:

(35)   a. Can I use your help!
         b. Can I help you?
         c. Could I use a drink!

Along the same lines, Searle has illustrated that speech acts can be conveyed indirectly by asserting one's sincerity about the act's being carried out, by questioning the propositional content of the act, and in various other ways.

There are three strategies one might follow in an attempt to handle indirect speech acts in a comprehensive theory of language. The first would be to consider, following Gordon and Lakoff (1971), that all the relevant generalizations fall under the domain of formal grammar. There are severe difficulties, however, with a strictly grammatical approach. The first is that any grammatical theory with rules powerful enough to incorporate all the generalizations pertaining to indirect speech acts would have to be so unconstrained that it would be incapable of distinguishing correct and incorrect grammatical generalizations. For example, Gordon and Lakoff's analysis of sentences like (33–35) requires grammatical devices that are so powerful that the rules they propose violate every constraint governing the application of rules whose syntacticity is not open to question. Second, as Morgan (1977) has pointed out, grammatical treatments incorrectly predict that the conditions governing indirect speech acts have the same logical status as semantic entailments. And, finally and most significantly, a strictly grammatical treatment misses the point that important generalizations involving indirect speech acts are linguistic manifestations of *general* strategies of human interaction, which need not even involve language (see Sadock 1974 for general discussion). Thus one can communicate a request to be fed every bit as well by looking famished and rubbing one's stomach as by saying *I'm hungry*.

One might suggest, then, that the facts pertaining to indirect speech acts should be explained *entirely* by pragmatic principles. To my knowledge, nobody has ever made such a proposal, and it is easy to see why. Even a rudimentary description of the phenomenon demands a reference to syntactic structure (i.e., to the syntactic differences between declaratives, questions, imperatives, etc.). Since no pragmatic principle has ever been proposed to explain, say, why (36a) is a well-formed question in English but (36b) is not, it seems safe to dismiss an entirely pragmatics-based account of indirect speech acts:

(36)   a.   Has she been working very hard?
        b.   *Has been she working very hard?

The explanation of indirect speech acts obviously demands a modular approach to language. Syntactic rules generate the well-formed sentences of the language; semantic rules describe their literal interpretation as declaratives, interrogatives, imperatives, and so on; and pragmatic principles such as Searle's, which interact with both but are stated in nonlinguistic terms, help predict the use of sentences with a literal interpretation as one type of speech act to convey a speech act of a different type.

1.4.4   The Interpretation of Anaphoric Elements

All approaches to pronominal anaphora in recent years have assumed some degree of modularity. For example, neither Kuno's (1972) discourse-based conditions on anaphoric interpretation nor Reinhart's (1981) structural conditions are sufficient by themselves to account for all antecedent-anaphor linkages in English, nor are they intended to be. Rather, a full explanation of whether a particular pronoun may be taken to have a particular antecedent depends on both types of conditions, as well as a number of others (see, e.g., Partee 1972 for a discussion of some of the semantic conditions involved). Interesting further support for a modular approach to language based on anaphora is provided by Hust and Brame (1976) and by Lust, Loveland, and Kornet (1980). Hust and Brame argue that still another distinction is at work in the interpretation of sentences with anaphoric elements. This is the distinction between the relation of *construal*, by which a term is associated with an anaphor, and the judgment of *coreference*, by which a term and an anaphor are understood to pick out the same referent. These relations can be understood only in terms of two interacting systems: observe that construal may exist without coreference, as in (37a), and coreference may exist without construal, as in (37b):

(37)   a. John gave *his Christmas bonus* to the United Way, but Mary kept *it*.
        b. *John* saw *him* (the murderer) and John was the only one who could have been present.

Hust and Brame argue that the nature of the two relations is distinct: construal is an essentially grammatical relation, based on structural principles; coreference assignment, on the other hand, is based on extragrammatical factors such as the discourse plausibility of a pronoun's being linked to a particular antecedent.

Lust, Loveland, and Kornet (1980) find additional evidence for the construal/coreference distinction from their studies of first language acquisition. They show that the distinction is supported by the fact that in early stages of acquisition construal is constrained by a principle—the directionality constraint—that has no effect on judgment of coreference. (The directionality constraint states that a pronoun must follow its antecedent.) In other words, it is even clearer in child speech than in adult speech that two distinct, though interacting, systems are at work. Lust, Loveland, and Kornet conclude:

> Our developmental results, summarized above, confirm that children appear to be sensitive to *both* syntactic and pragmatic factors in anaphora from the early stages of language development. Although these factors are independent, our developmental results suggest that the interrelation of these independent domains may change with development. The syntactic factor which constrains directionality of anaphora at early stages of language development is modified at later levels when the child learns to modulate direction of anaphora in accord with the syntax of the specific language being heard. . . . When this specific syntactic acquisition is achieved, it may override the effects of pragmatic context on interpretation of anaphora, as it may in adult grammar. (1980, 388–89; emphasis in original)

1.5   Some Troublesome Concepts

This section treats those central concepts of grammatical theory for which generativists have received the most criticism over the years. I hope clarifying them will (at least) remove whatever share of resistance to the theory is based on misunderstanding rather than principled disagreement.

1.5.1   Competence and Performance

Probably no notion within grammatical theory has aroused more controversy than the competence/performance distinction. Criticism of the distinction ranges from the assertion that it is "almost incoherent" (Labov 1972a, 110) to the conclusion that it is coherent enough, yet "too confining" (Clark and Haviland 1974, 92), since so many systematic aspects of language do not fall under the generativists' conception of competence. Indeed, it seems fair to say that the typical attack on grammatical theory both begins and ends with the competence/performance distinction.

"Linguistic competence" is no more than the name for the nonreducible core of language—those aspects of language that form the autonomous purely *linguistic* system characterized by a formal grammar. In other words, our competence is our tacit knowledge of the structure of our language. Let me emphasize that many things we "know" about language do not fall under competence as thus defined. For example, we know that saying *I'm hungry* can convey a request to be fed, and we know we should devoice our consonants and vowels when speaking in a library. This sort of knowledge is *not* competence, because it is not strictly linguistic. The generalizations underlying this knowledge undoubtedly fall within the domains of cooperative communication and proper social behavior.

"Linguistic performance" refers to "the actual use of language in concrete situations" (Chomsky 1965, 4).[11] There hardly exists an aspect of performance to which competence does not contribute. One could not describe fully (much less explain) a particular instance of whispering in a library without reference to the speaker's grammar any more than without reference to the social convention of silence in libraries. Even memorized formulaic expressions (for discussion see Fillmore 1979; Vihman 1982) are not free from the effects of linguistic competence. As Cooper and Ross (1975) demonstrate, the order of elements in frozen conjuncts (*bigger and better, fore and aft, kit and caboodle*, etc.) is determined in part by highly abstract grammatical conditions—conditions that productively constrain newly coined expressions.

Just as all nonmarginal linguistic phenomena demand a theory of competence for their explanation, it seems inconceivable that any aspect of language use could owe its explanation *only* to competence. After all, competence simply represents the speaker's *knowledge* of linguistic structure. Explaining speech production therefore requires a model of lan-

11. Confusingly, generativists have also used "performance" in a much more restricted sense. At times it has been used to refer only to the perceptual and processing mechanisms facilitating the use of grammars (see Chomsky 1965, 15; Kean 1981a, 175). This ambiguity has created problems (see section 5.2.3).

guage in which the competence model is supplemented with other explanatory devices. Thus it seems odd that many critics of grammatical theory seem to feel one can refute the theory simply by demonstrating that there is more to language than competence. For example, Oller (1977) gives an example of a syntactically well-formed but semantically deviant sentence (*the theory of relativity is blue*) and shows how it can be given a metaphorical interpretation. He concludes from the fact that this interpretation is dependent upon the context of utterance that he has refuted the generativist claim "that meaning is independent of settings" (45). But it seems to me, rather, that his example *supports* the claim. The point is that if our competence did not supply a "normal" reading for that sentence, how would we even recognize it as metaphorical? How would we know that it differs fundamentally from *the book is blue*? The notion of "metaphor" depends crucially on the conception of the autonomy of certain aspects of meaning with respect to extralinguistic setting. Without question, any adequate theory of metaphor must deal with the interaction of linguistic competence with whatever human faculties are involved in symbolic behavior.

Once these points are understood, it seems that another pervasive objection to competence (represented in the following quotation) simply disappears:

> many linguists have come to find the study of linguistic competence . . . too confining. There are simply too many interesting linguistic phenomena that do not fit under this rather small umbrella, yet are amenable to linguistic investigation . . . problems such as the structure of conversations . . . , the relation of meaning to context . . . , the perceptual difficulty of surface structures . . . , the production of speech errors and speech hesitations . . . , and other similar phenomena. (Clark and Haviland 1974, 92)

Clark and Haviland's remarks are typical of a class of arguments used against generativists having (very roughly) the following structure:

First premise: Generativists believe everything that is systematic about language falls under the heading of "competence."

Second premise: Many aspects of language are highly systematic, yet fundamentally different in their nature from those things generativists have wished to encompass under "competence."

Conclusion: The traditional generativist notion of "competence" must be expanded to the point where it all but equals performance, or else rejected entirely.

While the conclusion is not unreasonable, given the premises, the argument nevertheless does not go through because the first premise is incorrect. Systematicity alone is not sufficient to qualify a phenomenon for a treatment wholly within the sphere of grammatical competence. Rather, as we have already seen, most complex phenomena (such as those described by Clark and Haviland) owe their explanation to the interaction of the competence model with the cognitive and other systems at work in giving language its overall character.

The quotation above also reveals another attitude that pervades the critical literature—that generativists consider *uninteresting* and unworthy of study any phenomena "that do not fit under this rather small umbrella." I will discuss the basis for this wholly mistaken attitude in chapter 5.

Another common dissatisfaction with the competence/performance distinction is that, for any given linguistic phenomenon, no hard-and-fast criterion exists to decide which aspects of that phenomenon should fall under competence. Some linguists (e.g., Naro 1980, 165) have explicitly avoided referring to the distinction for that reason. But it is unlikely that such a criterion will *ever* exist. As new phenomena are discovered (and as the implications of old ones become better understood), the relevant theories will no doubt be modified, and a phenomenon that at one time was granted a competence explanation might well at a later point be subsumed under performance (or vice versa). But, still, *enough* is known about the systems interacting in language that the role competence plays in a particular phenomenon is often clear. It hardly seems likely, for example, that the fact that in most English dialects two modal auxiliaries do not follow each other pertains to anything but competence, or that the fact that one does not normally shout obscene expletives in church has any explanation but a performance one. It is not surprising that there exist many borderline cases, such as the variation phenomena discussed by Naro, given the state of development of linguistic theory. They pose an exciting challenge to researchers—a challenge whose resolution might well involve redrawing the boundaries of linguistic competence.

Dissatisfaction with the generativist characterization of "competence" and "performance" has led a number of linguists to apply the notion of a speaker's "competence" to a far broader range of abilities than the sort of grammatical knowledge outlined above. In particular, the term "communicative competence" has become fashionable. I believe it was Dell Hymes who first coined it as "the most general term for the speaking and hearing capabilities of a person" (1971, 16). A broadened notion of competence (communicative or other) was soon applied to such capacities as the ability of bilinguals to switch languages appropriately (Gumperz 1972); the proper control of stylistic registers (White 1974); the ability of readers to fathom aspects of literature properly (Culler 1975);[12]

---

12. Culler (1975) extends, metaphorically, virtually all of the technical vocabulary of linguistic theory to literary analysis, including "structural description" and "descriptive adequacy."

the use of language by doctors in emergency wards (Candlin, Leather, and Bruton 1976); and much more.

"Communicative competence" is an unfortunate term because it creates a pernicious ambiguity where none existed. In general, the least productive debates imaginable are those over terminology, and no one would deny, given the ordinary English sense of the term, that successful communicative behavior reflects "competence" in certain types of knowledge and ability. But the question naturally arises whether a model of "communicative competence" is intended to replace or simply to complement a "competence model" in the generativists' sense.[13] Hymes and, I believe, most others who write of "communicative competence" reject the idea of a narrower, strictly grammatical competence. However, a number of others who use this term do not do so. As I understand their positions, Widdowson (1971), Corder and Roulet (1973), Fraser (1977), Spolsky (1978), and Allen (1978) posit *both* types of competence. Since in the generativist view the question of the existence and nature of grammatical competence is central, the use of a technical term that, through its ambiguity, glosses over this question introduces a confusion of the highest order.

1.5.2   Linguistic Universals

The term "universal grammar" is used to refer to that which is true of language by biological necessity.[14] Hence universal grammar is "taken to be the set of properties, conditions, or whatever that constitute the 'initial state' of the language learner, hence the basis on which knowledge of language develops" (Chomsky 1980, 69).

Particular aspects of universal grammar have typically been motivated by reference to the poverty of the stimulus available to the child language learner.[15] How could the child have learned such-and-such a principle inductively, one reasons, given its abstractness, the limited amount of relevant information provided, and the speed of acquisition?

To give a concrete example, consider Chomsky's argument (1975b) that the structure-dependent nature of grammatical rules is an aspect of

13. See Canale and Swain (1980) for discussion of this problem.

14. As James McCawley has pointed out (personal communication), something can be true by biological necessity without being universal, just as there is biologically determined individual variation in the fine details of all anatomical structures. However, at present no concrete evidence exists for such individual variation in biologically determined aspects of grammars.

15. Generativists have also referred to the *degeneracy* of the data available to the child, though they have never considered this crucial. Commentators have consistently exaggerated the degree to which Chomsky attributes degeneracy to the data. For example, Labov (1970b, 36) claims Chomsky believes that "95 percent" of the sentences the child hears are ungrammatical. Labov puts this figure in quotation marks but without an accompanying citation. The truth is that Chomsky has never published such a figure.

universal grammar. Chomsky reasons as follows: Suppose one observes that a child learning English unerringly forms questions such as (38b) and (39b) from declaratives such as (38a) and (39a):

(38)   a. The man is tall.
       b. Is the man tall?

(39)   a. The book is on the table.
       b. Is the book on the table?

Two incompatible hypotheses suggest themselves to account for this behavior:

(40)   *Hypothesis 1*: The child processes the declarative sentence from its first word (i.e., from "left to right"), continuing until the first occurrence of the word 'is' (or others like it: 'may', 'will', etc.); the child then preposes this occurrence of 'is', producing the corresponding question (with some concomitant modifications of form that need not concern us).

(41)   *Hypothesis 2*: The child analyzes the declarative sentence into abstract phrases; then locates the first occurrence of 'is' (etc.) that follows the first noun phrase; and then preposes this occurrence of 'is', forming the corresponding question.

However, one further observes that the child forms question (42b)—never (42c)—from declarative (42a):

(42)   a. The man who is tall is in the room.
       b. Is the man who is tall in the room?
       c. Is the man who tall is in the room?

Thus the child makes use of the structure-dependent rule postulated in hypothesis 2, rather than the simpler structure-independent rule of hypothesis 1. Why should this be?:

> There seems to be no explanation in terms of "communicative efficiency" or similar considerations. It is certainly absurd to argue that children are trained to use the structure-dependent rule, in this case. In fact, the problem never arises in language learning. A person may go through a considerable part of his life without ever facing relevant evidence, but he will have no hesitation in using the structure-dependent rule, even if all of his experience is consistent with hypothesis 1. The only reasonable conclusion is that [universal grammar] contains the principle that all such rules must be structure-dependent. That is, the child's mind . . . contains the instruction: Construct a structure-dependent rule, ignoring all structure-independent rules. The principle of structure-dependence is not learned, but forms part of the conditions for language learning. (Chomsky 1975b, 32–33)

Thus the attempt to overthrow the notion of "linguistic universal" (or render it uninteresting) by hypothesizing the possible common origins of all languages (see Putnam 1967; Hiż 1967) simply misses the point. Whether the extant languages of the world have one ancestor or four thousand, the problem for the child is the same: to construct a grammar on the basis of the limited input available (for more discussion of the issues raised by structure-dependence for a theory of linguistic universals, see section 4.2.2).

Since conclusions of universality are drawn from hypotheses about the nature of language acquisition, it does not thereby follow that any feature common to all the languages of the world is a property of universal grammar. As Lightfoot has pointed out: "There may be universals which arise independently of innate principles: it may be a universal that every language has a word for 'arm' or that no language has more than 30 monosyllabic palindromes, but it would be wrong to attribute these universals to properties of Universal Grammar" (1981, 165).

The structure dependence of rules is a property for which evidence in fact *can* be found in every language in the world. Does it follow that every putative universal *must* be instantiated in every language? Not at all. For example, for each type of grammatical rule (transformations, deletions, filters, etc.) there may well be universal properties governing the behavior of rules of that type. Yet it may be that not all languages manifest all rule types. If a language had no deletion rules, one would hardly wish to conclude that the facts of that language "falsify" some claim about the universal properties of such rules.

Another logical possibility is that a universal hypothesized on the basis of examining one or more languages may actually seem to be *counterexemplified* by another. Indeed, it is difficult to find a single issue of a journal devoted to theoretical linguistics that does not contain an article purporting to show that some proposed constraint on grammars (C) does not work for some language (L). Needless to say, there could be many reasons why C seems not to apply to L. One might be simply that C is incorrect—a different principle might handle the same range of facts in the languages first investigated that does not overgeneralize to make incorrect predictions for L. Or perhaps the analysis of L is faulty, being based on a too-superficial look at its structure (I believe this is a common occurrence—see chap. 2 for discussion). Or, as a third possibility, perhaps C is a correct linguistic universal and L *does* counterexemplify it. Naturally the burden would fall on one taking this position to show that those aspects of L inconsistent with C pose "special" problems for the language learner, which might manifest themselves (for example) in terms of a high rate of production errors or late acquisition. The next decade is likely to see quite a bit of research addressed to this possibility (for a discussion of some of the problems involved, see Smith 1981).

1.5.3   Simplicity and Evaluation

Science, by definition, is the search for order in nature. Scientists take it for granted that their goal is to formulate the most elegant (i.e., the most order-reflecting) hypotheses possible, consistent with the data, about the particular area under investigation. Although philosophers extensively debate scientific methods and the ontological status of scientific constructs, this general point has hardly been questioned.

Linguistics, then, is the search for order in language. The goal of linguistics is to formulate the most elegant hypotheses possible about how language works, consistent with the data. No formula exists for how to do this, nor is there an automatic decision procedure for picking out one of several competing theories as more elegant than the others. Yet certain points, I think, are uncontroversial. One is that, given two theories that cover the same range of facts, the one in which the facts follow from a small number of general principles is better than the one that embodies myriad separate statements and auxiliary hypotheses. Another is that it is methodologically correct to reduce redundancy *within* a theory; to reduce the number of postulates while preserving the scope of the predictions.

Scientists (including linguists) often talk about "simplifying" a theory or about constructing a theory with greater "simplicity." Generally they mean a less redundant theory, as described above. "Simplicity" in that sense is distinct from the "simplicity measure" (or "evaluation metric") as used within linguistic theory. The "simplicity measure" is a construct of the theory itself and is evaluated like any other construct (a proposed constraint, a substantive universal, etc.). To be specific, the "simplicity measure" is the function that, within a particular theoretical framework, picks out a particular grammar from the set of possible grammars compatible with the data. For example, the idea of a "simplicity measure" is often implicit in the choice of notational conventions. The parentheses notation for collapsing rules is a good example. This notation was devised so that, given two analyses—one employing parentheses and one not—the former would be more directly reflective of linguistic generalizations and also be shorter. What sort of rule-collapsing notations to employ is a wholly empirical question. Kiparsky (1968a) pointed out that a convention could be devised to shorten the derivation (43) to the simpler (in length) statement (44):

(43)   A→B
       B→C

(44)   A→|B|→C

As Kiparsky noted, no such convention should be incorporated into the theory because the "| |" notation is an *incorrect* evaluation metric. In this case the shorter derivations that result from its use do not reflect true generalizations about linguistic processes.

Just as the choice of the best simplicity measure is an empirical question, it is an empirical question whether such a measure can be devised for all rule subsystems within a grammar. While recent developments in the theory of markedness (see, e.g., Kean 1975, 1981b) have led to some progress in answering this question, much remains to be accomplished.

Quite often, what superficially appears to be a critique of the simplicity measure turns out on close examination to be a rejection of scientific linguistics itself. The following quotation lends itself to such an interpretation:

> The Chomskian school, developing an economic metaphor, has implied that exceptions to grammatical rules should be very "costly," and therefore, rules should be constructed so as to yield the smallest number of exceptions possible. Like latter-day counterparts of Karl Verner, transformational grammarians have implied that actual language can be wholly generated by rules; our task is to find them. There have, however, been many schools of linguistics which have [correctly] rejected the Chomskian cost-benefit analysis of language. (Baron 1981, 84)

Baron's phraseology suggests that she is opposed to some particular evaluation metric internal to grammatical theory. But consider the *content* of the rejection of the idea that "rules should be constructed so as to yield the smallest number of exceptions possible." It is no less than the rejection of the goal of finding as much systematicity as exists in language. Perhaps some linguists would be content with a description of a language in which rules were stated with large numbers of exceptions, even though it could be demonstrated that the exceptions disappear given an alternative statement of the rules. But such an attitude, it seems to me, represents the abandonment of a scientific perspective on language.[16]

1.5.4   Psychological Reality

Any theory that is based on psychological data and has as its principal goal the explanation of those data is ipso facto a psychological theory. A theory that does this *correctly* is a theory with "psychological reality"; a theory that fails to accomplish this lacks psychological reality.

Now where does grammatical theory fit into this picture? Largely, but not exclusively, its data base has been speakers' introspections about the well-formedness and interpretation of sentences (see chap. 2 for extensive discussion of introspective data). Surely introspections count as psychological data if anything does. If that were all there were to it, then

---

16. For a survey of, and replies to, various critiques of the simplicity measure, see White (1980, 1981).

the constructs of grammatical theory could be considered psychologically real to the extent that they correctly explained such data.

But that is *not* all there is to it. Introspections are only one of many potential sources of psychological data about language. Data from studies of speech perception and sentence processing also count as psychological data. So do data gleaned from observations of aphasic speech, speech errors, and the acquisition of language by native and nonnative speakers. And so, one might add, do the results of any experiment carried out in the psychology laboratory exploring some aspect of verbal behavior. A psychologically real theory of grammar must therefore be judged on more than its ability to explain speakers' intuitions; it must be shown to be compatible with *all* these sources of data.[17]

Unfortunately, one finds in the literature—especially in the literature critical of generativist theory—the notion of "psychological reality" used in an extremely narrow way. As Wexler and Culicover have observed, it is common practice to label a concept " 'psychologically real' [only] if it plays a particular kind of role in a particular kind of experimental procedure (or perhaps psychological process like remembering)" (1980, 44). A paper by Steinberg and Krohn (1975) exemplifies this practice. Their goal is to test the psychological reality of the Vowel Shift Rule of Chomsky and Halle (1968). They claim (without providing justification) that if the rule is psychologically real, then subjects will perform in a particular way in a particular experiment they have designed. After discovering that subjects do *not* perform in that way, they conclude that "C & H's claim that the VSR is a psychologically real and general rule is therefore highly dubious" (252). No explanation is given of why this procedure should tap the reality they seek any better than an observation of language change, a conclusion that might be drawn from a speech error, a linguist's introspective judgment, or whatever. This is not to say that their results might not be relevant to grammatical theory. Rather, one must question why they feel their experimental results should be given *primacy* over the multitude of other pieces of evidence that bear on the question of the correct (i.e., psychologically real) theory of grammar.[18]

The question, then, is whether psychological data in general tend to bear out the essential claims of grammatical theory, or whether only introspective data do so. Since the mid-1960s, a great number of psycho-

17. Which is not to say that all these sources of data must necessarily be referred to when *constructing* a theory of grammar. How one should go about constructing a theory, and how one should evaluate it, are two very different questions (see Chomsky 1957, 49ff. for discussion of this point).

18. Cena (1977), on the other hand, claims to have demonstrated on the basis of an experiment *he* carried out that the Vowel Shift Rule *is* "psychologically real" (for discussion, see McCawley 1979). Fromkin (1975), Kiparsky (1975), and Black and Chiat (1981) discuss the general problems of experimental testing for "psychological reality."

linguists have concluded that the evidence from studies of language processing suggests that grammatical theory is *not* psychologically real. I will review this evidence below, then discuss how the results might be interpreted without leading to such a negative conclusion.

The challenge to the psychological reality of grammatical theory based on the facts of language processing has depended in large part on a presumed hypothesis of the relation between the grammar and the parser known as the "derivational theory of complexity" (DTC). The DTC posits an isomorphic relation between the grammatical steps involved in generating a sentence and the real time steps of the processing mechanism. In this view, if a certain sequence of operations (say, transformations) applies in the grammar in a particular order, then the processor's operations will mirror those steps.

Many investigators have pointed out ways that the DTC appears to be incompatible with particular generativist claims. For example, Fodor and Garrett (1967) showed that phrases with prenominal modifiers such as *the red book* take no more time to parse than *the book that is red*, despite the then-current syntactic analysis of these phrases, in which two more transformations applied in the derivation of the former. Likewise, Fodor and Garrett (1967) and Watt (1970) found that short passives such as *John was seen* are no more difficult to process than long passives such as *John was seen by someone*, despite the generativist analysis that derived the former from the latter by transformation. And Slobin (1966b) found that, despite the hypothesized existence of a passive transformation, subjects took no longer to respond to scenes depicted by passive sentences than to those depicted by actives. Since, at least initially, neither the DTC nor the specific grammatical analyses were questioned, these experimental findings tended to cast doubt on the psychological reality of the theory incorporating these analyses.

More recently, other sorts of experimental data have been cited as evidence that grammatical theory is at odds with processing facts and hence lacks psychological reality. For example, Bransford and Franks (1971) presented subjects with sentences such as (45):

(45)   Three turtles rested on a log and the fish swam beneath them.

In a subsequent recognition task, subjects believed they heard (46a) as often as (46b):

(46)   a. The fish swam beneath the log.
        b. The fish swam beneath the turtles.

Since the deep structure of (46a) is not represented in the deep structure of (45), Bransford and Franks concluded that meaning was inferred by use of extralinguistic knowledge such as real-world spatial relations, rather than being based on a stored grammatical representation.

A set of experiments conducted by Tyler and Marslen-Wilson (1977) have been interpreted as a challenge to the generativist autonomy hypothesis. Essentially, they showed that subjects' decisions in tasks involving the completion of a sentence are influenced both by their knowledge of the syntactic structure of the sentence and by the sentence's meaning. Subjects showed greater hesitation in completing (47b) than (47a), a reflection, it seems, both of the semantics of the context clause and the structural ambiguity of the initial portion of the following clause:

(47)   a. If you walk too near the runway, landing planes are . . .
         b. If you've been trained as a pilot, landing planes are . . .

By the mid-1970s these results had led many psycholinguists to conclude, with Watt (1974), that the psychologically real "mental grammar" must necessarily differ from the "linguistic grammar" proposed by generative grammarians. This conclusion, of course, tended to enlarge the gulf between generativists and psycholinguists. As Thomas Roeper has observed, "when psychological evidence has failed to conform to linguistic theory, psychologists have concluded that linguistic theory was wrong, while linguists have concluded that psychological theory was irrelevant" (1982, 468).

It seems to me, however, that the negative conclusions based on processing studies about the psychological reality of grammatical theory are not compelling. To begin with, even granting the correctness of the DTC, the arguments related to prenominal adjectives and short passives have ceased to have any force. This is because virtually no syntacticians today wish to derive prenominal adjectives by transformation from relative clauses or short passives by transformation from long passives (see Williams 1975 for arguments against the former transformational derivation and Bresnan 1972 for arguments against the latter). The derivations assumed for these constructions today are not in conflict with the DTC.

But, more fundamentally, there is no reason to take it for granted that the DTC is correct. Berwick and Weinberg (1983) discuss at length several alternative views of the grammar/parser interface that are compatible *both* with claims about the grammar that are widely accepted by generativists and with what is known about how speakers process sentences. In particular, they show that Slobin's findings, discussed above, can easily be accommodated if the computational power of the processor is expanded to allow a certain amount of nonseriality (concurrent processing), a hypothesis argued for on independent grounds in Marcus (1980). Furthermore, Berwick and Weinberg argue that the Tyler and Marslen-Wilson (1977) results show only that the sentence *processor* might have simultaneous access to syntactic and semantic representations; their results have no bearing at all on whether the syntactic and semantic components of the *grammar* are discrete—that is, they have no bearing on the autonomy hypothesis (this point is also made in Dresher and Hornstein 1976 and Valian 1979).

Carlson and Tanenhaus (1982) discuss a distinction whose implications challenge the conclusions of Bransford and Franks (1971) referred to above. This is the distinction between "on-line" and "off-line" experimental tasks. On-line tasks are performed simultaneously with sentence processing, while off-line tasks are performed after the sentence has been presented. Carlson and Tanenhaus present evidence that the contribution of formal grammar is manifest only during on-line tasks; after a certain (short) period, extragrammatical factors predominate. Hence, Bransford and Franks's off-line experiment may not be relevant in determining whether speakers utilize grammatical representations when processing a sentence.

Furthermore, there are experimental results suggesting that the principal components of a generative grammar *are* reflected by distinct processing components. For example, Forster (1979) reports that when subjects are presented with a class of sentence pairs that differ in some minimal way, their response times in determining that the sentences are different show a significant effect of grammaticality, but not of plausibility. Thus there is some evidence for distinct syntactic and semantic processors. Other experimental tasks, Forster has found, are insensitive to *both* syntactic and semantic variables and rely only on an autonomous lexical parser. This is in accord with the findings of Tanenhaus, Leiman, and Seidenberg (1979), who have investigated lexical ambiguity in syntactic contexts. They presented ambiguous words in a context that selected either a noun or a verb reading (e.g., 'they all *rose*', 'they bought a *rose*'). Immediately after this presentation, subjects were presented with a target word related to either the appropriate or the inappropriate reading of the ambiguous word (e.g., *flower* or *stood*). Under these conditions, subjects showed equal facilitation of both the related and the unrelated readings. After a short delay, however, only the appropriate reading continued to show facilitation. This seems to suggest the existence of an autonomous lexicon, in which lexical items are stored independent of their meanings. It takes a speaker some time to coordinate the information stored in this lexicon with information drawn from the extralexical context.

As is testified by the spate of recent articles in journals like *Cognition, Cognitive Psychology,* and *Journal of Verbal Learning and Verbal Behavior,* and by collections like Halle, Bresnan, and Miller (1978) and Cooper and Walker (1979), interest in probing the grammar/processor interrelation is greater than ever before. The results of this work are certainly relevant to the psychological reality of the grammarian's constructs, but they have no privileged status. To reinforce this point, let

me conclude with a perceptive cautionary statement by Carlson and
Tanenhaus:

> The field [of psycholinguistics] has occasionally labored under the
> illusion that psycholinguistic evidence has some special properties
> which can decree the validity of given linguistic theories or analyses.
> But this is, quite simply, the wrong level of comparison. What psycho-
> linguists must look for are interesting convergences between linguistic
> theory and a theory of sentence processing. In order to make this
> comparison, one must, obviously, have reasonably well-elaborated
> theories to compare. While there are such linguistic theories presently
> available, there are at present no theories of processing that can be
> meaningfully compared to the linguistic theories. . . . It is the task of
> psycholinguistics to develop processing theory along lines that will be
> comparable to linguistics. When such theories become available, then
> and only then can serious connections be made between psychology
> and linguistics—only at this level of abstraction will any significant
> convergences be discovered. Once this level is achieved, we feel the
> result will be a set of insights into natural language not otherwise
> attainable. (1982, 57–58)

2 The Data Base of Grammatical Theory

2.1 The Value of Introspective Data

The typical practice of generativists has been to use themselves as informants in collecting data about the acceptability and interpretation of grammatical constructions. Indeed, personal introspection more often than not represents the *sole* source of data for a linguist doing syntactic work in his or her native language. This method of collecting data has been subject to heavy criticism, from both inside and outside the field of linguistics. More than a few commentators have concluded that the nature of the data base renders suspect all generativist theoretical claims and even vitiates grammatical theory's claim to be a science. Others recognize the usefulness of introspective data collection in principle but feel that it has been relied upon too heavily and that the time has come to take a more "experimental" approach to the primary data.

In this chapter I will defend the normal generativist practice of using oneself as an informant. Bowing to popular usage, I will reserve the term "introspective data" for the results of such self-informant work. Data collected through experiments with linguistically naive subjects will be referred to as "experimental data," though one must keep it in mind that the purpose of many experiments is to elicit the subjects' "introspections" about acceptability and interpretation.

The use of introspective data is hardly a generativist innovation, nor are present-day generativists alone in relying on it.[1] In fact, dismissing such data is tantamount to dismissing work ranging from the ancient

1. Joseph Emonds has pointed out (personal communication) that the intensive exploitation of introspectively collected *unacceptable* sentences for theoretical purposes does seem to have originated with the generativist model.

Sanskrit and Greek grammarians to every modern school of linguistics. If generativists seem more "extreme" in their reliance on introspection than followers of other schools, it is only because they use it more intensively and creatively and with greater positive effect. Even the most vocal critics of introspective data have been happy to acknowledge the positive consequences of its use:

> This methodological revolution [of giving priority to introspective evidence] has gained support on the positive side from the great success of generative grammar in discovering new facts about English syntax, developing new grammatical formulations, and uncovering deeper theoretical problems. (Labov 1971, 438)

> This standard method [of data collection] has been enormously successful: Linguists have produced precise and interesting theories about syntax and semantics; and the bulk of the data on which these theories depend is undisputed and, we believe, undisputable. (Carden and Dieterich 1981, 1)

The number of things we can honestly say we *know* about grammar has increased astronomically since 1957. Consider, for example, the following ten generalizations about syntactic processes in English. The "methodological revolution" of intensive use of introspective data, not experimentation or naturalistic observation of performance, led to all of them:

1. No verb occurs in the dative passive construction unless it independently occurs both in the dative and in the passive.
2. Structural conditions limit the cases in which a pronoun can be interpreted as coreferential to a noun phrase it precedes.
3. The grammaticality of sentences like *John is believed to have left* and the ungrammaticality of **John is believable to have left* is related to the fact that the suffix on *believe* in the former is inflectional, while that in the latter is derivational.
4. No element in a relative clause may be questioned: *the man who ate poison died*, but **what did the man who ate die?*
5. The "easy-to-please" construction is impossible if the adjective is followed by *both* a dative phrase and a subject *for*-phrase: *the hard work is pleasant for the rich to do*, but **the hard work is pleasant for the rich for the poor to do*.
6. Contraction of *want* and a following *to* to *wanna* is blocked under structurally specifiable conditions.
7. There are far more grammatical processes that manifest themselves only in main clauses than only in subordinate clauses.
8. Passive noun phrases of the form NP_1's N by NP_2 are more restricted in their distribution than corresponding passive sentences of the form NP_1 was Ved by NP_2: *the answer was known by John* but **the answer's knowledge by John*.

9. Adjective-complement constructions do not have corresponding adverb-complement constructions: *fond of his children*, but **fondly of his children*.
10. In a subordinate clause with an understood (i.e., nonpresent) subject, the antecedent of that subject is normally the closest noun phrase in the main clause.

This list barely scratches the surface of the positive results of introspection; I suspect that any generativist could come up with an entirely different list given fifteen minutes' thought.

A second—and uncontroversial—reason for using introspective data is that they are the *easiest* data to obtain. There are no complex experiments to design and carry out, no sophisticated apparatus to buy and maintain, no subjects to recruit and instruct, and no time-consuming statistical analyses to perform. Generativists working on their own language can collect as much relevant and interesting data by introspection in an hour as it would take a psychologist (say) to collect by experiment in a month.

Finally—and highly controversially—generativists have typically felt that introspection is the *most reliable* source of data. I will argue that this feeling is probably grounded in truth and show that the defects attributed to introspective data have been vastly exaggerated while the reliability—and relevance—of the experimental data collected to date is itself highly suspect.

2.2 Conflicting Analyses, Not Conflicting Judgments

Are the grammarian's introspective judgments about the well-formedness of sentences to be trusted as data? A view popular among—though not limited to—sociolinguists holds that they are not. William Labov, for example, believes that "the studies of introspective judgments carried out so far show that variation in this field is widespread, uncontrolled, and chaotic" (1975, 14) and that "intuitive data has been found increasingly faulty as a support for our theoretical constructions" (6). When we look carefully at the examples cited to support these assertions, however, we find that they fail to establish a case for the unreliability of personal introspection. The vast majority of the examples that superficially appear to reflect disagreements about the data (and hence an unreliable data base) turn out on close inspection to reflect disagreements about the correct *analysis* of the sentences in question.

2.2.1 *Grammaticality and Acceptability*

Before I discuss concrete examples of supposed data disagreements, an important theoretical distinction must be made absolutely clear: that between *grammaticality* and *acceptability*. "Grammaticality" is a theoretical term; a sentence is "grammatical" if it is generated by the grammar, "ungrammatical" if it is not. In other words, the question of a sentence's grammaticality makes sense only with respect to a particular formal representation of an individual's competence, every bit as much as do the questions whether a particular rule is ordered before another or whether a lexical item has a particular subcategorization feature. Since "grammaticality," as thus understood, is a theoretical construct, it is not directly accessible to the intuitions of the speaker of the language. A speaker no more has intuitions about the grammaticality of a sentence than about whether the sentence *John gave Sue the book* is formed by a lexical rule or a transformational rule, or whether the proper level to state conditions governing antecedent-anaphor relations is surface structure. For this reason it is a mistake to refer to a "grammaticality judgment"—a mistake generativists make as often as anyone else.[2] While *as linguists* we might very well have an intuition (i.e., a hunch based on professional experience) that a sentence is grammatical, just as a chemist, say, might have an intuition that an unanalyzed compound contains zirconium, there is no such thing as a *native speaker's* intuition about grammaticality.

"Acceptability," on the other hand, is the appropriate term for the feelings speakers have about the well-formedness of sentences in their language. That is, speakers *do* have intuitions about acceptability and are able to make acceptability judgments. Judgments of acceptability, like other forms of complex behavior, are influenced by a multitude of factors. One of these factors, of course, is the speaker's internalized grammar (competence). That most speakers of English would (I suspect) find the sentence *the squirrel climbed up the tree* acceptable and the sentence *tree the up climbed squirrel the* unacceptable no doubt reflects fairly directly their linguistic competence. However, speakers are also prone to give acceptability judgments that depart both from their linguistic competence and from their everyday use of language. Thus people will find sentences unacceptable if they contain taboo words or nonstandard forms, and so on even though they commonly use such sentences. Conversely, speakers have been known to give favorable judgments to sentences that are demonstrably not part of their (nonstandard) dialects or that belong to stylistic registers they do not control.

Whether a sentence is generated by one's grammar, then, is only one of many factors involved in determining whether one will judge it acceptable. In addition to the attitudinal factors described above, cognitive and pragmatic systems also interact with the grammar to prevent the relationship between the two concepts from being one-to-one. As we saw in

---

2. Generativists have also been rather sloppy in their use of the asterisk to mark deviant sentences. While many are careful to precede with an asterisk only those sentences they claim to be ungrammatical, many others use the asterisk before *any* unacceptable sentence.

section 1.4, it makes sense to postulate the grammaticality of certain unacceptable sentences (*the rat the cat the dog chased ate died; I'm worried, aren't I?*), since the most elegant account of their ill-formedness involves the interaction of general linguistic principles with principles from outside the domain of grammar proper. By the same token, one need not assume that any acceptable sentence is ipso facto grammatical. Speakers might well have reasons for using sentences that are not generated by their grammars. For example, Otero (1972) argues that acceptable and widely heard Spanish sentences such as *se alquilan los apartamentos* are ungrammatical, and Langendoen and Bever (1973) make the same claim for sentences in English containing the *not un-* construction (as in *a not unhappy person entered the room*).

Only in the simplest cases does the conclusion that a sentence is ungrammatical follow directly from a judgment that it is unacceptable. While one can often assume that the syntactician regards as acceptable the sentences claimed to be grammatical and as unacceptable the sentences claimed to be ungrammatical, this does not have to be so. As a consequence, if two linguists disagree about the grammaticality of a sentence, it is incorrect to conclude that they necessarily disagree about the data (about the sentence's acceptability), though that might be a point of contention as well. But it is very likely that the heart of their disagreement is whether some crucial property of the sentence should be explained by a grammatical principle or an extragrammatical one.

To take a concrete example, consider the contrast between sentences (1a) and (1b):

(1)   a. That he left is a surprise.
        b. He left is a surprise.

Sentence (1a), which contains an embedded sentence in subject position headed by the complementizer *that*, is of unquestioned acceptability and grammaticality. Sentence (1b), which is identical to (1a) except for the nonpresence of *that*, is of unquestioned *un*acceptability. Is (1b) also ungrammatical? Some theoreticians have said yes and some have said no. Chomsky and Lasnik (1977), for example, propose the following grammatical principle to explain the deviance of this sentence:

(2)   *$[\alpha NP$ tense VP], unless $\alpha \neq NP$ and is adjacent to and in the domain of $[+F]$, *that*, or NP

Hence, in the Chomsky-Lasnik treatment, the unacceptability of (1b) is directly reflected in its ungrammaticality.

In the analysis of Bever (1970), on the other hand, (1b) is a *grammatical* sentence. He suggests that its deviance be attributed to an extragrammatical (processing) principle like (3):

(3)   The first N . . . V . . . (N) . . . sequence is processed as the main
          clause unless the verb is marked as subordinate.

In other words, following principle (3), the language user would take *he
left* to be the main clause and would thus be unable to process the rest of
the sentence.

To conclude, while Chomsky and Lasnik on the one hand and Bever on
the other disagreed about the grammaticality of a class of sentences,
there was no disagreement among them over the data. They each shared
the intuition that (1b) is unacceptable. Their only conflict involved the
proper means of accounting for this. One simply needs more evidence
than differing assignments of grammaticality to conclude that there is a
data dispute. And such evidence—particularly in what many commentators have taken to be the classic data disputes in linguistic theory—is
typically lacking.

2.2.2   Unclear Cases: Letting the Grammar Decide

It is hardly news that languages contain vast numbers of sentences of
indeterminate acceptability. Chomsky, in *Syntactic Structures*, suggested
a strategy for dealing with such sentences. It was his opinion that for any
issue there would be enough clear cases, where acceptability or interpretability was *not* open to dispute, that the residue of unclear cases would
not hinder the linguist's progress. He suggested that if rules were formulated with only the clear cases in mind, the resultant grammar would
thereby "decide" into which category the unclear cases would fall: "In
many intermediate cases we shall be prepared to let the grammar itself
decide, when the grammar is set up in the simplest way so that it includes
the clear sentences and excludes the clear non-sentences. This is a familiar feature of explication." (Chomsky 1957, 14).

While generativists have rarely alluded to Chomsky's suggestion in
their day-to-day work, it has in fact guided some of the most creative
refinements in the theory. A good example can be drawn from the
discussion surrounding the applicability of certain transformational rules
in nonroot (i.e., embedded) clauses. Ross (1968) noted that applying the
rules of Topicalization and Left-Dislocation in nonroot clauses often
results in sentences of marginal acceptability:

(4)   a. ?I believe that an A, you'll never get in that class.
          b. ?I acknowledged that my father, he was as tight as a hoot owl.

Ross's final formulation of the two rules assigns strings such as (4a–b) to
the class of grammatical sentences. His theory of unbounded movement
rules saw such rules as unrestricted by particular conditions. Hence his
grammar "decided" that unclear cases such as (4a–b) would be grammatical. The only alternative in his framework would have been to stipulate a

special condition on each rule to prevent it from applying in embedded contexts.

The theory of Emonds (1976), on the other hand, predicts (4a) and (4b) to be *ungrammatical*. The issue between Ross and Emonds was emphatically *not* a data dispute. Rather, Emonds, in developing a model of grammar with a somewhat different structure from Ross's, found that the most elegant description of the clear cases led to the prediction that Topicalization and Left-Dislocation should apply only in root clauses. Thus an analysis based on clear cases only led to the opposite prediction from the one Ross made about the unclear cases. Emonds, in fact, was fully aware of the desirability of explaining *why* a class of sentences should be of intermediate acceptability and, on page 28, even proposed (rather sketchily) a performance principle that interacted with the grammar to result in just such a prediction.

Unfortunately, most generativists have not been as forthright as Emonds in their handling of unclear cases. It is surely much more standard to fail to call attention to obviously unclear cases when one's theory makes a definite prediction about them, even if the prediction differs from that of earlier work. To take a typical case, consider the status of phrases like (5), which contain the derived nominal *likelihood* followed by an infinitival complement:

(5)   John's likelihood to win the prize

The lexicalist model presented in Chomsky (1970a) predicts that such phrases are ungrammatical, while the transformationalist model defended in Newmeyer (1971) predicts their grammaticality. And, in fact, Chomsky cited the "ungrammaticality" of (5) as an example of a correct prediction of the lexicalist theory, while Newmeyer cited the "grammaticality" of an analogous phrase as an example of a correct prediction of the transformationalist.

I do not believe it would take a great deal of experimental data to demonstrate that (5) is indeed an unclear case. The problem is that both Chomsky and Newmeyer presented their analyses as if there were no uncertainty at all about the data. By not calling attention to the marginal acceptability of the examples under contention, each mistakenly implied that they *are* clear cases. They should have stressed their theories' predictive power with respect to the uncontroversial examples, then mentioned that they were following the principle of letting the grammar decide in their handling of (5). By not doing so, they left themselves (and generativists in general) open to the charge of having a cavalier attitude toward the data. Given their presentation of the material, it is easy for a critic to conclude that they were adopting their intuitions to accord with their theoretical claims. But in fact there is no reason to believe that Chomsky's and Newmeyer's intuitions differed in the slightest.

I believe (and will demonstrate further in section 2.2.4) that very often what superficially appear to be conflicts in introspective judgments between two linguists are in reality different analyses of what both agree are unclear cases. That is, they have put into practice, but without calling attention to it, the idea of letting the theory decide. The problem, then, is not with introspective data per se, but rather with the way so many generativists have chosen to present theoretical claims that are grounded in such data. Given a modular approach, of course, it is perfectly understandable that one linguist's grammar might rule a sentence of unclear acceptability "grammatical" and another's might rule it "ungrammatical." For it is exactly in the sphere of unclear cases that we most expect to find the complex interaction of the grammar and some independent system to cloud speakers' judgments.

Once again, it is important to stress that a reader must exercise extreme care in concluding that a data dispute exists between two linguists because they disagree about the grammaticality of a sentence.

2.2.3   The Problem of Context

It is not uncommon to discover that one's judgment about the acceptability of a sentence does not correspond to the grammaticality assignment in the syntax paper one is reading. Entire journal articles—Bolinger (1968) and Ney (1975), for example—have been devoted to documenting this en route to the inevitable allegation about the flimsy empirical basis of some specific theoretical proposal or of the theory itself.

The examples cited in the critical literature to illustrate the capriciousness of introspection are overwhelmingly of one particular type: sentences that have been claimed to be ungrammatical but that, with a little imagination, can be given a context in which they sound perfectly acceptable. For example, Ney objected to the ungrammaticality assignments the following sentences had received:

(6)   a. I am lurking in a culvert.
        b. Cats eat fish in the morning but not onions at night.
        c. John knows that the Knicks didn't win, did they?
        d. You mother resembles herself.

Ney points out, quite correctly, that it is not terribly difficult to imagine contexts in which each might be uttered, and he concludes, naturally enough, that generativists seem rather arbitrary in their approach to the data.

Why sentences (6a–d) were regarded as ungrammatical can be answered only with reference to certain assumptions that were held by generativists in the late 1960s and early 1970s, when these sentences appeared in the literature. Most generativists at that time, particularly those who were influenced by the predominant generative semantics framework, assumed that sentences were not grammatical in isolation, but only with respect to particular *contexts* in which they might or might not be uttered. But since practically no elaborative work was done on the conditions involved in sentence-context pairings, most linguists simply ruled a sentence ungrammatical if it sounded odd in some (never defined) "normal" context. Hence the ungrammaticality assignments of (6a–d).

The attitude that grammaticality was context-dependent was inevitable given that, as recently as ten years ago, not even a rudimentary theory of sentence use was generally available. If a sentence was odd in some way—and the linguist wished to account for its oddness—there was little alternative but to rule it ungrammatical. Hence we find the literature from this period full of asterisked sentences whose only defect seems to be that nobody would be likely to have a reason to say them. Today, primarily as a result of recent work in the pragmatics of cooperative discourse (for foundational work, see especially Austin 1962; Searle 1975; and Grice 1975), virtually no generativist sees it as the grammar's task to filter out such sentences. Rather, generativists see context as one of many factors that *interact* with grammaticality to determine a sentence's acceptability or appropriateness. Consider (6a) again. Why is it an odd sentence? Certainly not because it violates any rule of English sentence formation. It is odd because normally one does not call attention to one's act of lurking.[3] One does not need a sophisticated theory of pragmatics to know that. Nor does one need a terribly clever imagination to come up with a self-directed discourse such as the following, in which (6a) might reasonably be uttered:

(7)   I just cannot believe the situation I have gotten myself into. Here I am. I am lurking in a culvert. God, I wish I could get myself to make an honest living and give up the life of a highway robber.

That (6a) can be contextualized is good evidence that it would be a mistake to regard it as ungrammatical. Its unacceptability in "normal" contexts is a consequence of the (properly formulated) pragmatic principle that one does not announce one's ongoing lurking. A high percentage of the challenged grammaticality assignments in the literature can be resolved in an analogous fashion. While the issues raised by grammatically impeccable but pragmatically odd sentences are highly relevant to the question of the boundary of formal grammar, the existence of such sentences neither challenges the value of introspective data collection nor leads to genuine disputes about the acceptability of linguistic data.

Bolinger, Ney, and others have performed a service by calling into question many generativist assignments of grammaticality and ungrammaticality—a service that goes beyond the demonstration that a great

---

3. See Harnish (1976) for an interesting modular treatment of *lurk*.

many more sentences are grammatical than had been thought. By calling attention to the pragmatic factors that affect acceptability, they have been instrumental in awakening generativists' interest in theories of language use, which in turn has led to the conclusion that the grammaticality of a sentence is most profitably regarded as independent of its discourse context. The conception of grammar and discourse context as distinct but interacting domains has resulted in a more elegant overall picture of language and at the same time has eliminated the basis for a major objection to introspective data.

There is good reason to think that idiosyncratic (i.e., nongeographical and nonsocial) dialects are nothing but artifacts of the now-abandoned view that grammaticality is dependent on context. Such hypothesized dialects include the quantifier dialects discussed by Carden (1970, 1973a) and G. Lakoff (1971); the crossover dialects discussed by Postal (1971); and the subordinate clause deletion dialects discussed by Elliott, Legum, and Thompson (1969). For example, Carden found that speakers differ in how they interpret sentences such as (8):

(8)   All the boys didn't leave.

For some speakers the *all* seems to have wider scope than the *not* (Carden's "NEG-Q dialect"), and for others the *not* seems to have wider scope than the *all* (Carden's "NEG-V dialect"). Carden thus came to the conclusion that dialects exist that have no obvious grounding in regional or social factors. But Baltin (1977) discovered that by embedding sentences like (8) in suitable contexts, any speaker of English can be shown to control *both* readings. In other words, both NEG-Q and NEG-V interpretations appear to be within the competence of all speakers of English, and the idiosyncratic dialects posited by Carden therefore do not exist. It would be interesting to ascertain whether *all* hypothesized idiosyncratic dialects are merely reflections of speakers' differing contextualizations of possible readings for sentences that are ambiguous in their grammars.[4]

2.2.4   Some Alleged Data Disagreements

How common then are *genuine* data disagreements, as opposed to the kind we have examined so far, in which the real (though hidden) point of contention is the structure of the theory itself? In the view of some commentators, "such disagreements [over introspective data judgments] are distressingly common and, if anything, more common on examples of theoretical importance" (Carden and Dieterich 1978, 1). Not only do I

---

4. Though Zwicky (1983) suggests that the indeterminacy of the data available to the child language learner might lead to the (idiosyncratic) construction of different grammars for the same data.

not believe this, but I believe that even the three *most famous* supposed
"data disagreements" in syntactic theory are nothing of the sort. The
issues involved in these three cases are the status of *colorless green ideas
sleep furiously* (section 2.2.4.1); the interpretation of actives and passives
with multiple quantifiers (section 2.2.4.2); and the acceptability of certain
sentences containing the verb *remind* (section 2.2.4.3). I will attempt to
show that, once again, the real point of contention is the analysis, not the
data.

2.2.4.1 *Colorless Green Ideas Sleep Furiously.* In *Syntactic Structures*,
as part of his general discussion of the independence of the notions
"grammatical" and "meaningful," Chomsky contrasted the following
two sentences:

(9)   a. Colorless green ideas sleep furiously.
         b. Furiously sleep ideas green colorless.

Chomsky wrote: "Sentences [(9a)] and [(9b)] are equally nonsensical,
but any speaker of English will recognize that only the former is grammatical" (1957, 15). In *Aspects of the Theory of Syntax*, however, *both*
sentences are treated as ungrammatical: "A descriptively adequate grammar should . . . distinguish perfectly well-formed sentences from [sen-
tences like (9a)], which are not directly generated by the system of
grammatical rules" (1965, 150). Did Chomsky change his intuitions about
(9a) between 1957 and 1965, as is implied in Spencer (1973)? No, of
course not. What changed was the grammatical model. In the earlier
model sentences like (9a), whose deviation from well-formedness lay
only in their violation of selectional restrictions, were generated by the
grammar. In the later model such sentences were blocked at the level of
deep structure by the selectional rules, which were stated as co-
occurrence restrictions holding between individual lexical items. The
understanding of the data remained the same—only the analysis differed.
Most generativists today would once again let (9a) be generated by the
syntactic rules and ascribe to the semantic component the task of characterizing its deviance.

2.2.4.2 *Passive and Quantifier Scope.* Chomsky, in *Syntactic Structures*, used the following two sentences to illustrate that the rule of
Passive could, in certain circumstances, change the interpretation of a
sentence:

(10)   a. Everyone in the room knows at least two languages.
         b. At least two languages are known by everyone in the room.

Chomsky wrote:

we can describe circumstances in which a "quantificational" sentence
such as [(10a)] may be true, while the corresponding passive [(10b)] is

false, *under the normal interpretation of these sentences*—e.g., if one person in the room knows only French and German, and another only Spanish and Italian. This indicates that not even the weakest semantic relation (factual equivalence) holds in general between active and passive. (Chomsky 1957, 100–101; emphasis added)

Katz and Postal, writing seven years later, claimed that both sentences are ambiguous:

[Chomsky] argued that in [(10a)] the languages known by different persons can both be different, while in [(10b)] it is the same two languages for each person. These examples are, however, unconvincing. *Although the facts are far from clear*, the active [(10a)] *seems* to be open to the same interpretation attributed to the passive [(10b)], and conversely, the passive is open to the same interpretation attributed to the active. (Katz and Postal 1964, 72; emphasis added)

What is going on here? Do we have a data dispute (over an issue of "theoretical importance") between Chomsky and Katz and Postal? I doubt it. As far as I can tell, the facts have been clear since day one: Both sentences *can* have both readings, yet they have different *preferred* readings. Chomsky says as much with his locution "under the normal interpretation." The "seems" in the Katz-Postal quotation appears to acknowledge (however implicitly) the same fact. The problem is that until very recently that fact defied incorporation into linguistic theory. The generativist was faced with two equally unsatisfactory choices. One was to generate (10a) and (10b) each with a single interpretation and ignore the fact that another can be contextualized. The other was to generate (10a) and (10b) each with both interpretations and ignore the fact that one is preferred over the other. Chomsky adopted the former choice, Katz and Postal the latter.

Recently linguists have attempted to explain the facts surrounding the interpretation of sentences with multiple quantifiers by probing the interaction of the grammar with extragrammatical systems. For example, Kempson and Cormack (1981) suggest that there is a tendency to interpret the first quantifier in the sentence with wider scope because the grammar interacts with Grice's theory of conversational implicature. In other words, their treatment captures what is right about both Chomsky's analysis and Katz and Postal's: the grammar generates both sentences with both readings; the pragmatics explains why, for each sentence, one reading is preferred.

A final point. It is not true, as Carden and Dieterich charge, that "neither side [i.e., neither Chomsky nor Katz and Postal] is willing to let this crucial piece of data 'be determined by the theory'" (1981, 2). As far as I can tell, that is *exactly* what both sides were doing. A principal theoretical claim of Chomsky's in *Syntactic Structures*, which he supported with page after page of evidence, was that grammatical processes are independent of semantic ones. He therefore, in this unclear case, let the theory decide that the active-passive relation is yet another manifestation of the independence of grammar. Katz and Postal, on the other hand, provided many arguments in support of the claim that transformational rules do not affect meaning. Again, in this unclear case, they let the theory decide—both sentences would be treated as ambiguous, and the rule of Passive would share with other rules the property of meaning preservation.

2.2.4.3   *Remind*. Carden (1973b) cites another example of a putative data disagreement over an issue of major theoretical importance. This involves the debate following the publication of Postal (1970), one of the most influential papers to argue for the generative semantics framework. Postal's paper is essentially a (long) argument that the verb *remind* can be analyzed correctly only within that framework. Within a year after the publication of Postal's paper, no fewer than four rebuttals appeared, each arguing that faulty data judgments led Postal to an incorrect analysis. For example, the following four sentences, all ungrammatical in Postal's analysis, were judged acceptable by his critics:

(11)   a. Harry reminds himself of a gorilla (from Kimball 1970).
        b. For some reason Larry reminds me of Winston Churchill
           although I perceive that Larry is not really similar to him at all
           (from Bowers 1970).
        c. Spiro's walk reminds me of a penguin (from Wolf 1970).
        d. Harry reminds me of myself (from Bolinger 1971).

Once again, I do not think a true data dispute was involved. The problem seems to be exactly that discussed in section 2.2.3—different ideas about the role of context. Postal's four critics found contexts in which sentences he predicted to be deviant could be plausibly used. Postal, in line with the rest of his generative semantics cothinkers, was simply restricting the assignment "grammatical" to sentences that seemed, in some intuitive sense, "normal." Reading the four rebuttals makes one appreciate how much Postal's paper—and, indeed, the entire generative semantics enterprise—depended on blurring the distinction between grammar and context.

2.3   Introspective and Nonintrospective Data

This section discusses some of the problems that arise from attempting to supplement or replace introspective data with experimental data.

2.3.1   On Investigating Acceptability Experimentally

There have been many attempts to replace personal introspection with experimentally based data-collection methods. To date, none has shown itself particularly successful.

The most common experimental approach to intuitive data has been the forced-choice questionnaire (for examples, see Labov 1970a and Stokes 1974). Subjects are asked to make "snap judgments" about acceptability, synonymy, interpretability, and so on. As Guy Carden points out in an overview and candid appraisal of experimental data-collecting methods, the results of this methodology have not been encouraging: "Forced-choice questionnaires are . . . difficult to construct, and have at best marginal reliability and very noisy data" (1976, 103). The overwhelming problem seems to be the difficulty of ensuring that naive subjects respond along the dimensions the questionnaire is designed to probe without at the same time biasing their responses. This problem should not be taken lightly. For example, when linguists ask themselves: "Is such-an-such an acceptable sentence of English?" they know *exactly* what they want. They understand that they do not seek an English teacher's approval for a particular usage; they understand how to control for context; they understand that the likelihood that the sentence would actually be uttered in a discourse is irrelevant; and so on. An experimenter interested in eliciting judgments "objectively" is obligated to ensure that each subject tested has exactly that understanding. I do not believe this has been true in any data-collecting experiment yet designed, nor am I optimistic that it will be accomplished in the near future.

Any attempt to restrict oneself to data gleaned from direct observation of performance seems particularly hopeless: "The complexity and resulting rarity of most of the interesting examples, the difficulty of reliably distinguishing slips from normal productions, and the problem of proving nonexistence combine to require a larger corpus than can reasonably be collected" (Carden 1976, 101). William Labov, in his fieldwork, employs a more focused naturalistic approach. The experimenter deceives the subject into believing that he or she is undergoing, say, an intelligence or memory test, when in reality the questions are phrased so as to (he hopes) elicit spontaneous productions of a form that interests the linguist. Shih, Carden, and Lane (1979) have pointed out the limitations of Labov's approach: "This works well for phonology, or for common syntactic structures; but the relatively complicated syntactic structures of interest to theoreticians usually do not occur often enough for this sort of direct observation of performance to be feasible" (1–2).

A third strategy for avoiding personal introspection of data is to give the subject performance tasks: "Repeat this sentence"; "Make this sentence negative"; "Passivize this sentence" (for examples, see Labov et al.

1968; Greenbaum and Quirk 1970). One then concludes from aspects of the subject's behavior in carrying out the task whether a particular construction is part of his or her grammar. Again, Carden has summarized the difficulties inherent in this methodology: "Performance tasks seem even less reliable than evaluation tasks, and are difficult to adapt to the more interesting syntactic problems" (1976, 103).

A fourth technique is the open-ended interview (see Carden 1973a, 7–11 for discussion). Interviews in general allow for much more interaction between the experimenter and subject than questionnaires—the task at hand can be explained at length, responses can be discussed to ensure that no misunderstandings were involved, and so on. And in fact open-ended interviews *have* produced cleaner results than questionnaires (see Carden 1976 for discussion). The question is why. One possibility is that "interview results are more valid, because more information can be exchanged—task definition can be more detailed, misunderstandings can be corrected, coding can be tuned to the informant" (Carden 1976, 103). But it seems at least as likely that the seeming "validity" is simply a consequence of the same sort of experimenter bias that many believe discredits the linguist's own introspective data collection. Heringer (1970) has observed: "In the casual interaction between linguist and informant, there are many opportunities for self-fulfilling prophesies to take effect, both ones conditioned by theoretical position and also ones conditioned by the linguist's own idiolect" (294).

A final technique is the "appropriate-response methodology" (see Shih, Carden, and Lane 1979). Here the interviewer produces the structures of interest and observes the subject's response. For example, if the subject fails to comprehend the sentence, does a double take, or responds in some inappropriate manner, the interviewer concludes that the sentence in question is deviant in some manner in the subject's dialect. Again we find difficulties: "Our results suggest that the method succeeds well in collecting unbiased data, but that its relative sensitivity to complexity and insensitivity to structural violations will limit its effectiveness in the complex and subtle cases where the theoretician is in most need of help" (Shih, Carden, and Lane 1979, 4).

In short, none of the experimental approaches to collecting data about well-formedness and interpretability of sentences has proved successful. This does not mean such approaches cannot *in principle* be designed to give reliable results. Nor can we thereby conclude that introspection wins by default; it is certainly logically possible that Carden is right that "the linguist's own intuitions are plainly untrustworthy" (1976, 103) and that therefore "in the short run, our best approach is to improve our instruments for evaluation tasks, first by improved pre-testing and questionnaire design, and second by testing interviews for reliability and bias effects" (104). Still, one point is clear: there does not exist at present an obvious replacement for introspective data.

2.3.2   The Studies "Disconfirming" Introspective Data

The first full-scale attack on the introspective data base of linguistic theory was a 1961 paper by Archibald Hill. Hill took issue with certain claims in Chomsky's *Syntactic Structures*, in particular the claim that speakers have the ability to distinguish well-formed from ill-formed sentences in their language.[5] His conclusion that speakers lack this ability was derived from the results of an experiment in which he presented the following ten sentences to ten informants, all of whom were native speakers of English (all but the last two sentences are cited from *Syntactic Structures*):

(12) a. Colorless green ideas sleep furiously. (= Hill's [1])
      b. Furiously sleep ideas green colorless. (= [2])
      c. Have you a book on modern music? (= [3])
      d. The book seems interesting. (= [4])
      e. Read you a book on modern music? (= [5])
      f. The child seems sleeping. (= [6])
      g. I saw a fragile whale. (= [7])
      h. I saw a fragile of. (= [8])
      i. Those man left yesterday. (= [9])
      j. I never heard a green horse smoke a dozen oranges. (= [10])

Why did Hill reject the idea that speakers have the ability to discriminate the sentences of their language from the nonsentences? I quote the discussion of his experimental design and results in full:

> The next request to the informants was to reject any sentences which were ungrammatical, and to accept those which were grammatical. In the results of this voting, (9) 'those man . . .' was the only sentence rejected by all ten informants. Sentence (2) 'Furiously sleep . . .' was rejected by seven, accepted by three. The voting on (8), '. . . fragile of.' was similar, seven rejecting, three (but not the same three) accepting. Sentences (5) 'read you . . . ?' and (6) '. . . seems sleeping.' were each rejected by three, accepted by seven. Sentence (10) '. . . green horse . . .' was rejected by three, accepted by seven. Sentence (1) 'Colorless green ideas . . .' was rejected by one, accepted by nine. Sentence (3) 'have you a book . . .' was accepted by all but one informant, who offered the qualification that it would be ungrammatical in his idiolect. This informant was one of the two linguists fully aware of differences in

5. A claim that Hill has adopted implicitly in all of his own work. For example, his major publication, *Introduction to Linguistic Structures* (1958), contains little data beyond that arrived at through personal introspection.

British and American dialects. Sentence (4) 'the book seems . . .' was hesitated over before final acceptance by one informant. All others accepted without hesitation. Sentence (7) '. . . fragile whale,' was accepted without hesitation by all informants. (Hill 1961, 3)

It seems to me that all we can conclude from Hill's experiment is that if one asks speakers whether sentences are "grammatical," without giving them any indication of what that term is intended to mean, one will get bizarre results. No doubt the six speakers who accepted (6) equated "grammatical" with "interpretable"; the three who accepted (8) might have contextualized *of* as a noun (having in mind, say, a neon sign with the letters *o* and *f*); the nine who accepted (3) might have interpreted "grammatical" to mean "possible in some (standard) English dialect"; and so on. But of course, this is mere speculation, since we have no way of reading the minds of Hill's ten subjects. I think, however, that one lesson can be learned from Hill's paper: if the results of personal interpretation are untrustworthy, then the results of an experiment like his are ten times more so.

The most often cited study whose findings seem to discredit introspective data is Spencer (1973). Spencer presented 150 example sentences from seven important publications[6] from 1968 and 1969 to forty-three "linguistically naive" and twenty-two "linguistically nonnaive" native speakers. She found that her subjects shared the intuitions of the linguists for only half of the examples, but agreed with each other 80 percent of the time. Spencer concluded:

> that this result indicates that linguists' intuitions should not be uncritically accepted as a secure data base for the derivation of a theory of natural language of the speech community. Intuitions of informants who are not linguists about the grammatical acceptability of exemplars which illustrate rules should be used to identify unclear cases and incorrect rules, if there is to be any confidence that the rules do reflect the formal structure of the common language being described. (1973, 97)

Spencer's results, however, are of as little value as Hill's. The reader is not even informed what the subjects' instructions were! All we are told is that each subject was asked "to make a decision on each statement as to whether it was complete [?] and well-formed or not," and that "there were a series of guidelines and examples as to what the [experimenter] meant" (91). But since Spencer does not tell us what these guidelines were, we have no way of knowing whether the subjects were being tested for the sorts of judgments that are (presumably) unreliable when they result from personal introspection. Furthermore, Spencer does not in-

---

6. The articles are Perlmutter (1968), Smith (1964), Postal (1969), Ross (1969a,b), Rosenbaum (1969), and R. Lakoff (1968).

clude a single example sentence from her list of 150. This is unfortunate, because the papers from which the examples were drawn were written in the period when most linguists considered a sentence grammatical only if it could be supplied with a normal context (see section 2.2.3). One suspects that her subjects' disagreements resulted from their supplying contexts for pragmatically odd sentences that the authors of the papers had ruled ungrammatical. But of course there is no way to be sure about this.

The most comprehensive critical discussion of the use of introspective data is Labov (1975). Labov bases his primary critique on the apparent fact that linguists' judgments tend to be influenced by their position on the theoretical issue they are discussing. For example, the "generative semantics" wing and the "interpretive semantics" wing of theoretical linguistics in the early 1970s made opposite predictions about the grammaticality of the following sentence:

(13)   John didn't leave until midnight, but Bill did.

As Labov points out, Grinder and Postal (1971), whose generative semantics approach predicted the ungrammaticality of the sentence, found it unacceptable. On the other hand, Chomsky (1972a), whose interpretivist model predicted its grammaticality, found it acceptable. And here we *know* that a data dispute was involved: the authors tell us explicitly that the data themselves are points of contention. Labov generalizes from this and a few other similar cases to conclude that "there is no basis for [linguists'] confidence . . . that the influence of their theory upon their judgments is only a minor problem at best" (1975, 30). He suggests as a remedy not the abandonment of the use of introspective data, but rather the adoption of "three working principles which offer a fairly sound basis for continued exploration of grammatical judgments" (31):

I.   THE CONSENSUS PRINCIPLE: if there is no reason to think otherwise, assume that the judgments of any native speaker are characteristic of all speakers of the language.
II. THE EXPERIMENTER PRINCIPLE: if there is any disagreement on introspective judgments, the judgments of those who are familiar with the theoretical issues may not be counted as evidence.
III. THE CLEAR CASE PRINCIPLE: disputed judgments should be shown to include at least one consistent pattern in the speech community or be abandoned.

Labov's three principles are not bad.[7] I suspect that our main point of contention is over how widespread *true* data disagreements, such as the

---

7. One has the uneasy feeling, however, that Labov's phrasing of the consensus principle indicates that he believes the grammars generativists write are intended to apply to entire speech communities rather than to capture the competence of individual speakers.

Chomsky/Grinder-Postal case, really are. That is, we disagree on how frequently one would need to advance to the Experimenter Principle. As I have stressed, the vast majority of supposed data conflicts have been essentially theoretical disagreements that are only superficially disagreements about the acceptability of sentences.

Labov also questions the intuitions of even linguistically naive speakers. He gives two examples that suggest contradictions between speakers' introspective judgments and their behavior. The first is the discovery by him and his co-workers that people will deny using positive *anymore* (as in *I go there anymore*) when in fact they use it regularly; or they may insist it means one thing when, as is clear from their usage, it means something else. The second is that speakers will insist two words are pronounced exactly the same (for example, *source* and *sauce* by many New Yorkers), when spectrographic studies show regular differences in their vowel nuclei.

Labov's examples are interesting, though they are tangential to the question of linguists' use of introspective data. The *anymore* case illustrates, I suspect, the dangers inherent in asking linguistically naive speakers to analyze language. It would be interesting to see whether professional linguists would display the same contradiction between their introspections and their behavior. Labov's *source/sauce* example is interesting for a different reason. It shows that there does not exist a perfect match between speech production and speech perception, but this hardly discredits introspection as data. Quite the contrary, it shows its importance! For if we chose to ignore introspective data, we would have no way of knowing that this theoretically significant imbalance existed. The introspective data and the spectrographic data, taken together, suggest the complexity of the interface between a speaker's phonology and the mechanisms involved in putting it to use.

2.3.3   The Validity Problem

Most of the criticisms of the use of introspective data are directed toward its reliability. One might instead (or also) question its *validity*. That is, one might ask how we know that, by basing our theories on data collected largely by introspection, we will be led to the reality we wish to describe. As Bever has phrased the problem, "a linguistic grammar may have formal properties that reflect the study of selected subparts of speech behavior (for example, having intuitions about sentences), but which are not reflected in *any* other kind of speech behavior. Other kinds of speech behavior may bring out additional aspects of the structure of language" (1970, 344). The fact is that we have no way of knowing if our theory might be "skewed" by too great a reliance on data collected in one particular way. But this problem is not unique to linguistics. Most sciences, in early stages of their development, have tended to be rather restricted in their sources of data. Early historical geology, for example, relied almost entirely on direct observation of the succession of strata and the fossil record. Improvements in "data collecting," made possible by twentieth-century developments in physics and chemistry, have led to revised theories of the history of the earth—in some ways drastically revised. So it is and will be with linguistics. As more reliable data become available that do not have their basis in introspection, we may find that our views about the structure of human language change accordingly. In fact, in the past few years there have been quite a few proposals for modifying linguistic theory based on nonintrospective data. To cite only a few examples, Lightfoot (1979a) utilizes data gathered from observations of language change in this way; Bresnan (1978a) and J. D. Fodor (1978) draw on results obtained in psycholinguistic experimentation; and Goodluck and Solan (1978), Baker (1979), Wexler and Culicover (1980), and Tavakolian (1981) suggest ways that facts drawn from studies of first language acquisition can be of use to grammatical theorists.

The results of a recall test or the observations of the verbal behavior of a two-year-old are in principle every bit as useful in determining the nature of a competence model as are a linguist's introspections about the acceptability of *John seems to the men to like each other*. As the implications of the former type of data become better understood, we can expect them to make an ever-increasing contribution to theory construction.

2.4   Is Grammatical Theory English-Oriented?

Most of the foundational work in grammatical theory, at least those portions dealing with syntax and semantics, has cited data drawn from English. A pervasive criticism of the theory is based on this fact. How dare generativists make *universal* claims about *human* language, the argument goes, when most of the four-thousand-odd languages of the world have not been examined at all, and the amount of work in one— English—equals that in all the others put together? Hasn't this distorted the structure of the theory to reflect the (incidental) properties of one language?

As I have pointed out elsewhere (Newmeyer 1980a, 48–49), one can easily exaggerate the dominant role English has played. Chomsky's earliest generativist work dealt with Hebrew, not English. Four out of the six faculty members at the Massachusetts Institute of Technology in the 1960s were known primarily for their work in languages other than English, and 61 percent of the dissertations written there in that period did not deal with English (the percentage is even higher today). If phonology is excluded, slightly over half of the pages in *Linguistic Inquiry*, the leading generativist journal, deal with English; if phonology is included, considerably under half. And in the past few years non-English papers have predominated at all major generativist conferences.[8]

Still, it cannot be denied that the most-cited books and papers—the ones with the major theoretical innovations—use mainly English data. This raises two questions: Why? and What effect has this had?

The Why? is easier to answer. Most of the first generativists were anglophones, as were their students. The sorts of subtle introspective judgments that have formed so much of the data base of grammatical theory do not come readily even to fluent nonnative speakers of a language. This, of course, has tended to discourage many generativists from working on languages other than their own (i.e., other than English). While nonnative speakers have published numerous successful generativist studies of Amerindian languages (generally with there being no time to wait for native speakers to be trained as linguists), I think most generativists feel more confident about the results they obtain from work on their native languages, where their command of the data is more secure.

It is not easy to do theoretically interesting syntactic work in a language one does not speak natively. Many centuries spent probing the structure of the well-studied languages (English, Japanese, and French, for example) have taught us to appreciate how *interconnected* grammatical phenomena are; how facts in isolation rarely bear directly on interesting hypotheses; how even the simplest generalization demands exhaustive analysis of dozens of seemingly disparate phenomena. And the sorts of data that have been found to bear most heavily on hypotheses about the nature of language simply cannot be found in a traditional grammar or be obtained in a few sessions with an informant.

Another reason English data have loomed so large in theoretical discussions is a consequence of the fact that until quite recently nonnative English speakers (non-Americans, more accurately) have been slow to adopt generativist theory. One can speculate about the reasons for this (the structure of academia in many European countries, political and economic factors that in many countries favor more "applied" approaches, etc.), but the fact remains that it is true. In the past few years, however, there has been a dramatic turnaround, to the point where I believe there are now as many generativists outside the United States as inside. The number of generativist papers on French, Dutch, Spanish, Japanese, and Italian in recent years bears witness to the internationalization of grammatical theory.

8. For example, at the First West Coast Conference on Formal Linguistics, held at Stanford in January 1982, only twelve of the thirty-nine papers presented cited primarily English data. And half of the twelve dealt more with the parsing and processing of sentences than with questions of formal grammar.

Finally, generativists have chosen to concentrate on their native languages (which, again, has typically meant English) because they believe that the *intensive* study of one language will yield far more insights into the basic nature of linguistic processes than the *superficial* study of many. If one assumes that children born into an English speech community are no different in their inherent capabilities from children born into others, then it follows that a detailed analysis of the properties of the grammar they acquire will reveal a great deal about the principles guiding language acquisition *in general*—that is, a great deal about universal grammar. For example, if the grammar of English seems to be constrained by some principle that is implausibly "learned" by the child, then a testable prediction follows: not just the grammar of English, but the grammars of *all* languages will be constrained by that principle. Here is where the advantages of studying one language in depth become most apparent: the principles found to constrain grammars are in general too complex and abstract to be discovered by a superficial look at a nonnative language. Chomsky (1972c) made this point clearly in a reply to Hiż (1967), who scolds generativists for paying too much attention to too few languages:

> Hiż objects to the fact that my proposals concerning universal grammar are based on detailed examination of a few languages rather than "examination of many cases." I certainly agree that one should study as many languages as possible. Still, a caveat should be entered. It would be quite easy to present enormous masses of data from varied languages that are compatible with all conceptions of universal grammar that have so far been formulated. There is no point in doing so. If one is concerned with the principles of universal grammar, he will try to discover those properties of particular grammars that bear on these principles, putting aside large amounts of material that, so far as he can determine, do not. It is only through intensive studies of particular languages that one can hope to find crucial evidence for the study of universal grammar. One study such as that of Matthews on Hidatsa [Matthews 1964] is worth one thousand superficial studies of varied languages from this point of view. If someone feels that the base of data is too narrow, what he should do is show that some of the material omitted refutes the principles that have been formulated. Otherwise, his criticism has no more force than a criticism of modern genetics for basing its theoretical formulations on the detailed investigation of only a few organisms. (1972c, 188–89)

What effect has the high reliance on English data had on the shape of grammatical theory? The answer is "Probably not much," though partly for reasons from which generativists will take small comfort. The overwhelming defect of grammatical theory is not that it is designed to handle only a small number of processes unique to English and a few related languages. The defect is exactly the *opposite*—the theory is far too *permissive*. That is, it allows the formulation of a wide variety of rules that are never found in *any* language, much less English. For example, the model presented in *Aspects of the Theory of Syntax* is consistent with a rule that allows a preposition (or postposition) to be extracted from its phrase in a subordinate clause and be adjoined to the subject of the main clause, even though such a rule (as far as I know) occurs in no human language. It is not easy to find evidence that the *Aspects* model is skewed toward English. Among other things, it permits the constituents of a sentence to be "scrambled" over each other as well as permitting agreement rules to be stated between any two items in a sentence, even though neither "scrambling" nor agreement rules are central to the grammar of English.

There have been cases, of course, where universal claims based largely on English data have been modified as evidence bearing on them has been brought forward from other languages. For example, Chomsky (1977b) modified his proposed "Tensed Sentence Condition" (see Chomsky 1973) to a revised "Propositional Island Condition" on the basis of certain facts about Korean discussed in Kim (1976). Or, again, Koster (1978) pointed out that the Complex Noun Phrase Constraint (see Ross 1968), which was proposed essentially on the examination of English data alone, was an artifact of a view of language that saw seemingly unbounded extraction rules as the norm in language. Koster then proceeded to propose a reanalysis of Ross's work that treated such extractions as the unusual phenomena they apparently are. And Chomsky (1981), following a proposal made by Hale (1981) on the basis of an examination of Australian languages, has adopted the idea that, contrary to the *Aspects* model, many languages have neither ordered base rules nor transformations. No doubt as more languages are studied in depth more revisions will be made. But why should that be disturbing? The construction of a grammatical theory is just as much an ongoing process as the construction of any other scientific theory, and a grammatical theory is just as likely to be revised as any other.

The major attack on the supposed English-oriented nature of grammatical theory, Hagège (1976), does not give a single example of a genuine negative consequence of most work's being in English. Hagège asserts, with great eloquence, that grammatical theory is a "lit de Procuste" that results in "les traitements générativistes dans lesquels les langues particulièrers ressemblent au modèle anglais" (45–46). But his examples illustrate nothing of the sort. The following remark is typical: "Si l'analyse des tags (type *you are a spy, aren't you?*) peut être utile pour les phrases interrogatives de l'anglais, quelle est sa pertinence pour d'autres langues?" (47). The answer is "Quite probably none." To my knowledge, no generativist has ever attempted to generalize the English tag rule to French, Samoan, or any other language. The conclusion one draws from Hagège's discussion is not that he genuinely believes generativists attempt to impose their analysis of English on other languages, but rather that he resents the fact that any work is done on English at all!

One frequently reads assurances that "one of the most productive directions of research lies in the collection of valuable facts from a diverse cross-section of languages and the discovery of generalizations based on them" (Li 1976, x–xi). But there is no evidence that "the collection of valuable facts" has ever led or could ever lead to the discovery of any generalizations other than the most superficial sort. For example, the seven-year-long Stanford University Language Universals Project (whose results are now published as Greenberg, Ferguson, and Moravcsik 1978) carried out Li's program to perfection yet has not led, as far as I know, to any substantial theoretical revisions. The problem is that the fairly shallow generalizations and statistical correlations described in the project's reports were far too sketchily presented to be of much use in ascertaining even the grammatical structure of the individual languages treated, much less shed any light on universal grammar.[9]

Lightfoot (1979b) has called attention to the implicit ethnocentric assumptions reflected in the feeling that one can draw insightful conclusions about a language based on the most casual acquaintance with it:

> There seems to be a general principle at work, perhaps appropriately referred to as the "Ebeling Principle," that the more exotic the language, the less need for precise analysis and the less controversy about correct descriptions. Ebeling (1960:43–4) noted that American structuralists were able to apply their phonemic theory successfully to Hopi, Navajo etc., but came across the most recalcitrant problems when analysing English. He, a Dutchman, found that it worked perfectly well for English, but that problems arose for Dutch: "I am convinced that when a Tübatulabal Indian masters the technique, he will soon notice that it works perfectly well for all languages except Tübatulabal." In short, "the results of phonemic analysis are often inversely proportional to the investigator's knowledge of the language." (384)

There is a tendency among many linguists (generativists included) to draw sweeping conclusions from a superficial examination of some poorly studied language; conclusions they would never dare draw from an equally superficial examination of, say, English, French, or German. This tendency, in my opinion, needs to be fought vigorously. Aside from the fact that it results, quite simply, in bad linguistic analyses, it has

---

9. Though Pullum (1979a) argues, perhaps with justification, that in those few instances where generativists *could* have made use of the project's results to help settle some pressing theoretical question they failed to do so.

negative social consequences as well. The poorly studied languages are spoken overwhelmingly by nonwhite inhabitants of the developing countries. By drawing hasty conclusions from a casual examination of such languages, a linguist stands (unwittingly, of course) to reinforce the idea that the Western languages—and by implication their speakers—are in some fundamental sense more sophisticated and advanced than those of the non-Western world.

3 | Grammatical Theory and Language Variation

3.1 Introduction

Many linguists who acknowledge that generativists have produced insightful analyses of particular grammatical constructions are nevertheless quite certain that their theory is inadequate as the nucleus of a *comprehensive* theory of human language. A major reason for their certainty is the belief that grammatical theory is in principle incapable of shedding any light on the complex problems that arise from the study of linguistic *variation*. This chapter challenges that belief. In sections 3.2, 3.3, and 3.4 I suggest that the widespread pessimism is derived in large part from what appear to be misunderstandings about certain fundamental generativist concepts. Section 3.5 describes at some length the ways the basic principles of grammatical theory have contributed to the explanation of aspects of variation.

3.2 On the "Ideal Speaker-Listener"

If a sampling of the critical literature is any indication, no paragraph in any generativist work has engendered as many misunderstandings as the following, from the beginning of *Aspects of the Theory of Syntax*:

> Linguistic theory is concerned primarily with an ideal speaker-listener, in a completely homogeneous speech-community, who knows its language perfectly and is unaffected by such grammatically irrelevant conditions as memory limitations, distractions, shifts of attention and interest, and errors (random or characteristic) in applying his knowledge of the language in actual performance. This seems to me to have

been the position of the founders of modern general linguistics, and no cogent reason for modifying it has been offered. To study actual linguistic performance, we must consider the interaction of a variety of factors, of which the underlying competence of the speaker-hearer is only one. In this respect, study of language is no different from empirical investigation of other complex phenomena. (Chomsky 1965, 3–4)

Conclusions drawn from this passage have ranged from the false (though perhaps natural) one that generativists have no interest in variation to the absolutely incredible one that Chomsky literally *believes* that speech communities are homogeneous and that speaker-listeners are unaffected by "irrelevant conditions." I interpret Cedergren and Sankoff's mocking of the generativists' fruitless "search for ideal speakers" (1974, 335) and Anshen's complaint that "one never seems to find the 'ideal speaker-hearer in the perfectly homogeneous speech community'" (1975, 6; see also Burling 1972, 236) as an indication that they have drawn the latter conclusion. Or again, Ringen's assurance to his readers that "there is evidence that actual speech communities are not homogeneous" (1975, 26) suggests that he has interpreted Chomsky's statement as a factual claim about the nature of speech communities rather than as a methodologically desirable idealization.

Insofar as Chomsky's remarks characterize the attitudes of grammarians from "the founders of modern general linguistics" to those of the present, they seem indisputable.[1] Surely they characterize the views of Ferdinand de Saussure, who explicitly advocated the identical idealization:

To summarize, these are the characteristics of language:
1) Language is a well-defined object in the heterogeneous mass of speech facts. . . .
2) Language, unlike speaking, is something that we can study separately. . . . We can dispense with the other elements of speech; indeed, the science of language is possible only if the other elements are excluded.
3) Whereas speech is heterogeneous, language, as defined, is homogeneous. It is a system of signs in which the only essential thing is the union of meanings and sound-images, and in which both parts of the sign are psychological.
4) Language is concrete, no less than speaking; and this is a help in our study of it. Linguistic signs, though basically psychological, are not abstractions; associations which bear the stamp of collective approval—and which added together constitute language—are realities that have their seat in the brain (1966, 14–15)

Or consider Saussure's statement that "synchronic linguistics will be concerned with the logical and psychological relations that bind together

1. This point is acknowledged by at least some of Chomsky's critics—see Weinreich, Labov, and Herzog (1968, 120–26) for discussion.

coexisting terms and form a system in the collective mind of speakers" (1966, 99–100). The "ideal speaker-listener" idealization is as old as the Western grammatical tradition and, as an inspection of papers from various twentieth-century frameworks will demonstrate, has underlain virtually all modern grammatical research (see, e.g., Joos's 1957 collection of papers in the post-Bloomfieldian framework; Vachek's 1964 Prague School collection, and Bazell et al.'s 1966 London School collection).[2] Now the truth, of course, is not decided by majority vote— the fact that the Great Linguists of the World have taken a stance on a particular issue hardly entails that it is correct. Yet the realization that Chomsky was simply reiterating a time-honored position does make one wonder why his remarks have constituted such a shock.

Another point worth stressing is that the opening words of the paragraph are "Linguistic theory is concerned," not "The field of linguistics is concerned." Chomsky has consistently used the term "linguistic theory" to refer to theories of grammar (i.e., theories of competence) rather than to refer to *any* work (theoretical or nontheoretical) involving language study. In other words, there is no substance to the charge that the passage indicates an ignorance (or, worse, a dismissal) of studies of language variation published before 1965. Again, the equation of "linguistic theory" (or an equivalent term) with "theory of grammar" was not Chomsky's innovation. Saussure explicitly distinguished the "science of language" (theorizing about grammar) from linguistics as a whole.

I think the greatest difficulties with Chomsky's remarks about the "ideal speaker-listener" result because they express two very different sorts of abstractions. One is an *empirical hypothesis*—the hypothesis that a central aspect of language is linguistic competence, which forms an autonomous system interacting with, but independent of, memory limitations, distractions, and so forth. The other is a methodologically expedient *counterfactual idealization*—the idealization that speech communities are homogeneous, that speakers know their language perfectly, and so on. Following a tradition that, at the time *Aspects of the Theory of the Theory of Syntax* was written, had rarely (if ever) been challenged, Chomsky hypothesized that the efficacious advancement of grammatical theory demanded abstracting from the effects of variation, just as progress in other sciences has gone hand-in-hand with analogous moves. But he was absolutely explicit that neither abstraction could in any way be thought of as imposing a boundary on the investigation of linguistic phenomena. On the contrary, as he pointed out, the understanding of

2. Even André Martinet, who has departed from mainstream "structuralist" practice in many respects, has adopted the same idealization: "To simplify our analysis, we shall assume that the language in process of evolution is that of a strictly monoglot community, perfectly homogeneous in the sense that observable differences represent successive stages of the same usage and not concurrent usages. . . . We must disregard these [social and geographical] variations as we did above in the case of descriptive linguistics" (1964, 164).

complex phenomena, including variation, will be understood only if one "consider[s] the interaction of a variety of factors, of which the underlying competence of the speaker-hearer is only one." That the modular approach to studying variation that Chomsky advocated has proved itself successful will be illustrated in section 3.5.

3.3 Optional Rules and Free Variation

Another misunderstanding that has led to negative conclusions about the ability of grammatical theory to help explain variation is the belief that generativists see optional grammatical rules as the proper device for describing free variation in language. Labov, in the following passage, expresses this idea succinctly (see also Fraser 1972, 1; Cedergren and Sankoff 1974, 333; Bolinger 1975, 23; Wolfram 1978, 9; and Fasold 1978, 87):

> In abstract linguistic discussions, we consider that rules may be obligatory, and always apply, or "optional," where the use or non-use of the rule is completely unrestrained. In the latter case, the two possibilities are said to be in free variation. (Labov 1973a, 104)

The fact is that the notions "free variation" and "optional rule" have absolutely nothing to do with each other. Two forms or constructions are said to be in "free variation" if they can be used interchangeably in discourse (for discussion, see Harris 1951, 29). The optionality of a transformational or phonological rule is simply a formal device for expressing the possibility that two derived structures originate from one underlying structure. The claim that passives, say, are derived by means of an optional rule from a structure that underlies both actives and passives entails no claim about whether the sentence types are in free variation or about any other aspect of their use in discourse. This should be clear from the way the passive construction has been treated within grammatical theory. In Chomsky (1957) passives were derived by an optional transformation; in Chomsky (1965) by an obligatory transformation; in Chomsky (1973) again by an optional transformation; and in Chomsky (1976) and later work by a general optional movement rule that subsumes passive as a special case. Today many generativists feel that passives should not be derived transformationally at all. The changing views on the grammatical nature of passivization have followed from changes in the theory of universal grammar, and not at all from novel observations about the degree of interchangeability of actives and passives in discourse.

Conversely, two forms can (in principle) be in free variation without being related in any way in the grammar, though there is little reason to believe that true free variation exists in language at all.

The widespread assumption that generativists desire to explain each instance of free variation by positing the optional application of a grammatical rule is the first step in a chain of argument that leads to the abandonment of a central hypothesis of grammatical theory—that of the discrete rule. Some linguists have reasoned that if the grammar incorporates directly *one* aspect of discourse variation (through the optional/obligatory distinction), then it stands to reason that it should incorporate directly *all* aspects. But, obviously, the standard generativist conception of rule formalization is incapable of expressing the nuances of variation. As Cedergren and Sankoff point out, simply labeling a rule "optional" gets one nowhere if one's goal is to capture variation grammatically:

> The notion of optionality fails to capture the nature of the systematic variation which exists even on the level of grammar of a single individual. It does not permit the incorporation of relativity or covariation between the presence of certain features in the linguistic environment of a rule and the frequency of operation of the rule. The label "optional" fails to convey any information as to how the elements of the structural description of a rule favor or constrain its operation. (1974, 333)

From such observations, Cedergren and Sankoff and others have gone on to conclude (quite naturally, given their assumptions) that the properties of grammatical rules have to be modified drastically. In particular, they have been led to hypothesize that rules must be allowed to encode directly a variety of aspects of linguistic variation. These "variable rules" will be the subject of the next section.

3.4   On Variable Rules

Variable rules were first proposed in Labov (1969)[3] as a means of describing the inherent variation involved in copula contraction in the Black English Vernacular (BEV) and have since been applied to phenomena as diverse as the placement of the future marker in New Guinea Tok Pisin (Sankoff 1973), the favored readings obtained in sentences with multiple quantifiers (Carden 1973a), and *r*-spirantization in Panamanian Spanish (Cedergren and Sankoff 1974). A typical example of a variable rule is discussed in Labov (1972b). Labov noted that words ending in consonant clusters in Standard English often appear in BEV with only the first consonant. Hence *bold*, *find*, and *fist* are frequently pronounced *bol'*, *fin'*, and *fis'*. However, since there are no speakers who *never* have the full clusters (nor are there any who always preserve them), Labov

---

3. Apparently Pāṇini, the great Sanskrit grammarian, included facts about variation in his rule statements and thus might be considered the originator of the variable rule. See Kiparsky (1979) for discussion.

deemed it reasonable to posit the full clusters in the underlying phonological representations of all speakers. If that were all there were to it, Labov argued, the facts could be handled by the following "optional" deletion rule:

(1)   a. $[-\text{cont}] \rightarrow \emptyset / [+\text{cons}] \underline{\quad} \#\# [-\text{syl}]$

However, there are facts about consonant deletion in BEV that are not directly reflected in this rule. First, speakers are more likely to omit the final consonant if no morpheme boundary intervenes between the two consonants; second, omission of the consonant is favored by the presence of a following nonsyllabic element. Labov chose to incorporate these facts directly into the formalization of the rule itself, as in (1b):

(1)   b. $[-\text{cont}] \rightarrow \langle\emptyset\rangle / [+\text{cons}]^{\beta}\langle\emptyset\rangle \underline{\quad} \#\#^{\alpha}\langle-\text{syl}\rangle$

The features in angle brackets represent variable effects or constraints; hence he termed rules like (1b) "variable rules." The Greek superscripts indicate the hierarchy of constraints that favor the application of the rule. Alpha constraints take precedence over beta constraints, reflecting the greater effect of the phonological condition over the morphological condition in the application of the rule.

Associated with each variable feature is a probability (i.e., a number between zero and one).[4] The probabilities are computed from the observed relative frequency of the applicability of the rule under particular linguistic and sociological conditions. Thus, for example, a probability might be influenced by age, group membership, and socioeconomic status as well as by purely linguistic factors such as the distinctive feature composition of a following segment or the presence of a word boundary. The calculation of a variable feature probability is not seen as presenting any theoretical difficulties—in fact, it has been compared to estimating the probability of a "full house" in poker by counting the proportion of full houses in a large number of randomly dealt hands (Cedergren and Sankoff 1974, 342–43).

It is difficult to determine whether advocates of variable rules regard their variable features as constructs of competence or of performance. Labov has written that "it is clear that variable rules are rules of production" (1972b; see also Labov 1971, 469 and Sankoff and Labov 1979, 202). Yet the opinion of Cedergren and Sankoff is that "the variable rules developed by Labov should, like other rules of generative grammar, be interpreted as part of individual competence" (1974, 335). If so, however, given that such rules conflate knowledge of linguistic structure (i.e., "competence" in the generativist sense) with a characterization of the

---

4. For discussion of the formal properties of variable rules, see Cedergren and Sankoff (1974), Sankoff and Cedergren (1976), Sankoff (1978), and Sankoff and Labov (1979).

likelihood of behaving in a particular way under particular conditions, it seems fair to conclude that conceiving of variable rules as competence constructs involves rejecting the idea of an *autonomous* linguistic competence. This conclusion gains credence from the following remark by Cedergren and Sankoff, in which competence appears to be regarded as a model *of* performance, not as one of many systems that contribute *to* performance: "The power of this [variable rule] approach lies in the uniquely well-defined and economical relationship which it posits between competence and linguistic performance, analogous to that between a probability distribution and a sample, or between a model and a simulation" (Cedergren and Sankoff 1974, 353).

The most forceful criticism of any theoretical innovation is the demonstration that an alternative approach provides a more insightful and explanatory treatment of the phenomena under consideration. In the case of several proposed variable rules, such a demonstration has been carried out. For example, Bickerton (1973a) argues, convincingly in my opinion, that the facts surrounding the deletion of the complementizer *que* in Montreal French can be handled much more elegantly through the interaction of discrete rules than by the variable rule posited in Cedergren and Sankoff (1974). Since Bickerton's general approach has been applied most creatively to the analysis of creole continua, I will present it in the next section.

However there are two specific criticisms of variable rules that, in my opinion, discredit them as motivated additions to grammatical theory. First, and most fundamentally, there is no sense in which such rules could be said to *explain* anything. Explanation involves a move from the concrete to the abstract; a variable rule is simply a data-displaying device, that is, it is a concrete summary of the concrete (as we have seen, rules of this type have explicitly been claimed to bear the same relation to the primary linguistic data as a model does to a simulation). An abstract discrete rule, on the other hand, through its interaction with other such rules, has the potential to reveal patterns and generalizations beyond the data base from which it was formulated. (For a good example of this, consider the *Syntactic Structures* Auxiliary Transformation. This rule was motivated solely on grounds of internal simplicity of the grammar, yet in conjunction with other rules was able to predict the occurrence of supportive *do*, as in *did he leave* and *he didn't leave*.) A variable rule cannot do this even *in principle*, since its stated purpose is to do no more than capsulize observed patterns in the data. As Kay and McDaniel have observed:

A variable rule analysis is closely related both mathematically and philosophically to an application of the statistical technique called analysis of variance. A typical application of analysis of variance would be to a situation in which one wanted to know which determining variables, such as soil type, available moisture, sunlight, fertilizer type, etc., were most important in producing a heavy yield of, say, corn. Analysis of variance is a technique that reduces a set of data giving, for example, the amount of corn produced under all combinations of determining factors to a set of measures of the relative importance of the determining factors (and their interactions). The results of such an analysis do not in and of themselves constitute a substantive theory of how corn plants grow, although perusal of such analyses may be valuable to the plant physiologist or economic botanist in attempting to form such a theory. . . . variable rule analyses should be viewed in much the same light, not as providing direct theoretical insight into the substantive processes that produce linguistic variation, but as a statistical tool that may be of considerable heuristic value to those searching to discover and understand such processes. (Kay and McDaniel 1979, 152)

Second, as Bickerton (1971, 1973a) argues, regarding variable rules as rules *either* of competence or of performance leads to an intolerable conclusion, since such rules represent statistical generalizations about the speech community as a whole yet are posited by their advocates to belong to the grammars of individual members of the speech community. But how, then, could a variable rule ever be learned? Since speech communities are clearly *not* homogeneous, different members of it would have to be assumed to have the ability to calculate identical probabilities for the variables involved on the basis of exposure to different frequencies![5] For example, speakers of BEV differ in the frequency with which they omit final consonants. But the probabilities associated with rule (1b) are determined from an observation of the entire community of BEV speakers. Variable-rule advocates seem to have placed themselves in the position of implicitly endorsing a theory of language acquisition that guarantees that any two speakers in the community will be led to hypothesize the same rule. Despite their superficially data-hugging appearance, the conception that variable rules are rules of individual grammars represents the reappearance of an extreme uncontrollable form of mentalism—taken literally, they demand the hypothesizing of a "group mind" (Bickerton 1971, 461).

3.5 Some Contributions of Grammatical Theory to the Understanding of Variation

In this section I document some of the ways the generativist hypothesis that linguistic rules are formal, discrete, and abstract has led to an understanding of aspects of linguistic variation.

5. At one point Cedergren and Sankoff comment that "the numerical quantities associated with the features in the environment of a rule are indications of the relative weight

3.5.1 Pidgins and Creoles

The best recent analyses of pidgin and creole continua assume the fundamental principles of grammatical theory. While there are differences in detail among them, the "dynamic paradigm" approach of Bailey (1973a), Bickerton (1973a,b,c, 1975), and Akers (1980, 1981), in which the surface complexities are shown to be a consequence of the interaction of a set of discrete rules, provides an elegant framework for the analysis of such continua.

The dynamic paradigm avoids the untenable assumption that all members of the speech community have the same set of rules. It does assume, however, that "polylectal grammars" exist for the community as a whole. It does not claim that such grammars have any independent psychological reality—that is, that they represent the competence of any individual speaker. It does, however, claim such reality for the subset of rules from this grammar that constitutes the grammar for each individual, different members of the speech community holding different subsets. In Bickerton's words: "The dynamic paradigm retains the concept of the autonomous grammar-forming individual at the cost of rejecting the principle (held tacitly or explicitly by virtually all other persuasions) that individual and community grammars are isomorphic"[6] (1973a, 25).

The most interesting claim made by advocates of the dynamic paradigm is that individual grammars are not randomly chosen from the "polylectal grammar." Rather, there exist implicationally ordered arrays of admissibility conditions that constrain individual grammars. Take the case of final consonant deletion. Akers, instead of describing the phenomenon by a variable rule, says that "a simple and general rule of final consonant deletion of the form $C \rightarrow \emptyset / C \_\_ \#$ applies categorically to all clusters not permitted by the admissibility conditions corresponding to any given [grammar] stage. Instead of the hierarchy of constraints on the application of final consonant deletion posited under the [variable rule] model, final consonant deletion applies to cluster-types of each grammar

---

which they contribute to the applicability of the rule, rather than the existence of discrete probabilities in the head of the speaker" (1974, 335; but see p. 343 of the same article, where they write that "these probabilities are properly part of competence"). Whether the speaker's head contains "relative weights" or "probabilities," the problem of acquisition remains the same.

6. Bickerton believes that Chomsky holds the view of individual-community grammar isomorphism and hence is critical of what he sees as the generativist approach to linguistic variation (see Bickerton 1975, 180ff.). In particular, Bickerton objects to Chomsky's apparent unwillingness (reflected in Chomsky's remarks about "the ideal speaker-listener") to regard the *interaction* of the creole continua rules—as opposed to the individual rules themselves—as part of linguistic competence. While Chomsky, to my knowledge, has made no explicit claim about such matters, it does not seem to me that regarding the rule interaction as a competence phenomenon runs afoul of any generativist principle. It is not at all clear whether the issue is a substantive one or whether it is essentially terminological.

stage, according to the implicational order between successive stages as defined by the admissibility conditions" (Akers 1981, 7–8).

Akers demonstrates that for speakers of Jamaican Creole a series of six increasingly permissive admissibility conditions is sufficient to describe the order of acquisition of acrolectal clusters by basilectal-dominant speakers. Consider the conditions he proposes to characterize the first four of these stages:

(2)   a. $\begin{bmatrix} + \text{consonant} \\ + \text{sonorant} \\ \left\{ \begin{matrix} + \text{nasal} \\ + \text{lateral} \end{matrix} \right\} \end{bmatrix}$ $\begin{bmatrix} - \text{sonorant} \\ - \text{voice} \end{bmatrix}$

       b. $\begin{bmatrix} [\; + \text{consonant}] \\ < + \text{sonorant}> a \\ \left< \left\{ \begin{matrix} + \text{nasal} \\ + \text{lateral} \end{matrix} \right\} \right> b \end{bmatrix}$ $[- \text{sonorant}]$

                                                                    $a \rightarrow b$

       c. $+ \text{plural} \rightarrow - Z$
       d. $+ \text{past} \rightarrow - D$

Speakers at the first stage (2a) have monomorphemic clusters consisting of a nasal or lateral followed by a voiceless obstruent. In the second stage (2b) the initial consonant can be any segment except [r] and the second can be any obstruent, voiced or voiceless. The first bimorphemic clusters (those containing the marker of plurality, possession, and person-number agreement) are added at the third stage (2c), and at the fourth stage (2d) we find the regular past tense marking of the acrolectal system.

Akers's approach is significant because there is no *logical* necessity for creole continua to be characterizable in terms of formal, discrete, implicationally ordered rules. It is through such unexpected results that a theory gains special plausibility. Akers also speculates that the admissibility condition analysis can characterize the notion "linguistic change in progress" and thereby help explain how synchronic grammars come to reflect their historical sources.

Of equal significance is the impressive battery of evidence that advocates of the dynamic paradigm have adduced for the *autonomy* of formal grammar. Bickerton gives several pages of arguments that "demonstrate the independence of grammar from context" and argue against "the incorporation of social or contextual factors in grammars" (1975, 184). For example, he shows that a speaker's choice of style is not linked mechanically to features of the social setting but is a function of *many* interacting phenomena. The importance of the fact that Bickerton's evidence is drawn from the study of a creole system cannot be over-emphasized. Many linguists have concluded that variation in general and the complex interactions of a number of phenomena one finds in pidgins and creoles in particular demonstrate the hopelessness of grammatical theory. When linguists like Labov ask rhetorically, "In what way then, can 'sociolinguistics' be considered as something apart from linguistics?" (1972b, 183), they have in mind the seemingly inseparable sociological and grammatical interplay one finds in a creole system. Bickerton has provided an answer to this question—the optimal description of the grammatical properties of a creole system makes no reference to sociological facts about the speakers. In short, a fundamental aspect of linguistics is not sociolinguistics.

Bickerton has recently (1981, 1982) suggested some further implications for linguistic theory that may be drawn from creole languages. He notes that two facts about such languages pose an interesting challenge to investigators of language acquisition. First, creolization typically involves adding grammatical features not present either in the historically antecedent pidgin language or in the substratum languages. That is, creolization, even more than "normal" language acquisition, involves learning without teaching. Second, creoles the world over share certain grammatical properties. To give one example, Hawaiian Creole English systematically marks the distinction between realized and unrealized complements (by the complementizers *go* and *fo*). This type of distinction was not marked in Hawaiian Pidgin English or in the major languages that came into contact in Hawaii: English, Hawaiian, Chinese, Japanese, Ilocano, and Tagalog. Moreover, the distinction *is* marked in other (completely unrelated) creoles: Jamaican Creole, Sranan, and Mauritian Creole. Bickerton concludes on the basis of these and a great number of related facts that the innately endowed program for language acquisition is even *more* highly structured than generativists have been wont to believe:

> There is only one hypothesis that will account for both phenomena: the hypothesis of an innate bioprogram for language, which, instead of imposing outer limits on possible forms of language, specifies a set of highly particularized, substantive structures which are accessible to the child in the event that linguistic input should be too limited and/or too unstable for an adequate human language system to be derived from it. (1982, 26–27)

3.5.2 Casual Speech Phenomena

A number of linguists examining "casual speech" varieties of language have also come up with evidence that vindicates the essential claims of grammatical theory. Zwicky (1972) demonstrates that the motivation for a variety of casual speech phenomena in English and Welsh cannot be merely "euphonic" (that is, they are not predictable solely on the basis of brevity, ease of articulation, etc.). Rather, these phenomena can be explained only through an abstract phonological or syntactic model. For example, in English casual speech there is a syncope rule that applies before liquids and nasals in words like *cam(e)ra* and *butt(o)ning*. Yet the rule is constrained *not* to apply before obstruents, even though it seems that its output in such cases (*typ(i)cal, Att(i)ca*) is equally as "natural" (i.e., pronounceable) as its output before liquids and nasals. Thus there is evidence that an *abstract rule* is learned. Along the same lines, Zwicky shows that casual speech processes are often sensitive to the position of morpheme boundaries (again, with no obvious "euphonic" explanation). For example, in Welsh casual speech a syncope rule eliminates many instances of word-initial *a-* (in *adroddiád* 'report', *afonýdd* 'rivers', etc.), but never when it is part of the negative prefix *an-*, as in *anallú* 'inability' (*gallu* 'power, ability') or *anorffén* 'endless' (*gorffen* 'finish'). One might think there is a "functional" explanation for this, such as that the non-deletability is an automatic consequence of a general principle whose function is to preserve the identity of semantically contentful prefixes. This appears to be false—the initial vowel of the prefix *ym-* can be deleted in casual speech in *ymweléd* 'to visit' (*gweled* 'see') and *ymddangós* 'to appear' (*dangos* 'to show'). English syncope is similarly sensitive to morpheme boundaries, as Zwicky shows. Consider words ending in [ərij]. One finds schwa syncope quite productively when the [ij] is not a separate morpheme, as in *machinery, shrubbery, hickory, slippery, Bowery*. However, syncope is rare when [ij] is a separate morpheme, as in *cindery, powdery, summery* (cf. *summary*), and *peppery*.

Hasegawa gives an example of a casual speech phenomenon in Japanese that is subject to a complex interplay of sociological and grammatical factors. In the casual speech of "a certain social group, e.g. gangsters . . . and the speakers of certain regional dialects" (1979, 129), a process called Vowel Fusion occurs, which Hasegawa formalizes as in (3):

(3) $\begin{Bmatrix} ai \\ oi \\ ae \end{Bmatrix} \rightarrow \bar{e} / C_1 \underline{\quad}$

Interestingly, this rule is sensitive to word or phrase boundaries. Vowel Fusion applies in (4a) and (b), but not in (c) or (d), illustrating that an explanation based on euphony or brevity alone is not sufficient.

(4)   a. atarimae $\rightarrow$ atarimē 'of course'
        b. sugoi $\rightarrow$ sugē 'great'
        c. ore ga iku $\rightarrow$ *ore gēku 'I go'
        d. ore mo iku $\rightarrow$ *ore mēku 'I also go'

The best-studied casual speech phenomena are those related to English contraction. Every study dealing with contraction has revealed phenomena that require postulating an abstract competence model. For example, the grammarian is faced with explaining why negative contraction is optional in declaratives but obligatory in questions:

(5)   a. John is not working.
       b. John isn't working.
(6)   a. *Is not John working?
       b. Isn't John working?

These facts fall out straightforwardly in the approach of Zwicky and Pullum (1983). These authors present considerable evidence that the properties of *n't* reveal that it is not a contracted word form (clitic) at all, but rather an inflectional affix. Thus the ungrammaticality of (6a) is an automatic consequence of the long-standing generativist assumption that only a constituent may be moved by a grammatical rule.

Consider also the contraction of *be* and other auxiliary verbs in English. As is well known, *is* in English contracts regularly under reduced stress:

(7)   a. There is this much wine in the bottle.
       b. There's this much wine in the bottle.
(8)   a. The concert is here at two o'clock.
       b. The concert's here at two o'clock.

But in certain circumstances contraction is impossible:

(9)   a. I wonder how much wine there is in the bottle.
       b. *I wonder how much wine there's in the bottle.
(10)   a. That's the way it is in real life.
       b. *That's the way it's in real life.

As it turns out, contraction is blocked just before a site from which some syntactic constituent has been removed—a fact whose statement even in English prose betrays the working of an abstract theory. For discussion, see the "global rule" account of King (1970) and G. Lakoff (1970), the word boundary treatment of Selkirk (1972), and the approach of Kaisse (1983a), which refers to the constituent structure of the elements both preceding and following the deletion site.

As Zwicky (1972) has demonstrated, the contraction of *will*, *are*, and *am* is even more severely constrained than that of *is*. These auxiliaries will not contract with words in a preceding relative clause, while *is* will do so:

(11)   a. Anyone who wants to go's [gowz] going to go.
       b. *Anyone who wants to go'll [gowl] have to go.
       c. *All of us who want to go're [gowr] going to go.

The conditions involved blocking this contraction involve reference to fairly abstract properties of constituent structure.

Kaisse (1981) shows that the cliticized form of the pronoun *who*, [(h)ə], can appear only in restricted syntactic conditions: roughly, when it is preceded by the head of the constituent that contains it. Hence the following contrast:

(12)   a.   The people-[həl] be there are very important.
           b.   *[həl] be there?

More exotic forms of contraction seem to involve even further conditions to be posited as part of linguistic competence. For example, Kaisse (1983b) shows that the contraction of *don't know* to *dunno* is blocked by the presence of a deletion site on either the left *or* the right ("∅" signifies a deletion site):

(13)   a.   I dunno what to do.
           b.   *I'm at a loss and ∅ dunno what to do.
           c.   *The procedure that I dunno ∅ involves some fairly sophisticated operations.

One of the most hotly debated recent topics in theoretical linguistics involves the conditions governing the casual speech contraction of *want to* to *wanna*, *have to* to *hafta*, and so on. Chomsky and Lasnik (1977, 1978), Bresnan (1978b), Postal and Pullum (1978), Pullum and Postal (1979), and Jaeggli (1980) are just a small fraction of the papers that have been devoted to this topic. While analyses have differed, they all posit the interaction of very abstract principles as an essential part of the explanation.[7]

3.5.3   Dialect Differences

Capturing dialect differentiation is another area in which the basic assumptions of grammatical theory have played a crucial role. For example, in his discussion of the material presented in the *Linguistic Atlas of the Eastern United States*, Keyser (1963) showed that certain differences in pronunciation between Winchester, Virginia; Charleston, South Carolina; New Bern, North Carolina; and Roanoke, Virginia, could be accounted for nicely if it were posited that the grammars of the dialects of those cities differed according to the presence or absence, and relative ordering, of two rules. In those dialects, the words *five, twice, down,* and *out* are pronounced with the following vowel nuclei:

	Winchester	Charleston	New Bern	Roanoke
five	[ɑ·ɛ]	[ɑ·ɨ]	[a·ɛ]	[ai]
twice	[ɐɨ]	[ɐɨ]	[a·ɛ]	[ɐi]
down	[æ·u]	[au]	[æ·u]	[æu]
out	[ɐu]	[ɐu]	[æu]	[æu]

---

7. For illuminating discussion of a number of casual speech deletions, see the introductory textbook by Akmajian, Demers, and Harnish (1979, 184–206).

In Keyser's analysis, the two relevant rules are ordered in the different dialects as schematized below:

(14)   a. Rule 1: a → ɐ / __ V   C
                                    [-voiced]
        b. Rule 2: a → æ / __ u

Winchester	Charleston	New Bern	Roanoke
Rule 1	Rule 1	—	Rule 2
Rule 2	—	Rule 2	Rule 1

An interesting feature of Keyser's paper is his demonstrating how, by comparing rules and their respective orderings from one dialect to another, it becomes possible to account for the formation of *new* dialect groups through the geographical dissemination of rules (for similar observations with respect to Spanish dialects, see Saporta 1965).

Bailey (1973b) gives dozens of examples of how differences between American dialects (both geographical and social) can be characterized by different orderings of identical rules. One example is of special interest because it reduces what superficially might seem to be profound differences between BEV and Standard English to a relatively trivial difference in rule ordering. Both dialects have the following informally stated rules (Bailey cites William Labov for the data; (15b) is normally a fast speech rule in Standard English):

(15)   a. [ə] is inserted before inflectional
           /d/ following apical stops and before inflectional
           /z/ following sibilants.
        b. t → Ø/___s

In Standard English (15a) precedes (15b); in BEV (15b) precedes (15a). Hence we find BEV pronunciations such as *tesses* and *desses* where Standard English has *tests* and *desks*.

There have likewise been numerous papers showing that *syntactic* differences between dialects are a product of the different orderings of identical (or nearly identical) rules. Possibly the first to do this—and certainly the best known—is Klima (1964b). Klima, for example, contrasted the dialect having the forms of (16) with that in which the sentences of (17) are grammatical:

(16)   a. You spoke with whom?
        b. He is the man with whom I spoke.
        c. The man *whom* I saw John with just left.

(17)   a. You spoke with whom?
        b. He is the man with whom I spoke.
        c. The man *who* I saw John with just left.

Klima reasoned that in the first dialect the rule of Case Assignment precedes *Wh*-Movement, while in the second dialect the reverse order holds.

A similar argument was put forward in Carden (1973b). Among other points, Carden argued that the difference between dialects that include sentences such as (18) and those that reject them is a product of the different orderings of the rules of Tag-Question Formation and Negative Raising in those dialects. If (18) is grammatical, Negative Raising precedes Tag-Question Formation; if it is ungrammatical, the reverse ordering obtains:

(18)   John doesn't think that Mary arrived until 6 P.M., does he?

It is important to point out that many of the specific analyses referred to above have been modified (in some cases drastically) as grammatical theory has advanced. But in no case to my knowledge has the modification undermined the basic point of this section—that differences in dialects are a function of the complex interaction of formal discrete rules (or rule components). And to my knowledge, no one working in theories that reject such rules has provided an explanation (or even anything more than an informal characterization) of the phenomena discussed.[8]

Napoli and Nespor (1979) draw some interesting conclusions about grammatical theory by examining a phenomenon present in two nonstandard varieties of Italian. This phenomenon, "raddoppiamento sintattico" (RS; literally "syntactic doubling"), involves the phonetic lengthening of the initial consonant of a word, as illustrated below:

(19)   *Fa caldo* 'It's hot'
        without RS [fá káldo]
        with RS [fá k:áldo]

Napoli and Nespor state the condition for RS as follows (1979, 824):

(20)   RS can apply between a word *a* and a following word *b*, where *a* is immediately dominated by the preterminal category symbol *A*, and *b* is dominated (not necessarily immediately) by the category symbol *B*, only if *A* is a left branch of the first node that dominates both A and B.

In other words, RS can apply as illustrated in (21):

---

8. The material discussed above also presents a challenge to theorists such as Ringen (1972); Koutsoudas, Sanders, and Noll (1974); and Pullum (1979b), who argue against extrinsic ordering of grammatical rules.

(21)

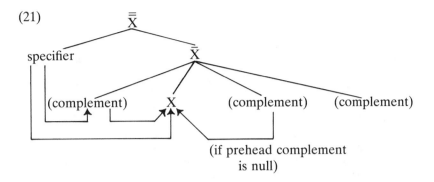

(if prehead complement
is null)

Napoli and Nespor conclude by pointing out the theoretical implications of their analysis of this aspect of Italian variation:

> Our analysis of RS gives serious support to generative grammar in general by making use of the notions "constituent" and "branch." In particular, it supports the status of the notion "major category" as defined in Chomsky 1965 and in Chomsky & Halle 1968, and it shows one more way in which the X̄ notation of Chomsky 1970 can be used to capture this notion. . . .
>
> Furthermore, this analysis claims that phonological rules can have access to syntactic structure, at least to surface structure. Thus the phonological and syntactic components of the grammar cannot be perfectly discrete. (1979, 839)

3.5.4 Speech Errors

Among the more common speech errors are those that involve the anticipation or perseveration of a phonological feature. Typical of the former are errors such as *grottal strain* for *glottal strain* and *a naval infix* for *a nasal infix*. Typical of the latter are *Kingston and Hamston* for *Kingston and Hampton* and *flipping his lib* for *flipping his lid*. "Spoonerisms," of course, involve simultaneous anticipations and perseverations: *fight a liar* for *light a fire* and *the queer old dean* for *the dear old queen*. Fry (1973) discusses the implications of such errors for grammatical theory:

> It is worth pointing out in passing that the occurrence of such phonemic errors makes it impossible to accept the hypothesis which has sometimes been advanced that language-users do not operate with phonemes and that we must regard the syllable or the word as the smallest functional unit for speakers and listeners. If this were true, then all the errors just given could not have occurred at all. To account for a spoonerism such as [ən isteip əv ski:m] for *an escape of steam*, we should be compelled to say that the speaker had, on the spur of the moment, coined a word-final syllable new to the language in [steip] and had followed this up by selecting the word scheme from the word store

in the face of all the constraints of semantic planning and sequential probability. To call such an explanation far-fetched would be an understatement.

Over thirty years ago, Twaddell in his monograph "On Defining the Phoneme" referred to a "mythological view of the linguistic process according to which a speaker reaches into his store of phonemes, selects the proper number of each, arranges them tastefully and then produces an utterance." All the evidence points to the fact that this is what the speaker does, if we discard the ironical adjective "tastefully," and far from being mythological, this view is the only one which allows us to account for many of the things which actually happen in speech, particularly the kind of errors in speech generation which have been cited above. (Fry 1973, 161)

Fromkin (1971, 1975) discusses other interesting conclusions about the nature of grammar that can be drawn from certain types of phonological errors. For example, the following errors, represented by the forms to the right of the arrow, have all been attested:

(22)   a. swing and sway → swin and sweyg
            [swĩŋ . . . swe] → [swĩn . . . sweg]
         b. Bing Crosby → Big Cronsby
            [bĩŋ krɔzbi] → [big krɔ̃nzbi]
         c. ring her neck → rink her neg
            [rĩŋ . . . nɛk] → [rĩŋk . . . nɛg]

The problem is to account for phonetic [g] in the errors, since the intended target utterances have no [g]. This is easily accomplished if one assumes that velar nasals are derived from phonemic /ng/'s—the analysis made by Sapir (1925) and by Chomsky and Halle (1968) but rejected by advocates of natural generative phonology (see Vennemann 1973; Hooper 1976).[9]

In discussing what might be learned from an analysis of these and similar errors, Fromkin makes the extremely strong claim that "behavioral data of the kind described here may not be necessary to validate hypotheses about linguistic competence, but they certainly are *sufficient* for such verification (1971, 30; emphasis added).

As Fromkin (1975) shows, speech errors give support to the existence of word-formation rules along the lines posited in Halle (1973). The following errors have been attested:

---

9. For discussion of the relative role that the constructs "distinctive feature," "phonetic segment," and "syllable" play in speech errors, and what might thereby be concluded about the nature of sentence processing, see Shattuck-Hufnagel (1982).

(23)   a. a New Yorker → a New Yorkan
        b. counter indicator → counter indicant
        c. resemblance → resemblancy
        d. untactful → distactful
        e. motivate → motify

Fromkin suggests that these errors can be explained if one assumes that the speaker selected a lexical morpheme but then applied the "wrong" word-formation rule.

As Zwicky (1982) points out, lexical errors (malapropisms, for example) "bear only at great remove and in a limited way on issues of linguistic theory" (131). However, his paper and Fay and Cutler (1977) both contain interesting speculations, based on speech error data, about what might be involved in accessing items from the lexicon in the process of speech production.

3.5.5   Language Play

Languages made up for purposes of play (or concealment) often reveal properties of the internalized grammars of their users. For example, Applegate (1961) described a secret language made up by three brothers in "a small New England community near Boston" (187). While this language exhibited syntactic and morphological differences from that spoken by the brothers' parents and playmates, its special linguistic interest arises from its phonological differences. It can be characterized as deviating from Standard English by possessing two additional rules: (1) in a word containing several identical stop consonants, all but the first of these are replaced by a glottal stop; and (2) all continuants are replaced by the cognate stops. Hence:

(24)   a. [ba?iy] 'Bobby'
        b. [pey?ər] 'paper'
        c. [pə?iy] 'puppy'
        d. [dəd] 'does'
        e. [takt] 'talks'
        f. [teykt] 'takes'

However, observe the following two forms:

(25)   a. [takɨ?] 'talked'
        b. [teykɨ?] 'took' (alternating with [tuk])

How can the barred-*i* in these examples be accounted for? Clearly, Applegate concludes, by assuming that the secret language rule creating glottal stops applies *before* the Standard English rule determining the phonetic features of positional variants. In other words:

> The rules that are peculiar to the children's dialect are not mere appendages to the grammar but are an integral part of the set of rules for generating sentences in that dialect. They are ordered not only in relation to each other, but also in relation to the other rules of the grammar. . . . On the basis of our observations, we may say that the children's speech does not represent a random attempt to imitate the language of the adult community. Instead, it is clearly an autonomous system with well developed rules. (192–93)

Halle (1962) has used Pig Latin to illustrate the importance for dialectologists of comparing *grammars* rather than merely the superficial characteristics of related dialects. As Halle points out:

> If we compared utterances in Pig Latin with their cognates in General American, we should be struck by the extreme differences between them:

General American	Pig Latin
/str´īt/	/´itstrē/
/str´īts/	/´itstrē/
/k´æt/	/´ætkē/
/k´æts/	/´ætskē/
/r´ōz/	/´ōzrē/
/r´ōzɨz/	/´ōzɨzrē/

> We observe that the distribution of phonemes in Pig Latin differs radically from that in General American, for in the former all words end in the vowel /ē/, and very unusual consonant clusters abound. We note also that infixation rather than prefixation and suffixation is the major morphological device. In view of this, we are hardly surprised to find that Pig Latin is incomprehensible to the uninitiated speaker of General American. Since these are precisely the observations we would expect to make if we compared the utterances in two totally unrelated languages, we are led to conclude that Pig Latin and General American are unrelated, or, at best, only remotely related tongues; a conclusion which is patently false. (1962, 342)

However, if instead of "hugging the phonetic ground closely" we compared the grammars of Pig Latin and "General American," we would find that they differ in a relatively trivial way—the grammar of Pig Latin, but not that of English, contains the following rule:

(26) Shift initial consonant cluster to end of word and add /ē/

As Halle concludes, "this result follows only if instead of concentrating on the utterances, we shift primary attention to the grammars that underlie the utterances" (343).[10]

10. Ferguson (1982) has pointed out that rules like (26) (and many other rules found in play languages) are not typical of phonological rules found in "normal" languages. However, they *do* bear a resemblance to the rules that characterize simplified speech registers.

Sherzer (1970, 1976) argues for abstract phonological representations on the basis of a language game called *sorsik sunmakke* 'talking backward' played by the Cuna Indians of San Blas, Panama. The game consists of moving the first syllable of a word to the end of the word. Thus:

(27)   a. [obsa] 'bathed' → [saob]
         b. [dage] 'come' → [geda]
         c. [mila] 'tarpon' → [lami]

However, at least one word appears to violate this rule:

(28)   [bíriga] 'year' → [gabir], not *[rigabi]

Sherzer points out that if the underlying phonological representation of [bíriga] is /birga/ (i.e., if the second [i] is epenthetic), then [gabir] is a perfectly regular form in *sorsik sunmakke*. What is the evidence for this move toward abstractness? In Cuna the stress usually falls on the penultimate syllable of the word, but [bíriga] appears to be an exception. However, if the [i] is epenthetic, the rule of stress placement will stress, correctly, the first vowel in the word. In other words, positing an epenthesis rule allows generalizations both about stress placement and about the rules of *sorsik sunmakke* to be preserved.

Along the same lines, Sherzer shows how *sorsik sunmakke* data can provide evidence about the underlying representation of geminate consonants. The Cuna word *in·a* 'chicha', pronounced backward, becomes *nain*. In other words, it seems reasonable to conclude that *n·* is represented phonologically as a sequence of segments.

The output of the rules of Pig Latin and *sorsik sunmakke* are forms that are typically, if not always, well-formed phonologically in the languages from which these play dialects are derived. Swintramont (1973) discusses the Thai word game *khamphuan*, in which, all other things being equal, the game rules would produce ill-formed sequences of segments.[11] In this game, in bisyllabic words everything except the initial consonant is exchanged between the two syllables. In one possible output of this rule (KP_1), the tone of the two syllables is exchanged, in the other (KP_2), the segmental portions are exchanged, but not the tone. Hence:

(29)
	Gloss	*Word*	KP_1	KP_2
a.	see movie	duu + năŋ	dăŋ + nuu	daŋ + nŭu
b.	dance	tên + ram	tam + rên	tâm + ren

However, there are words in which only KP_1 may be used, as illustrated in (30):

---

11. What follows is based wholly on the material presented in Churma (1979).

(30)   *Gloss*   *Word*   *KP₁*   *KP₂*

a. Friday   wan + sùg   wùg + san   *wug + sàn
b. touch head   càb + hŭa   cŭa + hàb   *cùa + hăb
c. attend temple   paj + wád   pád + waj   *pad + wáj

Churma (1979) summarizes Swintramont's explanation of the above data as follows:

> This explanation concerns "the distribution of tone in Thai syllables," which (p. 126) "can be stated in this way: syllables [which do not end in a stop or short vowel] can have any of the five tones. . . . But syllables [which end in a stop or short vowel] are always restricted to one of three tones: low, high, or falling." He continues (p. 127) that "this condition on tone distribution of . . . syllables [which end in a stop or short vowel] places a constraint on KP as well. When a final of a live syllable, 'X', is exchanged with the final of a dead syllable, 'Y', . . . the final X must carry its own tone. . . ." That is, only KP₁ may be used when KP₂ "would generate an impermissible structure." (1979, 101–2)

In other words, the forms actually used in playing *khampuan* are determined by the interaction of the grammatical rules of Thai and the rules of the word game.

3.5.6   Bilingual Code Switching

As is well known, bilinguals often produce utterances in which the two languages they speak appear to be mixed. For example, consider the following instances of midsentence code switching, cited from the speech of Spanish-English bilinguals by Pfaff (1979):

(31)   a.   No van a bring it up in the meeting.
              'They are not going to bring it up in the meeting'
         b.   Todos los Mexicanos were riled up.
              'All the Mexicans were riled up'
         c.   Estaba training para pelear.
              'He was training to fight'
         d.   Some dudes, la onda is to fight y jambar.
              'Some dudes, the in thing is to fight and steal'

Quite a few linguists have addressed the nature of the grammatical principles constraining code switching. For example, Sankoff and Poplack (1980) hypothesize that, in addition to their separate monolingual grammars, bilinguals have a third, code-switching grammar. This third grammar is considered to consist essentially of the free union of all portions of both monolingual grammars, subject to certain constraints, such as Poplak's (1980) bound-morpheme constraint (which prohibits code switches between a bound morpheme and the rest of a word) and an equivalence constraint (which prohibits code switching between any two phrase structure nodes that occur in an order unique to one of the languages).

A number of recent treatments of code switching have taken a more modular view of the interaction of the two grammars than did Sankoff and Poplack. Woolford (1981), for example, suggests that the possible forms produced result from the interaction of the components of each of two monolingual grammars. The phrase structure rules from both grammars are freely mixed in the construction of trees, but the lexicon and word-formation component of each grammar remain entirely autonomous:

(32)

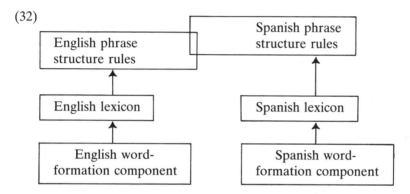

Poplack's bound-morpheme constraint follows directly from the fact that the word-formation components (in the sense of Aronoff 1976) remain autonomous. Woolford's model also predicts that nodes created by a phrase structure rule unique to one language must be filled by the lexicon from that language (i.e., forms like *I went to the house chiquita 'I went to the little house' are impossible).

In the treatments of Doron (1981), Joshi (1983), and Muysken, di Sciullo, and Singh (1982), the two grammars are regarded as *completely* distinct. Doron and Joshi propose parsing principles sensitive to constituent structure that allow or disallow switches from one language to the other. For Muysken, di Sciullo, and Singh, the most important principles governing code switching are entirely grammatical. They argue that certain concepts from the framework for syntactic description known as the government-binding theory (see Chomsky 1981), in particular that of "government," are crucial to explaining when it is possible to switch from one language into another.

4

Formal Grammar and Extragrammatical Principles

4.1 Introduction

The alternative to the generativist conception of an autonomous formal grammar is the hypothesis that grammatical facts can, in large part or in totality, be reduced to facts derivable from the properties of some *general* human attribute (i.e., an attribute not specific to language). For example, a popular view holds that much of what generativists would incorporate into the grammatical model is, in fact, a consequence of some general principles governing human *communication*. Advocates of this view share "a conviction that the structure of language cannot be fruitfully studied, described, understood, or explained without reference to communicative function" (Givón 1979a, xv).

There is a fairly wide spectrum of opinion that shares such a conviction. It ranges from the theory of "form-content linguistics" (García 1975; Diver 1980), which maintains that a communicative orientation renders unnecessary traditional notions like "constituency," "syntactic category," and "grammatical rule," to frameworks that take a "discourse-based" approach to grammar and attempt to derive such constructs largely or entirely from their function in discourse. Most varieties of "textlinguistics," a leading European approach (see Dijk 1972, 1977; Petöfi 1973), stress communicative function as a determinant of structure, as do most "functional(ist)" approaches to language.

A complementary approach attempts to ground as many properties of language as possible in principles that govern some aspect of human cognitive functioning. Generally, proposals along these lines involve hypothesizing a "perceptual strategy" or "processing strategy," whose effect is to eliminate the need for a principle or principles assumed by generativists to be internal to grammatical theory. A typical example is

96

the perceptual principle proposed in Bever (1975) to explain why grammatical processes that occur in main clauses but not subordinate clauses are very common, while those that occur in subordinate but not main clauses are rare (see Emonds 1970, 1976 and Ross 1973 for examples). Bever argues that this is a consequence of a general principle governing the processing of foreground and background material within one's perceptual space—a principle that he argues applies to visual perception as well as language. Therefore, in Bever's view, the generalization need not be stipulated as part of grammatical theory.

My purpose in this chapter is to point out what I see as some of the principal limitations of the attempt to replace formal grammar in its entirety by a set of communication- or cognition-based principles. I do not intend to analyze comprehensively even one branch of this extremely diverse school of thought, though in section 4.3 I will review two books that I take to be representative: Dwight Bolinger's *Meaning and Form* and Talmy Givón's *On Understanding Grammar*.

While the view that grammar is grounded in discourse-based principles is immensely popular, an immediate problem faces anyone wishing to scrutinize its implications. This is the universal lack of a clear formulation of the specifics involved in deriving grammatical facts from such principles. Most discourse-based approaches repudiate, at least for the time being, the need to construct a formal theory. In the words of a leading advocate of discourse-based grammar: "The lack of concern with formalism . . . represents [the] recognition of the fact that our knowledge and understanding of the languages of the world is far from sufficient for postulating adequate generative systems or for debating the nature of generative mechanisms, or even for determining whether the generative approach to the study of language is indeed correct" (Li 1976, xi).

Another obstacle to evaluating the claims and consequences of discourse-based approaches is the extreme fuzziness of most of the notions to which it appeals. Reference is typically made to discourse-oriented constructs like "topic," "comment," "old information," "new information," "theme," "empathy," "point of view," "informativeness," "mental effort," and so on. Yet no comprehensive theory of discourse exists in which even one of these terms is given an explicit characterization. The result is that we find the same term used differently by different authors (see Li 1976, x for discussion of the "elusive" nature of the notion "topic"), and, as far as I can determine, even individual authors are not completely consistent in their use of terminology.

Before beginning my discussion, I must stress that advocating the autonomy of syntax in no way suggests that the appropriateness of a sentence can be understood without reference to its function in discourse, and it *certainly* does not entail the absurd view that "transformational grammar thus discounts the possibility that certain characteristics of a sentence may simply be consequences of the larger discourse of which it is a part" (García 1979, 24). On the contrary, in keeping with a modular approach to language, generativists are happy to posit *any* combination of factors, discourse-based or other, at work in the determination of "certain characteristics of a sentence."

The way syntax and discourse interact can be shown by examining English sentences containing both a direct and an indirect object. Verbs such as *give* and *sell* regularly occur in both the $V\frown NP_1\frown to\frown NP_2$ and the $V\frown NP_2\frown NP_1$ ("double-object") constructions, as illustrated below:

(1)   a. John gave the book to Mary.
        b. John gave Mary the book.
(2)   a. John sold a bicycle to Bill.
        b. John sold Bill a bicycle.

However, if NP_1 is a definite pronoun and NP_2 is not, the double-object construction sounds peculiar:

(3)   a. John gave it to Mary.
        b. ?John gave Mary it.
(4)   a. John sold it to Bill.
        b. ?John sold Bill it.

Why should this be? The earliest generativist treatments simply built into the rule relating the two construction types the stipulation that NP_1 in the double-object construction cannot be a pronoun. However, Erteschik-Shir (1979) has laid the basis for a treatment of the unacceptable forms that removes from the syntax the burden of accounting for their deviance. She provides a number of examples to illustrate that NP_1 in the double-object construction is always understood as being what she terms "discourse-dominant." Essentially, an element in a sentence is discourse-dominant if and only if the speaker intends to direct the attention of the hearer to the semantic content of that element by uttering the sentence. Since discourse dominance, as thus characterized, cannot be a property of an unstressed pronoun, it follows that (3b) and (4b) will be unacceptable.

If something along these lines is correct, then a narrow condition referring to pronouns can be replaced by a general one referring to any element with a particular discourse property. But, as Erteschik-Shir goes on to observe, the oddness of (3b) and (4b) might be a consequence of an even deeper principle—*in general* it seems that, in English, one does not find discourse-dominant material in sentence-final position. While she is careful not to make sweeping claims about such matters, given the difficulty of characterizing precisely the notion of "discourse dominance," her approach holds out the hope that no condition at all need be imposed on the rule that derives the double-object construction. That is, the deviance of (3b) and (4b) might be a simple consequence of the interaction of this rule and the discourse principle.

There is no hope, however, of attributing the properties of the English double-object construction *entirely* to one discourse principle, or to a set of them. As is demonstrated in Fischer (1971), Green (1974), and Oehrle (1976), the V⁀NP⁀NP construction is associated with numerous discourse (and semantic) functions, few (if any) of which are unique to it. Thus there is no obvious discourse-based principle that would predict the acceptability of (1b) and (2b) above and (5a–b) below, yet rule out (6a–b):

(5)   a.   I consider John my friend.
       b.   We elected her president.

(6)   a.   *I regard John my friend.
       b.   *We overthrew him king.

It seems to be the case, then, that neither grammatical principles alone nor discourse-based principles alone suffice to characterize the acceptability of sentences of the form NP⁀V⁀NP⁀NP.

Quite a few linguists have done creative work on the interface between syntax and discourse without abandoning the generativist autonomy hypothesis (for specific examples of such work, see Kuno 1975; Prince 1978; and Horn 1978). Kuno is explicit about the compatibility between the goals of formal syntacticians and those whose principal interest is in determining how discourse factors influence the acceptability of sentences:[1]

> Each theory of grammar must have a place or places where various functional constraints on the well-formedness of sentences or sequences of sentences can be stated, and each theory of grammar can benefit from utilizing a functional perspective in analysis of concrete syntactic phenomena. Therefore, in theory, there is no conflict between functional syntax and, say, the revised extended standard theory of generative grammar. Given a linguistic process that is governed purely by syntactic factors, this process will be described in the syntactic component of grammar both by pure syntacticians and by functional syntacticians. On the other hand, given a linguistic process that is governed by both syntactic and, say, discourse factors, the syntactic aspect will be formulated in the syntactic component, while discourse factors that interact with this syntactic characterization will be de-

1. Though I find infelicitous Kuno's phrase "the discourse component of grammar," which implies that the same sorts of formal devices suitable for stating syntactic and phonological generalizations are also appropriate for discourse. There is certainly no reason to believe that.

scribed in, say, the discourse component of grammar. Pure syntacticians would concentrate on the former characterization, and functional syntacticians, on the latter. There need not be any disagreement between the two. (1980, 117–18)

The thrust of Kuno's work has been the attempt to replace complex constraints on syntactic rules by generalizations rooted in discourse, thus "making the theory of syntax less powerful, and hence, more desirable" (1978, 280). While perhaps not all generativists feel that Kuno has been entirely successful in his undertaking, none dispute the desirability of his goals.

In the following three sections I will scrutinize three beliefs typifying approaches that advocate the replacement of formal grammar in its entirety by principles derived from communication or cognition or both: the function of language is communication (section 4.2.1); grammatical form is derivable from extragrammatical principles (section 4.2.2); and communicative function explains linguistic form (section 4.2.3).

4.2   Three Popular Beliefs about Language

4.2.1   First Belief: The Function of Language Is Communication

What is the function of human language? In the opinion of many this terse question has an even terser answer: "The function of language is communication." Obviously, communication is a function of language—perhaps, according to some plausible but still undevised scale, its most important function. But communication does not appear to be the *only* function of language. Language is used for thought, for problem solving, for play, for dreaming, for displays of group solidarity, for deception, for certain specialized literary modes such as represented speech (Banfield 1982), and possibly to fulfill an instinctive need for symbolic behavior (Langer 1942); in fact, language plays an integral role in virtually every conceivable human activity. Now one might, of course, choose to call all these attributes and abilities "communication." But doing so, it seems to me, takes from the word "communication" any meaning other than "acting human." Surely, given the ordinary English use of the term, there are linguistic aspects of these activities that do not count as "communication." If so, then the answer given above is simply false. Communication is *a* function of language, not *the* function. And it therefore follows that a theory whose methodology is derived from the idea that communication is *the* function of language must be considered suspect.

While the origin and early evolution of language are problematic, there is certainly no positive evidence that language arose to fulfill a need to communicate. And even if it did arise primarily for that function, it would not therefore follow that its structural development would have progressed in lockstep with its functional development. For example, Mattingly (1972) and Liberman (1974) speculate that grammar may have originated primarily as an interfacing system linking the several mismatched components of transmission and intellect common to language (long-term memory, intelligence, the properties of the ear and vocal tract, etc.), rather than as a direct reflection of external communicative needs.

4.2.2   Second Belief: Grammatical Form Is Derivable from Extragrammatical Principles

If linguistic form were in any sense a *direct* reflection of extragrammatical principles, then there would be no need at all for language-particular syntactic statements. One presumably would need do no more than derive grammatical effects from the relevant principles. However, this is impossible. At every level of investigation we are impressed with the incredible *diversity* of grammatical structures among the languages of the world. All six possible orders of subject, object, and verb have now been definitely attested (for a catalog of languages with some of the rarer constituent order types, see Pullum 1981). There are languages in which the topic of the utterance is marked by word order and languages in which the topic is marked by morphology (see Givón 1979b, 82). There are languages with rich inflectional systems and those with no inflections. There are languages with rigid word order and languages in which word order is practically free. Now, obviously, the degree to which languages may vary *is* constrained by the circumstance that language is used to perform a variety of vital human functions, communication among them. No doubt the fact that no language consists only of voiceless sounds or lacks some device for conveying "plurality" has a "functional" explanation. But that virtually every plausibly necessary function of language can be manifested grammatically in many different ways gives the lie to the most simplistic view of the form-function relation.

To take a concrete example, consider the various ways that relative clauses may be formed in the languages of the world. Let's assume a "functional" characterization of such clauses: their function is to modify a noun while preserving to some degree the rudiments of propositional structure (which would distinguish them, say, from pre- or postnominal adjectives). Let's also assume (without any independent evidence) that this function is "necessary" for communication.[2] What can we conclude, then, about the form a relative clause will take? Absolutely nothing. Givón (1979b, 146–52) illustrates the great diversity of existing "strat-

---

2. The evidence, in fact, suggests that this function is *not* necessary. The language Hixkaryana has nothing that could properly be called a "relative clause" (see Derbyshire 1979).

egies"[3] of relative clause formation in the world's languages: among other ways, relatives may be formed by complete nonreduction of the clause (as in Bambara), by gapping the coreferent noun phrase (as in Japanese), by changing word order (as in English), by nominalization (as in Turkish), by use of a resumptive pronoun (as in Hebrew), by use of a relative pronoun (as in Spanish), or by coding the verb (as in Philippine languages). While, as Givón demonstrates, the strategy a particular language may employ correlates with other structural properties of that language, it seems to be literally the case that in general *any* strategy is possible, consistent with the general (function-independent) properties of universal grammar. The one/many relation between the function of relativization and the form relative clauses may take not only makes the claim that form reflects function (or other external factors) seem dubious, it also calls into question the much weaker hypothesis that the former even correlates in any interesting way with the latter.[4]

Conversely, we find what appear to be true structural universals of language not admitting at all (as far as I can tell) to extragrammatical explanations. A good example is "Wackernagel's law" (see Wackernagel 1892 and, for recent discussion, Klavans 1980; Kaisse 1982; Baltin 1982). Wackernagel was apparently the first to notice that sentential clitics always occur in "second position"—that is, after the first stressed word or phrase in the sentence. Hence, as is illustrated in (7) and (8), the Pashto clitic *xo* 'indeed' and the Tagalog clitic *ko* 'I' regularly occur in second position, regardless of the nature of the element occupying first position (the data are taken from Kaisse 1982):

(7)   *Pashto*
   a.   Tor   xo   de   nən   xar   nə   rawali
        Tor   indeed   should   today   donkey   not   bring
        'Tor   really   shouldn't   bring   the   donkey   today'
   b.   nən   xo   de   xar   nə   rawali
        today   indeed   should   donkey   not   bring
   c.   xar   xo   de   nə   rawali
        donkey   indeed   should   not   bring
   d.   nə   xo   de   rawali
        not   indeed   should   bring
   e.   rawali   xo   de
        bring   indeed   should
        'Indeed,   he   should   bring   it'

---

3. Advocates of discourse-based grammar frequently use the term "strategy" when it appears that they mean "rule." Apparently "strategy" has a more discourse-flavored communicative sound to it than "rule."

4. Sankoff and Brown (1976), in their interesting study of relative clauses in New Guinea Tok Pisin, show how such clauses have developed since the earliest stages of pidginization from structures that had broader discourse functions. But their claim to have demonstrated that "syntactic structure, in this case, can be understood as a component of, and derivative

(8)   *Tagalog*

a.	nakita	ko	siya	ngayon		
	have seen	I	him	today		
b.	hindi	ko	siya	nakita	ngayon	
	not	I	him	have seen	today	
c.	bakit	ko	siya	hindi	nakita	ngayon
	why	I	him	not	have seen	today

There is no obvious reason why the exigencies of communication or the structure of the human perceptual apparatus would demand second position as opposed to third, fourth, or last; or, for that matter, why there should be sentential clitics at all. Those taking a reductionist approach to grammar have the obligation to demonstrate that, in some sense, the occurrence of sentential clitics in second position "reflects" the function of such clitics.

The more abstract the universal, the more implausible an external explanation appears to be. For example, in several publications Chomsky has called attention to the implications of the structure-dependent nature of grammatical rules (see section 1.5.2). No language exists in which grammatical processes do not make reference to abstract constituent structure. Yet surely it is not true that communicative need *demands* that processes have this property.[5] Chomsky comments:

> [Structure-dependence] seems to be a general property of an interest-ing class of linguistic rules, innate to the mind. . . . [L]et us try to account for [this property] in terms of communication. I see no way of doing so. Surely this principle enters into the function of language; we might well study the ways in which it does. But a language could function for communication (or otherwise) just as well with structure-independent rules, so it would seem. For a mind differently consti-tuted, structure-independent rules would be far superior, in that they require no abstract analysis of a sentence beyond words. I think that the example is typical. Where it can be shown that structures serve a particular function, that is a valuable discovery. To account for or somehow explain the structure of [universal grammar], or of particular grammars, on the basis of functional considerations is a pretty hopeless prospect, I would think. (1975b, 57–58)

---

from, discourse structure" (631) is highly misleading. They present no explanation of why a particular "discourse structure" (itself a misleading expression, given the informality of their discussion of discourse roles) should have led to a particular syntactic structure.

5. Sampson (1978) attempts to provide an external explanation for both structure dependence and the cyclic application of grammatical rules (see below). He suggests that they follow from Herbert Simon's hypothesis (1962) that there is evolutionary pressure toward making natural systems hierarchical in structure. Yet the gap between Simon's extremely general observations and the intricacy of the phenomena Sampson proposes to explain is so great that the latter's remarks, it seems to me, have very little content. Also, for reasons that are unclear to me, Sampson regards Simon's hypothesis as supporting an empiricist approach to language.

Or consider the cyclic property of transformational rule application. Evidence from a number of languages indicates that transformations apply cycling from the most deeply embedded sentence to the topmost one. That is, given an underlying structure like (9) below, transformational rules apply first on the domain S_4, then on S_3, then on S_2, and finally on S_1 (for thorough discussion of the cyclic principle, see Pullum 1979b):

(9)

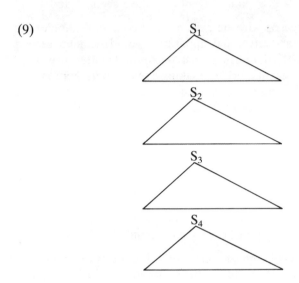

While the cycle apparently cannot be motivated for the grammars of all languages, there are no languages for which it has been counterexemplified (that is, there are no languages in which a rule must apply in a higher clause before another rule in a lower clause). Why should this be? What theory of discourse or perception predicts the transformational cycle?

There have been quite a few attempts to remove various proposed constraints on grammatical rules from the grammar per se and attribute them to the functioning of the human perceptual apparatus, to the problems involved in accessing certain syntactic structures in discourse, to communicative strategies designed to minimize confusion, and so on (see Bever 1970; Grosu 1972; Kuno 1976; Marcus 1980). Such attempts seem eminently reasonable. So consider, for example, the following unacceptable sentence of English (*who* is to be interpreted as the object of *bit*):

(10)   *The man who I saw the dog that bit fell down.

Generativists have typically proposed *structural* explanations for the unacceptability of sentences of this type, though specifics have differed.

One such explanation is Ross's (1968) Complex Noun Phrase Constraint. According to Ross, no element may be extracted from a sentence that is dominated by a noun phrase with a lexical head noun. As one can see by examining the structure underlying (10), *who* is in a position that, by Ross's constraint, prevents its extraction from the sentence that dominates it:[6]

(11)

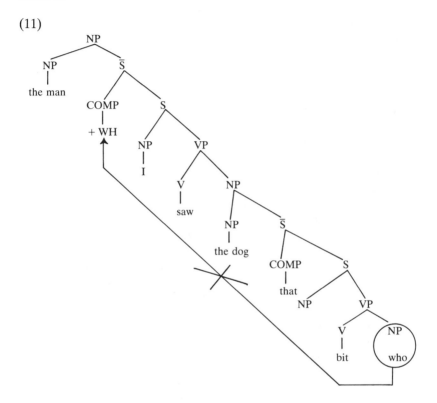

Instead of attempting to block (10) by a syntactic constraint, one might explore the possibility that its deviance results from some principle outside the domain of formal grammar. Recall from section 1.4.1 that the unacceptability of multiply center-embedded constructions is essentially a product of the limitations of the human sentence-processing mechanism. One might hypothesize, then, a similar explanation for Complex Noun Phrase Constraint violations. At an intuitive level, at least, (10) does seem as though it might present processing difficulties. Indeed, Givón (1979b) has proposed an explanation along those lines. He has

6. Notice that the A-over-A Principle (see section 1.4) also blocks (10). For a general overview of recent approaches to constraints on grammars, see Newmeyer (1980a, chaps. 6 and 8).

suggested that sentences such as (10) "are difficult to process because the grammatical-functional relations in the deeply embedded clause are hard to reconstruct, given the deletion, the lack of morphological indicators, and the fact that there is a large gap between the head noun *the man* (object of *bit*) and the verb of which it is the object" (17). Givón's case for a processing explanation is bolstered, as he points out, by the fact that sentences like (12), in which the "grammatical-functional relation" in the embedded clause is marked by a resumptive pronoun, are fully acceptable in some dialects of English, and (one assumes) easier to understand than (10) for all speakers:

(12)   The man that I saw the dog that bit him fell down.

Critics of the generativist autonomy thesis have been extremely zealous in their attempts to demonstrate that *all* proposed syntactic constraints are in reality derivable from extragrammatical principles. The goal seems to be, in effect, to remove so much from formal grammar that it is "constrained" out of its very existence.

There are, however, severe problems with any *general* attempt to relieve grammatical theory of the responsibility of accounting for sentences whose deviance results from a putative constraint violation. Consider the Complex Noun Phrase Constraint again. To begin with, any theory that attempts to derive its effects *solely* from its property of facilitating communication would be hard pressed to explain why sentences that "violate" it are perfectly acceptable—and understandable— in Swedish (the data are taken from Allwood 1976):

(13)   a. Vad ser jag en hund som gnager på?
            'What do I see a dog who is gnawing on?'
        b. En kyss känner jag till en flicka som gav en pojke på Röda Torget.
            'A kiss, I know of a girl who gave a boy in Red Square.'
        c. Stina som jag hade en stille undran om verkligen sett Pelle. . . .
            'Stina who I had a quiet wonder if really had seen Pelle. . .'

Given the assumption that Swedish speakers do not differ from speakers of English in their intrinsic capabilities to process discourse, one must wonder how contentful the claim is that the Complex Noun Phrase Constraint reflects (or is an artifact of) its discourse function to facilitate comprehension. It seems quite clear that English and Swedish speakers learn different *structural* possibilities, which only indirectly reflect their discourse functions.

The nonapplicability of a constraint on the grammar of one language to that on the grammar of another is common. For example, it is well known

that structures of the form [$_S$ *that* ___ VP] are unacceptable in English
(see Perlmutter 1971; Chomsky and Lasnik 1977; Chomsky 1981):

(14)   *Who do you think that ___ came?

Do the facts surrounding this construction demand a structural account,
or are they rooted in (or replaceable by) a statement derivable from the
general properties of discourse or perception? The latter hardly seems
likely, since sentences analogous to (14) are perfectly acceptable in
Icelandic (see Maling and Zaenen 1978 for discussion):

(15)   Hver sagðir þú, að ___ væri kominn til Reykjavíkur?
        'Who did you say that had come to Reykjavik?'

Faced with the nonuniversality of grammatical constraints that are
plausibly derived from perceptual principles or from the processing of
discourse, one could retreat to the position that *for each language* grammatical structures reflect external factors, though different languages
might make use of different strategies for the effects of such factors to be
realized. This retreat results in a *far* less interesting theory, since now the
strategies involved, it seems, would have to refer to language-specific
grammatical information—that is, this retreat makes a fundamental concession in the direction of formal grammar. To an advocate of autonomous syntax, there is nothing disturbing about a constraint at work in
one language but not in another, though naturally one is pleased to
discover universal constraints on grammars. But how could one who
believes that formal grammar is artifactual help but be disturbed, after
postulating that a sentence type in one language is unacceptable "because" of some extragrammatical principle, to find that the same sentence type in another language is perfectly acceptable? It seems, then,
that one would have to lower one's sights merely to search for *correlations*
between grammatical constructions in a particular language and some
external principle.

Even at the language-particular level, the correlations seem in general
too weak to allow proposed constraints on grammars to be attributed
entirely to extragrammatical principles. Given the Swedish facts, let's
assume that Givón's perceptual explanation for the deviance of (10) and
relative acceptability of (12) follows from facts about how *English* speakers process sentences. Even there we run into trouble. As Van Valin
(1981) points out, there are sentences like (16), in which there is deletion,
no morphological indication of grammatical relations, and a large gap
between the *wh*-word and the verb of which it is the object, that are fully
acceptable; and there are those, like (17a–b), that employ the resumptive
pronoun strategy and are quite unacceptable:

(16)   What do John and the other boys really believe that the old drunken sailor actually saw?

(17)   a. *What do you believe the claim that John saw it?
         b. *Who did you see the dog that bit him?

Along the same lines, consider the status of the Nested Dependency Constraint, which J. D. Fodor (1978) motivates and formulates as in (18):

(18)   The Nested Dependency Constraint (NDC)
        If there are two or more filler-gap dependencies in the same sentence, their scopes may not intersect if either disjoint or nested dependencies are compatible with the well-formedness conditions of the language.

The NDC rules out i-j-i-j filler gap dependencies such as the following ("$\triangle$" indicates a gap, that is, a position from which the filler—marked by the same subscript—was removed):

(19)   a. *What$_i$ are boxes$_j$ easy to store $\triangle_i$ in $\triangle_j$?
         b. *This form$_i$, foreign students are required to list $\triangle_j$ on $\triangle_i$ [the dates of all previous visits to the United States]$_j$
         c. *[Which of the guests]$_i$ did you have to ask Mother who$_j$ to introduce $\triangle_i$ to $\triangle_j$?

The deviance of the sentences of (19) seems a likely candidate for a perceptual explanation. Is the NDC then simply an artifact of the human (or of English speakers') ability to process certain types of complex sentences?[7] The crucial evidence comes from sentences of the form of (20):

(20)   *[Which boy]$_i$ did you shout $\triangle_j$ to $\triangle_i$ [that there was a bull in the field]$_j$?

Sentence (20) violates the NDC and is judged not fully acceptable by speakers of English. Yet, as Fodor reports, it is not in the least *uninterpretable*. Speakers have no difficulty in linking the fillers and the gaps properly. In other words, the NDC is a *grammatical* (i.e., structural) constraint. Whatever its historical origins, it now only imperfectly carries out the function of promoting understanding by reducing the number of possible filler-gap pairings.

7. Apparently NDC violations are perfectly acceptable in Italian (see Rizzi 1978). Sentences like (i) pose no problem for Italian speakers:

(i)   l'uomo [che$_i$ [non so [chi$_j$ [$\triangle_i$ conosca $\triangle_j$]]]]
       the man who$_i$ I don't know who$_j$ $\triangle_i$ knows $\triangle_j$

Hence the NDC cannot be *merely* an artifact of the communicative process.

Fodor concludes her paper by questioning the communicative need for *any* gap-leaving movement rules (i.e., "chopping rules") and speculates that the existence of such rules strikes at the very heart of the idea that linguistic form reflects communicative function:

> Of course, the sentence producer is concerned with more than merely generating well-formed sentences; communication must be served as well. But the movement and deletion rules do not seem to be critical to any of the expressive functions of language. Perhaps it is preferable, for producer or perceiver or both, to have certain particularly important constituents at the front of a sentence or clause. But copying rules can serve this function as well as chopping rules can. And the fact that copying rules are not subject to the NDC or to the standard island constraints suggests that they could serve the expressive function much more cheaply.
>
> Having reviewed, and at least presumptively eliminated, all of the alternatives, there appears to be only one conclusion left. This is that gap-creating rules are widespread in natural languages because the format of our mental representations of the well-formedness conditions on sentences is such that these rules are more highly valued than other conceivable types of rules that would have made life easier for the language-using mechanisms. This doesn't make any sense at all, however, on the assumption that the language-using mechanisms are all there is. (1978, 471–72)

Why *do* syntactic constraints exist, then? There are enough examples of constraint-violating sentences that seem (intuitively) to present processing difficulties that it seems reasonable to assume that constraints arose historically to facilitate the production and comprehension of sentences. But what has apparently happened is that, in the course of time, the processing-derived constraints have taken on a grammatical "life of their own," so to speak. Now some constraints do seem to have a confusion-reducing effect and some seem not to. But whether they have this effect or not, they have one fundamental property in common: their formulation involves such notions as "syntactic category" and "constituent structure"—that is, their formulation is in terms of the primitives of grammatical theory.

Some interesting data relevant to the form-function debate are provided in Smith (1981). Smith notes that some recorded children's utterances seem to violate proposed syntactic constraints. Two examples are (21a–b), which were uttered by a four-year-old and a three-and-a-half-year-old respectively:

(21)   a. What's this for doing?
        b. What else are there signs that say?

Smith regards these sentences as Complex Noun Phrase Constraint violations, as is illustrated for (21b) in (22):[8]

(22)

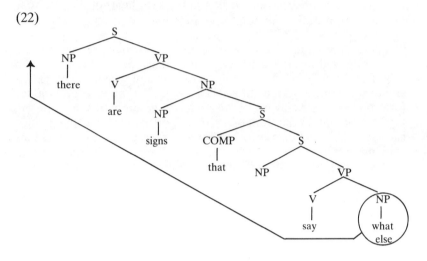

Smith's remarks are not addressed to the *syntacticity* of constraints like the Complex Noun Phrase Constraint, but rather to their *innateness*. He cites the sentences above to rebut a suggestion in Chomsky (1977b) that constraints are innate, though they may nevertheless be "overridden" by positive evidence in a particular language. That is, he attacks Chomsky's position that the speaker (unconsciously) expects rules to obey the constraints, but is capable of learning rules that violate them if presented with positive evidence that such rules exist. In Smith's opinion, the Chomskyan view has two consequences: "first, that a child should not spontaneously produce sentences whose analysis violates 'universal' principles if such principles are not already violated by particular sentence types in the language he is exposed to; second, that in a language where such principles are violated, constructions crucially involving such violation should be learned later" (Smith 1981, 46). The errors of (21) seem to be at odds with both consequences. While I find considerable merit in Smith's argument, it is based on what seems to me a highly questionable assumption—the assumption that exactly the same constraints that govern adult grammars also govern child grammars. But holding the position that constraints have a genetic basis does not necessarily force one to assume that this is so. For example, it is logically possible that humans

8. Though James McCawley has argued (in unpublished work) that these sentences do not contain deep structure relative clauses and thus that the Complex Noun Phrase Constraint (or some similar constraint) is not responsible for their deviance. Notice the greater degree of unacceptability of (ii) below (which is a true constraint violator) than (21b):

(ii)   What else can you see signs that say?

might be preprogrammed so that a particular constraint does not make its effects apparent until age five (or older). If this is true, then Smith's conclusions are without force. But attested child utterances like (21) seem to me to be *extremely* problematic for a theory that attempts to ground constraints extragrammatically. Now we are talking not about maturationally determined permissible operations on grammatical structures, but rather about facts that should be an immediate consequence of the human ability to process discourse. One would think that, given their lack of experience in the conscious manipulation of language, small children would be much *less* likely—and able—than adults to circumvent the principles that make sentences like (21) impossible. These sentences put those who advocate an extragrammatical account of constraints on the horns of a dilemma—either they can maintain that such constructions *are* difficult to process (which would account for their deviance in adult language) and leave them with no explanation for why children utter them, or acknowledge that they are *not* difficult to process and thereby concede that syntactic constraints are not directly rooted in communicative function.

Wherever we look, though we might find *correlations* between grammatical structures and their discourse functions, we only rarely find *direct reflections* of the latter by the former. So, for example, a "left-dislocated" noun phrase in English can represent either old information or new information, as the following illustrates:

(23)　a. Tell me about your boss.
　　　b. My boss [old information], she's a real slave driver.
(24)　a. What's the matter?
　　　b. My boss [new information], she's been harassing me.

Or, conversely, one discourse function can be performed by several different structural configurations. Creider (1979), for example, lists no fewer than nine rules of English that perform a topicalizing function and five that perform a focusing function. In short, there is a many/many relation between form and function.

No generativist denies the interest of determining the discourse function (if any) of a particular syntactic construction or constraint, nor, once again, does any generativist deny the plausibility of the hypothesis that aspects of formal grammars might have their origins in an adaptation to the needs of communication.[9] But generativists are hardly surprised to

9. No generativist, to my knowledge, has ever disparaged the study of the interaction of form and function. For example, Chomsky has written: "I have never suggested that 'there is no interesting connection' between the structure of language and 'its purpose,' including communicative function, nor have I 'arbitrarily assumed' that use and structure do not influence one another. . . . Surely there are significant connections between structure and function; this is not and never has been in doubt. . . . Where it can be shown that structures serve a particular function, that is a valuable discovery" (1975b, 56–58).

discover that grammatical systems, in keeping with all other known natural systems, exhibit a mismatch between form and function.

4.2.3   Third Belief: Communicative Function Explains Linguistic Form

Each purported "explanation" of linguistic form in terms of communicative function that has come to my attention is one of two types. The first type attributes whatever structural property is being discussed to informally described human states, drives, needs, abilities, and such that have no basis in any existing formalized theory of human behavior or cognition. The other type simply proclaims that a phenomenon has been "explained" if it is shown to correlate, however loosely, with some discourse function.

The modern pioneer of the first type of "explanation" was George Zipf. Zipf attempted to account for a wide variety of phenomena, from the fact that there is a correlation between the length of a word and its frequency in discourse, to the fact that in languages with both aspirated and unaspirated voiceless stops the latter tend to be more frequent, to the arrangement of a sentence in terms of its immediate constituents by appeal to what he called the "underlying law of economy of effort" (1935, 129). This law can be paraphrased roughly: "The easier something is to do, the more likely one is to do it." But Zipf had no theory of mental processes or speech production that provided an independent characterization of the notion "degree of effort." As is clear from the examples he cites, he simply concluded from the fact that something *was* done frequently that it *must have been* easy to do. Hence his argument was circular and he failed to explain the phenomena he described.

A more characteristic approach to the question of explanation is found in Creider (1979). Creider presents evidence that, apparently without exception, the function of rules in English that move constituents to the left is topicalizing, and the function of rules that move constituents to the right is focusing. Why should this be? In Creider's view: "Construction of the extrasentential contexts in which sentences derived with these rules are appropriate leads to the conclusion that discourse factors are probably the major force responsible for the existence and shape of the rules" (1979, 3). In other words, discourse factors explain the form the rules take. But demonstrating a correlation does not constitute an explanation. One can be said to have "explained" why leftward movements are topicalizing only when one has successfully defended a theory within which one can deduce that the first part of an utterance will be reserved for topics. Not only does no such theory exist, but, as advocates of discourse-based grammar themselves admit (Li 1976, x; Keenan and Schieffelin 1976, 380), there is not even agreement on what constitutes a "topic."[10]

---

10. See Reinhart (1982) for interesting recent discussion of the notion "topic."

Chomsky (1980, 229ff.) has discussed some of the problems of constructing functional explanations for grammatical structures and rules. As he points out, a child learning English does not learn to reserve the first position in the utterance for the topic "because" there is some natural reason for topics to occur there. The child places topics first because that is the way English is. Why is English that way? One possibility is that this property reflects a biological universal—that languages are preprogrammed to place topics first. In that case we would naturally ask how it came to be that the process of human evolution dictated such a form-function correlation. Another possibility (the correct one) is that this property is not universal, and therefore must be learned. That would lead us to ask what functional demands determined that English and similar languages would evolve in that particular way, but not languages that lack that particular correlation. In either case, as Chomsky points out, "the functional explanation applies on the evolutionary level—either the evolution of the organism or the language. The child does not acquire the rule by virtue of its function any more than he learns to have an eye because of the advantages of sight" (Chomsky 1980, 23).

4.3   Two Discourse-Oriented Approaches to Grammar

4.3.1   Bolinger's "Meaning and Form"

Dwight Bolinger is renowned for the acuity of his introspective judgments about grammatical constructions, his sensitivity to the nuances of meaning and intonation contours, and his remarkable ability to characterize the (intuitively) correct discourse context for any English sentence. It is an uncontroversial statement, I think, that Bolinger has the greatest feel for linguistic data of any living grammarian. He is also known for his obvious delight in debunking generativist proposals and his concomitant lack of interest in himself contributing to the formal theory of grammar. His book *Meaning and Form (MAF)* admirably illustrates both qualities.

The goal of *MAF* is to "reaffirm the old principle that the natural condition of a language is to preserve one form for one meaning, and one meaning for one form" (x), and to mount a "frontal attack on the theory that it is normal for a language to establish a lunacy ward in its grammar or lexicon where mindless morphs stare vacantly with no purpose other than to be where they are" (ix). In his opinion, transformational generative grammar is just such a theory, so it is generativists who receive the brunt of his frontal attack. The running theme of *MAF* is that demonstrable meaning differences between particular sentence types falsify generativist claims that they share deep structures and can be related by optional transformational rules. So, for example, two chapters are devoted to illustrating that elements commonly posited to be transformationally introduced and non-meaning-bearing—expletive *it* (chap. 4, pp. 66–89) and existential *there* (chap. 5, pp. 90–123)—make definite contributions to the interpretations of the sentences in which they occur. Other chapters illustrate the effect on meaning of putatively optional transformations such as Some-Any (chap. 2, pp. 21–36), Raising-to-Object (chap. 6, pp. 124–34), and Imperative Deletion (chap. 8, pp. 152–82); the rest of the book discusses the discourse factors determining the appropriateness of *not any* and *no* (chap. 3, pp. 37–65), ergative *of* and the infinitive of specification (chap. 7, pp. 135–51), and imperatives and analogous constructions with *do* (chap. 9, pp. 183–200).

Actually, Bolinger's views on the symmetry of form and meaning in language turn out to be considerably more temperate than the quotation above suggests. First, he is careful to point out that phonological differences do not ipso facto entail communicative differences:

> one may find an identical system being used by another speaker, but with the physical traits of each signal differing slightly in ways that mark him as an individual or as the speaker of a different dialect, but with each unit still having the same communicative value as before. It is not too farfetched to claim that cases like these are identical linguistically but different sociologically. The deviations can reasonably be defined out of the field. (3)

Morphology is exempt as well: "with morphology it still makes sense to think of the plurality of *geese* and the plurality of *hens* as the same entity despite the difference in ways for forming the plural" (3). And even at the lexical level, Bolinger is ready to concede that a single form may bear multiple meanings that, at least to a degree, are discontinuous (his examples are locative and existential *there* and demonstrative and relative *that*). While he posits for these items "two meanings related at their base" (120) (reflecting, obviously, their single historical roots), he acknowledges in principle the possibility of semantic divergence. So it is only *syntactic* constructions, really, that one is said to never meet in one's visit to the linguistic lunacy ward.

Bolinger has no trouble demonstrating the nondiscourse equivalence of whatever two constructions he decides to compare. To take a typical case, he notes (128) the following pattern of acceptability for sentences manifesting the infinitival construction:[11]

---

11. Bolinger's asterisks should not be interpreted as assignments of ungrammaticality in the generativist sense. Rather, they indicate that the sentences are, in some intuitive sense, not likely to be uttered. Bolinger differs from most of the generativists' critics in that he explicitly advocates the use of introspective data:

> The test that I want to apply is suggested by two points of generative doctrine: (1) that the intuitions of the native speaker are the guide to grammaticality, and (2) that a grammar must account for sentences that have never been heard before. These tenets put a premium on inventiveness. They require the grammarian to sit down and assiduously

(25) a. I understood that to be the reason.
      b. I understood that explanation to be the right one.
      c. *I understood that explanation to be the wrong one.
      d. *I understood the natives to be unfriendly.
      e. I understand this solution to be the simplest.
      f. *I understand this solution to be the most complicated.

He illustrates that a different pattern emerges when we look at the corresponding construction with *that*; for example, the sentences corresponding to (25c,d,f), namely (26a–c), are fully acceptable:

(26) a. I understood that that explanation was the wrong one.
      b. I understood that the natives were unfriendly.
      c. I understood that this solution was the most complicated.

Bolinger takes this as prima facie evidence that sentences of the form of (25) and (26) cannot be derived from identical deep structures (i.e., there cannot be a transformational rule of Raising-to-Object). Why are (25c,d,f) unacceptable? Because of the generalization that the infinitive construction with *understand* "is normal only if what is referred to is correct and intellectually ascertainable, and *understand* plus the noun is compatible" (128). Hence (25d), for example, is unacceptable because it brings in a nonintellectual meaning of the verb—one does not literally "understand" a person.

At the lexical level, Bolinger gives examples of the discourse role played by what might be taken to be "meaningless" elements such as the *it* in (27) to (29) below. As the minimal pairs indicate, *it* has a greater function than serving as a syntactic place holder:

(27) a. I can understand it that the election hurt him.
      b. *I understand it that the election hurt him.
(28) a. *She hid that she was involved.
      b. She hid it that she was involved.
(29) a. When will we know?—It's tomorrow that we'll know.
      b. When will you tell me?—*It's tomorrow that I'll tell you.

Bolinger assigns a general "neuter definite" meaning to the *it* in (27a), (28b), and (29a), which he then attempts to link with the "ambient" *it* of the following constructions, where, again, *it* is said to have "a referent, in

---

concoct sentences to the limit of his capacity, to try to see everything that can be done with the resources of his language in the linguistic area in question. It is not enough to skim a few examples from the handbooks, and add a few more invented on the spur of the moment. One must improvise situations, imagine conversations for them, judge, and finally accept or discard; then reinvent, and repeat the whole process many times. Only by going in this way as far as ingenuity will carry one is it possible to discover what the real boundaries of a construction are—and to justify the appeal to intuition and originality, which I believe is profoundly correct. (153)

this case precisely the 'environment' that is central to the whole area" (78):

(30)   a. It's scary in the dark.
       b. It's threatening a storm.
       c. It's her graduation next week.
       d. It's not much fun, when you have to work all the time.

While I find Bolinger's characterization of the function of *it* a bit vague, there is no question that he has succeeded in showing that it contributes to the interpretation of the sentences in which it appears.

Bolinger's foil throughout *MAF* is the generativist who

> has carried the fantasy [of mindless morphs staring vacantly] to new heights, and expanded it with a new version of an old vision, that of synonymy: not only are there mindless morphs, but there are mindless differences between one construction and another. The transformation of that old vision is, literally, transformations: in its original form, one construction could be converted into another; in its newer form, an abstract structure could be converted into *x* number of surface structures—in either case without gain or loss of meaning. The resulting structures were the same; only the guise was different. (ix)

Did Bolinger's generativist ever exist? True, most generativists from the mid 1960s to the mid 1970s attributed the property of meaning preservation to transformations. However, their conception of "meaning" was *so* fundamentally different from Bolinger's that his running criticism throughout *MAF* loses virtually all its force. To understand why, we must first examine what exactly it is that Bolinger calls "meaning":

> Linguistic meaning covers a great deal more than reports of events in the real world. It expresses, sometimes in very obvious ways, other times in ways that are hard to ferret out, such things as what is the central part of the message as against the peripheral part, what our attitudes are toward the person we are speaking to, how we feel about the reliability of our message, how we situate ourselves in the events we report, and many other things that make our messages not merely a recital of facts but a complex of facts and situations. (4)

In short, for Bolinger anything that can make a conceivable contribution to understanding a sentence or the appropriateness of its use is considered part of that sentence's "meaning." Thus, in Bolinger's analysis, the following two sentences differ in meaning:

(31)   a. She bought a red dress, a green one, and a blue one.
       b. She bought a red dress, she bought a green dress, and she bought a blue dress.

Since after hearing (31b), but not (31a), the hearer is led to "infer that she bought excessively" (7), the sentences, by Bolinger's criteria, clearly differ in meaning.

However, the early work in generative grammar that led to the hypothesis that transformational rules are meaning preserving (the "Katz-Postal hypothesis") used the term "meaning" in a *far* more restricted sense than Bolinger did. For example, the seminal generativist treatment of semantics, Katz and Fodor (1963), explicitly excluded from the domain of semantic theory those aspects of interpretation that might be classified as emotive, affective, context-influenced, and so forth. Katz and Fodor's use of the term "meaning" was restricted, essentially, to those factors involved in determining analyticity, contradiction, entailment, and such—those involved in determining a sentence's truth conditions.[12] It was those aspects, and those alone, that Katz and Fodor claimed remained constant under transformation. Without exception, about those aspects of meaning that Bolinger successfully demonstrates *do* change under transformation, the early generativists made no explicit claim at all.

It seems to me that Bolinger's one explicit objection to generativist theory boils down to a terminological difference about what to call "meaning." While Bolinger may well feel that the notion "identity of truth conditions" is of no linguistic interest—and hence the Katz-Postal hypothesis is of no interest either—he has not, in *MAF*, presented any evidence to refute this hypothesis.[13] As far as I can tell, there is nothing in *MAF* that refutes *any* generativist claim. Bolinger's work, focusing as it does on the pragmatic presuppositions borne by lexical items and the discourse appropriateness of sentence types, bears only in the most

---

12. This point is perhaps made more clearly in later generativist writings than in the original Katz-Fodor paper. For example:

Take an active-passive pair such as (7.15a,b):

(7.15)   a. David killed Goliath.
           b. Goliath was killed by David.

These two sentences derive from the same underlying form and differ only in that the optional rule of Passive has applied in the derivation of (7.15b). In one sense these may differ in meaning, for the first is "about" David and the second "about" Goliath, and thus they may differ in emphasis, etc. But in most important respects they have the same meaning. In particular, they have precisely the same *truth conditions*—i.e., there is no state of affairs that could make one true and the other false—and thus we may say they are *cognitively synonymous* (or have the *same cognitive meaning*). If we concentrate only on cognitive meanings, as defined loosely above in terms of truth conditions, then as far as examples (7.15a) and (7.15b) are concerned, the Passive Rule is consistent with the form of the Katz-Postal Hypothesis given in (7.14). The application of the Passive Rule to derive (7.15b) has made no change in meaning. (Akmajian and Heny 1975, 238)

13. The hypotheses had, of course, been abandoned by many generativists even before *MAF* appeared. See, for example, Chomsky (1971) and Jackendoff (1972), and, for general discussion, Newmeyer (1980a, 123–27).

marginal way on the debates of the 1960s and 1970s over the interface between the syntactic component and the semantic component within a generative grammar.

Where Bolinger takes on *theoretical* questions, as opposed to purely analytical ones, his discussion unfortunately lapses into much of the apriorism that typically characterizes the search for "external" communication-based explanations for linguistic principles. So, for example, he writes that "if a language permits a contrast in form to survive, it ought to be there for a purpose. . . . It is not normal for a language to waste its resources" (19). It is hard to know what to make of such a statement—as is well known, language is full of redundancy. For example, why isn't the redundant plural morpheme in *three books* a waste of the resources of English, or the redundant case marking in the phrase *den alten Jungen* a waste of the resources of German? Language seems replete with features that seem implausibly a reflection of the resource-husbanding organism that Bolinger pictures. As Maratsos and Chalkley have noted:

> Gender systems, verb conjugation systems, and similar systems thus in many ways comprise systems of luxurious waste. They serve little function, probably require some effort to acquire and use, yet are very common. Such systems seem to be the sign of a species that has more than limited resources available. At any rate, such systems do not display a linguistic system molded by the constraints of a fierce and well-directed competition for channel resources for the expression of important meanings. (1980, 188–89)

Bolinger recognizes, of course, that "the fact that a contrast that we carry in our competence is relevant does not mean that it is relevant all the time. It means only that it is there when we need it" (19). But that does not help us at all; no theory exists that elucidates either the "need" for a linguistic contrast or its "purpose," nor is there any systematic explication of what determines the preservation of linguistic resources. The understanding of the nature of language is not advanced by an appeal to either.

MAF is a remarkable achievement in lexicography and impressionistic semantics. One would like to be able to close this discussion on that positive note. But one is left with the uneasy feeling that Bolinger believes it is not necessary for linguistics to go *beyond* the casually described observations of the sort that fill the pages of his book. To be sure, he never explicitly denies the need for a formal theory of syntax.[14] Yet by constantly calling into question particular generativist claims

---

14. Though in other publications he has come close to doing so: "'Anecdotal' is no longer a dirty word in linguistics, and 'rigor' contains a high percentage of rigormortis—quite applicable to the semantically dead part of language, phonology, but not so well to other parts" (Bolinger 1977b, 511).

without proposing a formal analysis to replace them, he certainly invites his readers to conclude that once a Bolingerian analysis is carried out, nothing more rigorous need be done. This is a shame, because if anybody could contribute to the increasing body of research devoted to probing the interaction between formal grammar and pragmatics (see section 1.4), Bolinger could. If there were reason to believe that this interaction cannot be characterized by fairly general principles, I would be content with Bolinger's informal listing of individual constructions and their discourse effects. But, ironically, his great achievement is the demonstration that the grammar-pragmatics interaction is *not* unsystematic. *MAF* makes one desire all the more to learn the *precise nature* of the principles that determine how the various components of semantics and pragmatics relate to syntactic structure. It is the generativist goal to formulate such principles within a comprehensive theory of language. However Bolinger himself might feel about formal theory, the observations in *MAF* and his other writings will be of value in helping to attain that goal.

4.3.2   Givón's "On Understanding Grammar"[15]

The publication of *Syntactic Structures*, besides ushering in a new era of linguistic research, also engendered a new era of belligerent polemics. Both generativists and their opponents indulged in rhetorical excesses; certainly no one would deny that some of the more vigorous defenses of generative grammar exceeded the normal bounds of partisan scholarship. But it seems fair to say that the reactive literature has not in general balanced its belligerence with positive content. Such work has devoted far more effort to toppling generative grammar than to motivating a coherent alternative. For this reason alone it has failed to sway many generativist practitioners or sympathizers. Talmy Givón's *On Understanding Grammar* (*OUG*) is very much in the tradition of the bellicose "definitive" reply to generative grammar. However, it differs from the other works of its genre in a way that demands that it be taken seriously— it supplements its hostile critique of the dominant theory with more than a cursory discussion of an alternative conception of language.

OUG has two goals: first, to demolish transformational generative grammar by showing that it is "a pseudotheory and useless methodology" (44); second, to motivate an approach to syntax based on "communicative function and discourse-pragmatics" (xiv). However, the book fails to attain either goal. Aside from containing numerous examples of linguistic phenomena that, properly elaborated upon, might be of interest to

---

15. This section has benefited from my discussions with G. N. Clements, Annie Zaenen, Robert Ladd, and—especially—Laurence Horn. An earlier version of the section was published as Newmeyer (1982a).

linguists and communications theorists,[16] *OUG* has little to contribute to an understanding of either the nature of grammar or the functioning of language in its communicative setting.

As its title suggests, chapter 1, "Methodology—On the Crypto-Structuralist Nature of Transformational Grammar" (1–44), is a vitriolic attack on what Givón sees as the goals and methodology of generativist theory. Chapter 2, "Grammar and Function: Toward a Discourse Definition of Syntax" (45–90), attempts to explain various properties of positive, active, declarative, main-clause sentences (including their putative simplicity and high text count) in terms of their low degree of presuppositional complexity. Chapter 3, "Logic versus Language—Negation in Language: Pragmatics, Function, Ontology" (91–142), attributes properties of sentences with negatives to the high presuppositional complexity of "negative speech acts."[17] Chapter 4, "Semantic Case and Pragmatic Function—Promotion, Accessibility, and the Typology of Case Marking" (143–206), attempts to explain the features of certain rules by appeal to the need to "recover the semantic function of the deleted coreferent argument in relativization" (144). Chapter 5, "Syntacticization—From Discourse to Syntax: Grammar as a Processing Strategy" (207–34), contrasts languages with topic-comment structure with those with subject-predicate structure and discusses how the two structural types can interact. Chapter 6, "Language Change—Where Does Crazy Syntax Come From: Diachronic Constraints on Synchronic Grammars" (235–70), defends the position that it is hopeless to try to understand synchronic grammar without understanding diachronic grammar. Chapter 7, "Language and Phylogeny—the SOV Mystery and the Evolution of Discourse" (271–309), attempts to ground properties of human language in phylogenetic evolution. Chapter 8, "Language and Ontology—On Construing a Universe" (311–52), is about "the relation between cognition and the universe, and what it all may mean" (xiv).

Givón's critique of generativist linguistic theory begins with the undefended assumption that the structure of language *necessarily* reflects a variety of external factors, from cognitive structure to ontogenetic development to phylogenetic evolution; that even a *description* of syntax and phonology (much less an explanation) that is not rooted in these "natural explanatory parameters" (5) must be fundamentally deficient. The a priori underpinnings of Givón's approach are established at the very beginning of *OUG*, where he supplies a long list of parameters that

16. The "properly elaborated upon" is crucial. Few of the examples Givón cites are elaborated upon in sufficient detail to justify even any of his more modest claims. He seems to feel that by citing a fact here from Hittite, there from Yoruba, here from Bemba, there from Bikol he can say something profound both about those languages and about language in general.

17. A "negative speech act" is, apparently, a sentence containing a negative element.

the structure of language "obviously must reflect" (3) and "cannot be understood without reference to" (4). Naturally then, Givón concludes that generative grammar, which describes syntactic phenomena partly in terms of a discrete system whose primitives are themselves syntactic, should not be taken seriously.

One's initial reaction might well be to reject Givón's assumption and give the book no further thought. Even if it were *correct* that all structure is ultimately artifactual, the conclusion that it is therefore misguided to characterize formal systems independent of the functional factors that shaped them is false. This point can be illustrated by developing further an analogy Givón himself introduces early in *OUG*. He writes:

> Imagine an anatomist describing the structure of the human body without reference to the functions of various organs. But this is precisely what happened in transformational-generative linguistics: By fiat, a priori, and with no visible empirical justification, an attempt has been made to describe the structure of human language, both syntax and phonology, without reference to natural explanatory parameters. (5)

Givón is apparently unaware that there *are* anatomists—histologists, for example—who do precisely what he finds so unthinkable; they "describ[e] the structure of the human body without reference to the functions of various organs." And they have good reasons for doing so. First, because they know that similar structures can perform very different functions, and that many anatomical functions are performed by diverse histological structures. Some structures (the appendix, for example) serve no useful function at all, while others (the gallbladder, for example) have phylogenetically been adapted to novel functions. And, second, because some anatomical structures serve *no known* function. Clearly, it would be unreasonable to postpone their study until their function is known. Indeed, through a detailed analysis of such structures, insight might be gained as to their function. The point is that the organs, tissues, and so forth, of the human body form *structural systems* that interact with the functional systems of the body (digestion, reproduction, etc.) in extremely intricate ways. Givón, to be consistent, would have to condemn structural studies of human tissue for the same reason that he condemns structural analyses of human language—they are not rooted in the body's "natural explanatory parameters."

Givón's casual dismissal of function-independent grammatical systems would have no serious consequences if it turned out that there were in language a one-to-one match between syntactic structure and communicative function. One could then, presumably, derive the syntax by a trivial algorithm from the relevant "natural explanatory parameters." But Givón himself gives page after page of evidence (the bulk of chaps. 5

and 6, to be specific) showing that syntax *cannot* be read off these parameters. For example, after discussing the common tendency of auxiliary verbs to develop into tense-modality markers, he remarks: "It is most likely that the main-auxiliary verb already carried—as one of its functions—the signal for some tense-aspect-modal notion. . . . But in the *syntacticized* construction, the erstwhile verb *has shed its other (earlier) functions* and has become specialized" (222; emphasis added). In other words, the language learner is presented with a construction whose form is not directly derivable from its function. For the most part, Givón proposes to explain such constructions diachronically—by appealing to the various "natural" diachronic processes that might have combined to yield the particular syntacticized construction. He is absolutely clear that he believes it absurd to write synchronic rules to characterize such constructions, since doing so would mask their explanation (see the discussion on 268–69 ridiculing a hypothesized generative rule of "Pronoun Hopping"). But nobody, not even Givón, would claim that a child language learner has access to linguistic history. Therefore, for Givón, what the child learns and what the linguist describes must *in principle* be disparate. What a strange view of language is presented in *OUG*, in which a child can learn a syntacticized construction but the linguist is discouraged from characterizing precisely the syntax that the child has learned.

In places, Givón appears to retreat somewhat from his sweeping condemnation of synchronic formal syntax:[18] "Does syntax exist, then? Yes and no. It does exist as a mode of linguistic communication, and it does have highly specific structural properties" (233). One wonders what it could possibly mean to speak of grammatical morphology, say, as a "structural property" of a "mode of linguistic communication" and how one goes about characterizing precisely the structural properties of such "modes" (Givón is completely silent on this crucial question). An answer to that puzzle will no doubt await an answer to a still more perplexing one: How can grammar be at one and the same time a mode of communication and (as we find out by reading the same paragraph) an "automatic processing strategy"? One would think that "strategies" and "modes" (not to mention "rules of grammar," to which Givón alludes at times) would be incompatible characterizations of the same phenomenon. While he is quite certain that generativists have found the wrong way to view grammar, he himself seems to have several mutually contradictory ideas about the right way.

18. One aspect of this hedging is his repeated use of theory-bound terminology from generative grammar. For example, he writes of an object that can "undergo dative-shift" (144) and refers to a grammatical relationship as describable by "a transformational operation . . . regardless of how these operations are formulated ultimately" (145). But see (232) where Givón refers to "so-called transformations."

Givón gives many examples illustrating that the asymmetry in language between form and function is not limited to marginal phenomena. One set of his assumptions about discourse leads him to predict that VO order should predominate among the world's languages. This is wrong; OV order predominates. He recognizes the problem this poses for his hypothesis: "somehow the SOV word-order, though seemingly the *earliest* attested in human language, is *not* the one most *compatible* with the currently extant discourse-pragmatic evolutionary stage of human language" (276; emphasis in original). This problem, which Givón never really deals with satisfactorily, underscores a basic point: however discourse, cognition, or any other external factors may ultimately have *influenced* the structure of language (and we may never know fully), there is no *deterministic relation* between any (or all) of them and the structure of language. In short, grammatical systems have an independent existence, and it is the job of the grammarian to describe them.

Even where Givón sees a deterministic relation, it is fairly easy to show that he is mistaken. For example, he attempts to explain away Ross's (1968) Complex Noun Phrase Constraint and similar syntactic constraints by regarding them as artifacts of "perceptual strategies of speech analysis" (17). This has a measure of plausibility—many sentences that result from constraint violations *are* confusing and no doubt difficult to process. But, as we saw earlier in section 4.2.2, *not all of them are.* Analogously, Givón thinks that through the "general explanatory principle of communication . . . that of avoiding irrecoverable deletion" (12), it follows that a Bemba verb will have an agreement marker when its subject is not present. But this is no explanation at all—other languages (Japanese, for example) freely allow nonpresent subjects *without* an agreement marker. The rule ordering solution that Givón rejects shows explicitly how Bemba differs grammatically from such languages, without recourse to unformalized (and no doubt unformalizable) notions such as "discourse irrecoverability."

No generativist has ever questioned or will ever question the value of studies of the interaction of linguistic structure and communicative function. What we learn from a careful reading of *OUG*, however, is that there is every good reason to formulate the *structural* properties of language in *nonfunctional* terms.

Do formal models explain anything? Givón is quite certain they do not: "In essence, a formal model is *nothing but* a restatement of the facts at a tighter level of generalization. . . . There is one thing, however, that a formal model can never do: It cannot *explain* a single thing" (5–6; emphasis in original). Naturally then, he sees the generativists' formal models as nonexplanatory: "The history of transformational-generative linguistics boils down to nothing but a blatant attempt to represent the

formalism as 'theory,' to assert that it 'predicts a range of facts,' that it
'makes empirical claims,' and that it somehow 'explains' " (6). But Givón
is mistaken; there are two types of formal models—descriptive (iconic)
models and theoretical (explanatory) models. The model of language
posited by many post-Bloomfieldian structuralists is a good example of
the former. Quite explicitly, many post-Bloomfieldians saw their goal as
simply to construct a "compact one-one representation of the stock of
utterances in the corpus" (Harris 1951, 366). And just as explicitly, they
rejected the idea of "explanation" as a goal for the model builder (see
Joos 1957, v, 96).

A theoretical model, on the other hand, is designed to *explain* the data.
In the words of the philosopher of science Rom Harré: "the function of a
[theoretical] model is to form the basis of a theory, and a theory is
invented to explain some phenomena" (1970, 52).[19]

A theoretical model is not a model *of the data*. The relation between a
theoretical model and the data is typically extremely indirect because the
complex phenomena of the real world owe their behavior to the *interaction* of many systems, each embodying its own theoretical model. To
borrow an example from geology, it takes literally dozens of interacting
theoretical models to explain the succession of strata one might find in an
outcrop—some chemical, some physical, and at least one metaphysical
(the principle of uniformitarianism). None of the models employed is in
any sense a model *of* the succession of strata.

The competence model of the generativists is an example of a theoretical model. Such a model does not "restate the facts at a tighter level of
generalization"; rather, it interacts with other models to *explain* the facts.
For example, as we have seen, the explanation of the unacceptability of
multiply self-embedded constructions like *the cheese that the rat that the
cat chased ate was rotten* involves the interaction of the competence
model with a model of immediate memory storage. Neither model alone
even describes the facts, much less explains them. The competence model
surely does not describe the facts—it characterizes this sentence as grammatical. And the memory model alone does not describe the facts either,
since even a rough description of the phenomenon demands a notion of
linguistic structure. *Combined*, however, the models *explain* the sentence's unacceptability.

Givón's belief that the generativists' model is intended to be a concise
description of the data leads him irrevocably to another error—that the
generativist view is that speakers use their grammars deterministically:
"the human communicator is not a deterministic user of an autonomous
subconscious grammar as Chomsky would have us believe. Rather, he
makes *communicative choices*. He uses rules of grammar for a com-

19. Harré (1970) contains a lengthy discussion of the various types of models employed
in science. Givón's view of a model is essentially that of logical positivist philosophy (see
Carnap 1956 for a view very similar to Givón's).

municative effect. He may choose to break the rule for an effect, such as poetics, metaphor, or semantic extension" (32; emphasis in original). Givón invites the reader to conclude that Chomsky believes that the "human communicator is . . . a deterministic user of a . . . grammar," though he omits any direct reference to Chomsky's writings. There is a good reason for this omission; Chomsky believes no such thing. Rather, Chomsky *agrees* with Givón that "rules of grammar" (though it is difficult to be sure what Givón has in mind by this phrase) may be "broken" for any number of reasons. Chomsky made this point clearly twenty years ago in response to critics who had exactly Givón's misconception about grammars and "determinism." For example:

> it is perfectly plain that deviation from well-formedness is not only tolerable, in prose or poetry, but can even be used effectively as a literary device. . . . There are circumstances in which the use of grammatically deviant sentences is very much in place. Consider, e.g., such phrases as Dylan Thomas' "a grief ago," or Veblen's ironic "perform leisure." In such cases, and innumerable others, a striking effect is achieved precisely by means of a departure from a grammatical regularity. (Chomsky 1961, 231, 234)

If the competence/performance distinction reflects *one* insight about language, it is the insight that what speakers know *about* their language (its structure) does *not* deterministically trigger what they will do *with* their language.

Givón cites a number of phenomena (26–31) that are intended to subvert the competence/performance dichotomy, but that on closer examination turn out to support it. For example, he argues:

> In many of the world's languages, probably in most [Krio is an example], the subject of declarative clauses cannot be referential-indefinite. . . . In a relatively small number of the world's languages [English is an example] . . . referential-indefinite nouns may appear as subjects. . . . When one examines the text frequency of such English sentences however, one finds them at an extremely low frequency: About 10% of the subjects of main-declarative-affirmative-active sentences (nonpresentative) are indefinite as against 90% definite. . . . But are we dealing with two different kinds of facts in English and Krio? Hardly. What we are dealing with is apparently the very same *communicative tendency*—to reserve the subject position in the sentence for the *topic*, the old-information argument, the "continuity marker." . . . And a transformational-generative linguist will then be forced to count this fact as competence in Krio and performance in English. But what is the communicative difference between a rule of 90% fidelity and one of 100% fidelity? In psychological terms, next to nothing. . . . it seems to me, the distinction between performance and competence or grammar and behavior tends to collapse under the impact of these data. (26–28; emphasis in original)

There is a sense in which Givón is right—the rarity of referential-indefinite subjects in discourse is probably a unified phenomenon. One hopes that a theory of performance embodying notions less fuzzy than "communicative tendency," "old information," and "continuity marker" will be developed to explain it. But there is another sense in which Givón is dead wrong—as far as the grammar of subject phrases is concerned, English and Krio are fundamentally different. English speakers know that referential-indefinites *can* be used in that position (however unlikely they are to use them), and Krio speakers know they cannot. This is reflected in the way the grammar of English differs from the grammar of Krio. In short, the two languages differ at the competence level.

An analogy might be helpful. Let us imagine two people who find chess boring—one of these people (E) rarely plays the game, and the other (K) never plays it. Let us also assume that (E) learned the rules of chess and that (K) never did. Givón, if he analyzes this situation with the same logic that he uses in analyzing language, would say *no more* than that (E) and (K) have the same "tendency" to avoid playing chess. In "psychological terms" their different states (knowledge versus lack of knowledge of chess) would count for "next to nothing"!

The bulk of *OUG* is devoted to an attempt to explain syntactic phenomena on the basis of the pragmatics of discourse. While some of Givón's explanations push the extreme limits of "creative speculation" (311), the bulk of them involve notions like "old information," "new information," "topicality," and others familiar from much recent work in discourse-based syntax. Givón makes use of the notion "presupposition" more than any other as the cornerstone of his explanations. For example, after characterizing "the main, declarative, affirmative, active sentence [as having] the lowest presuppositional complexity in discourse, as compared to all other types" (49), he claims that more presuppositional constructions exhibit greater syntactic complexity than less presuppositional ones and that more presuppositional variants exhibit greater distributional restrictions than less presuppositional ones. Givón illustrates the former claim by pointing to the greater syntactic complexity of "more presuppositional" clefts and relative clauses than simple actives, and he illustrates the latter claim by pointing to the well-known fact (see Emonds 1976) that main ("less presuppositional") clauses allow a far greater range of syntactic constructions than embedded ones.

Givón proposes to *explain* these observations by appealing to the processing of presupposition-bearing and non-presupposition-bearing items in discourse. For example: "It is reasonable to assume that clauses which are more presuppositional and therefore not a critical part of the new information will also tolerate more syntactic—and thus probably more *perceptual*—complexity" (88–89; emphasis in original). Presuppositional clauses have greater distributional restrictions because "in terms of the freer distribution of meaning-bearing elements, obviously the clause type which carries the bulk of new information is precisely the one where maximal elaboration is to be expected. . . . On the other hand, the communicative loss emanating from less elaboration and less specification in presupposed clauses is more easily offset by the fact that they represent background information already accessible to the hearer" (88).

But Givón in reality explains nothing because his notion of "presupposition" is incoherent. He cannot even decide whether a presupposition is something a *speaker* has, a *discourse* has, or a *syntactic construction* has. On page 50, presuppositions are "defined in terms of assumptions the speaker makes about what the hearer is likely to *accept without challenge*" (emphasis added). On page 92, speakers still have presuppositions, but now "they involve what the speaker assumes that the hearer *tends to believe*, is *likely to be leaning toward*, or is *committed to by a probability higher than 50%* (emphasis in original). On page 64 and elsewhere, we find reference to "discourse presuppositions"; on page 67 "constructions" have presuppositions, on page 69 verbs have them, and on page 84 a "sentence type" can be presuppositional. Perhaps there is some way these various characterizations can be reconciled, but it should not be the reader's responsibility to figure out how.[20]

Givón seems unaware that the attempt to characterize presupposition has been one of the main preoccupations of linguists and philosophers of language over the past decade. His only references to the literature on the nature of presupposition are to Keenan (1971) and Karttunen (1974). Yet literally *dozens* of studies of this topic appeared in the early and mid-1970s that contain material bearing directly on Givón's hypotheses, including (most important) Garner (1971), Horn (1972), Landesmann (1972), Katz (1973), Kempson (1975), Wilson (1975), and Gazdar (1977). If Givón had been familiar with the literature on the topic that bears so heavily on his hypotheses, he would at least not have committed such elementary errors as making a blanket characterization of relative clauses as "presuppositional" (77) (for discussion, see Kempson 1975) and equating the felicity conditions of speech acts with presuppositions (54–55) (for discussion, see Gazdar 1977).

Givón's treatment of presupposition reflects his general ignorance of formal logic and of the vast literature on the logical properties of grammatical constructions. He confuses truth value with paraphrase, claiming that the "truth value" of *John read a book* is *there exists a book, and John*

---

20. *Whatever* Givón ultimately decides a "presupposition" is, its ontological status will need clarification. On the one hand, it is certainly not for him a theoretical term within an explanatory model. But on the other hand, it is not an observational term either. One does not measure presuppositions the way one measures voting results or the height of mercury in a cylinder. To make matters worse, at one point Givón speculates that presuppositionality may not be a categorial matter but may have to be "quantified over a continuum" (56).

read it (94). He calls *someone doesn't love Mary* the "internal negation" of *someone loves Mary* (113), not realizing that the internal/external dichotomy does not map onto the narrow scope/wide scope dichotomy. He cites Bickerton (personal communication) (95) for the observation that in example (32), but not in (33), one gets a reading that allows for an interpretation of *both* sense and reference, despite the fact that practically identical sentences, and their implications, are discussed in Partee (1972):

(32)   John met a girl yesterday,
         and Fred met one too (SENSE).
         and Fred met her too (REFERENCE).

(33)   John didn't meet a girl yesterday,
         and Fred didn't meet one either (SENSE).
         *and Fred didn't meet her either (*REFERENCE).

A particularly muddled section of *OUG* begins with the citation of (34), where ⊃ is explicated first as a logical entailment, then as a logical presupposition, apparently without any change of direction (106–7):

(34)   He didn't run as fast as he could ⊃ He ran, though not as fast as he could.

Givón then writes:

This apparent logical contradiction may be summarized as:

(39)   a. $p \supset q$
        b. $\sim (\sim p \supset \sim q)$
        c. $\sim p \supset q$

where (39b) is a correct inference from the premise (39a), but (39c) is not. (107)

He then proceeds to offer a Gricean explanation for the "seemingly contradictory (39c)" (107), which he credits to Robert Kirsner (personal communication). Now, unless these familiar symbols are in fact meant to be interpreted according to a nonstandard logic that Givón fails to delineate, (39b) is *not* a correct inference from (39a), and (39c) is not internally inconsistent, nor is the conjunction of it and (39a) a logical contradiction. In any event, it was argued in Horn (1972, 29) that the relation in examples like (34) cannot be *either* entailment *or* logical presupposition.

    Even if some sense could be made out of Givón's notion of presupposition, he would still not have been successful in explaining the subject matter under discussion. This is easily demonstrated by a thought experiment: Assume that the facts are exactly the opposite from what Givón claims them to be. That is, assume counterfactually that the clauses containing constructions generated by Emonds's root transformations are *more presuppositional* than main, declarative, affirmative active clauses and assume, also counterfactually, that relative clauses are *less presuppositional* than main, declarative, active affirmatives. Givón would not have to change his "explanations" *one bit* to accommodate these counterfacts. He could "explain" why clauses containing the output of root transformations are syntactically more complex than main, declarative, affirmative, active clauses; since root transformation clauses are "more presuppositional and therefore not a critical part of the new information, [they will] tolerate more syntactic—and thus probably more perceptual—complexity" (89). And he could "explain" why relatives are less restricted in their distribution than main, declarative, affirmative actives, since "in terms of the freer distribution of meaning-bearing elements, obviously the clause type which carries the bulk of new information is precisely the one where maximal elaboration is to be expected" (88).

A theory that can accommodate a fact and its counterfact with equal ease is no theory at all. Yet such a state of affairs is hardly likely to bother a linguist like Givón who, when confronted with an obvious counterexample to the hypothesis that communicative function is paramount in language, can write blithely: "The answer [to this problem] seems to be that speakers make communicative choices which are *not ideal*, but rather are a matter of judgment" (39; emphasis in original)! What a shame for Givón that reality should so consistently depart from his "ideal."

5 | The Applicability of Grammatical Theory

5.1 Introduction

The great appeal of Chomsky's *Syntactic Structures* cannot be explained exclusively by the fact that it presented a convincing theory of grammatical description. After all, the correct form of the theory of grammar is a topic of little interest to the nonspecialist. No, the theory presented in that book captured the imagination of scholars and pedagogues in numerous fields because it seemed likely to promote solutions to long-standing problems in *every* area in which language plays a role.

The implications of Chomsky's approach for learning theory were perceived immediately. Robert B. Lees's review, published almost simultaneously with *Syntactic Structures* in 1957, pointed out that, if Chomsky's views are correct, then "our notions of human learning are due for some considerable sophistication" (1957, 408). More "sophisticated" approaches to learning were presented within a few years, both in Chomsky's review of Skinner's *Verbal Behavior* and in Miller, Galanter, and Pribram's important book *Plans and the Structure of Behavior* (1960). As Judith Greene put it: "Chomsky's theory of generative transformational grammar was the first to force psychologists to reconsider their whole approach to the study of language behavior, and so heralded the psycholinguistic 'revolution' " (1972, 15).

Attempts to apply the theory to the solution of practical problems were made soon afterward. The early results of this work were felt to be promising—by the mid-1960s many agreed with Owen Thomas that "transformational grammar has significant application to the teaching of all languages, including English, at all grade levels and to both native and nonnative speakers" (1965, 1). The publication of Chomsky's *Aspects of the Theory of Syntax* in 1965 accelerated adoption of the concepts and technical vocabulary of grammatical theory in solving a wide variety of language-related problems. The late 1960s saw attempts to apply the theory to areas as diverse as literary criticism, the structure of music, and kinship terminology.

But as the 1970s progressed the star of transformational generative grammar began to wane. Increasingly it was realized that the earlier applications were inadequate, premature, or based on a faulty understanding of the theory. The seeming inability of the theory to lead to payoffs in a wide variety of areas led to the suspicion that the Chomskyan view of language was fundamentally flawed; naturally, a misconceived theory could not be expected to lead to fruitful applications. Certainly the repeated schisms *within* transformational grammar, including some, like generative semantics, that in later stages challenged almost every basic assumption of *Syntactic Structures* and *Aspects*, did little to bolster the confidence of those who looked to the theory to provide direction for their particular concerns. By the late 1970s many researchers had come to the same negative conclusion—the theory was of no use to them at all. At best they saw its insights as no more than artifacts, derivable from some more general (not specifically linguistic) system. At worst they saw it as a malicious distraction from the necessary task of explaining the functioning of language in its social, cultural, and interpersonal context.

In the past few years there has been a slow but unmistakable readoption of generativist principles by many outside the study of formal grammar proper. Nevertheless, it seems safe to say that a majority still react to generativist theory with feelings ranging from skepticism to hostility.

The rest of this chapter is organized as follows. Section 5.2 attempts to explain the circumstances that led to the theory's falling into ill-repute in many quarters in the 1970s. I hope to demonstrate that the negative conclusions were based primarily on an imperfect understanding of the theory or on unrealistic expectations of the insights it might provide. Section 5.3 reviews the positive contributions the theory has made and can reasonably be expected to make to the solution of "practical" problems.

5.2   Three Reasons for the Disillusionment with Generativist Theory[1]

There are three principal reasons why the work of generative grammarians began to fall into disfavor among applied linguists in the early 1970s: the peculiar conception of the nature of "applied linguistics" created unrealistic expectations of what grammatical theory might contribute to

---

1. An earlier version of much of the material in this section (and in section 5.3.1) was published as Newmeyer (1982b).

the solution of practical problems (section 5.2.1); many attempted applications were naive and therefore led ultimately to failure (section 5.2.2); and many applied linguists felt that the generativist goal was to redefine linguistics so as to trivialize their own interests (section 5.2.3).

5.2.1 The Unrealistic Expectations of Many Applied Linguists

For unclear reasons, "applied linguistics" has come to be identified with almost any area of research or pedagogy involving language outside grammatical theory proper (though in Britain the term is often restricted to the application of linguistics to language teaching—see Corder 1973a, 7). For example, the Center for Applied Linguistics, the institutional nerve center for much language-oriented work in America,

> was established in order to serve as a national clearinghouse and catalyst in the following loosely related areas: (1) teaching and research in English as a foreign language; (2) teaching and research in the major languages of Asia and Africa, and other languages not commonly taught in the United States; (3) the application of linguistic science to practical language problems; (4) the availability of trained linguists for various teaching and research tasks; (5) cooperation among various governmental agencies concerned with language problems; (6) similar cooperation and coordination of information among various units of the academic community, and between government agencies and the language teaching profession in general. (*Linguistic Reporter*, vol. 7, no. 2 [1965])

Along the same lines, the American Association for Applied Linguistics, founded in 1977, "consists of scholars interested in and actively contributing to the field of applied linguistics, which for the purposes of the Association, is defined as 'a multidisciplinary approach to language problems and issues'" (*Linguistic Reporter*, vol. 20, no. 8 [1978]).

Apparently one can do "applied linguistics" without drawing, even vaguely, on what is normally considered to be "linguistics." For example, two papers in Perren and Trim's *Applications of Linguistics* (1971) deal with the tensions of preparing courses for television and with the necessity for cost-effectiveness studies for language teaching programs.

Going to the other extreme, much of what seems to be, in its crucial respects, theorizing about grammar is also labeled "applied linguistics." For example, Selinker's work on "interlanguage" (1972) is generally considered applied linguistics, presumably because his grammatical model results from language contact.

"Applied linguistics" contrasts sharply with applied everything else. James B. Conant writes that the primary goal of applied research is "the application of the existing conceptual schemes to solution of practical problems" (1951, 305). Certainly applied physics, applied chemistry, applied mathematics, and so forth are consistent with Conant's characterization. But, as Bowen and Stockwell have correctly observed: "Much of the work . . . that has gone under the name of applied linguistics either has only the most tenuous links with linguistic theory of any variety or has grown, in the cases where linkage does exist, from inadequate comprehension of the nature of the linkage" (1968, viii).

It is interesting that the *original* use of the term "applied linguistics," by the great nineteenth-century linguist Jan Baudouin de Courtenay, was entirely consistent with Conant's characterization of applied science: "applied linguistics, whose subject is the application of the results of pure linguistics to questions pertaining to other sciences" (quoted in Stankiewicz 1972, 60). Baudouin went on to give examples of the application of contemporary theory (historical reconstruction) to the solution of certain philological problems.

So what's wrong with an idiosyncratic use of a term? Inherently nothing, of course. People should be free to designate their work as they see fit. But the use of the term "applied linguistics" in too broad a sense has led to the desire (often unconscious) that the central theoretical core of linguistics—in the 1970s, transformational generative grammar—provide more of a contribution than could realistically be expected.[2] If one is an applied scientist, then one naturally looks to the results of science for application. But the results of generativist theory seem intrinsically inapplicable to much of what is considered applied linguistics. How could these results possibly help provide solutions to the problems encountered in areas of "applied linguistics" like national language planning? The inherent lack of applicability to numerous problems involving language has, I believe, resulted in increasing frustration with the theory—a frustration engendered ultimately by a peculiar conception of what characterizes an applied science (or at least an applied linguistics).[3]

2. To be sure, many linguists and applied linguists have prescribed caution about drawing overhasty conclusions about the immediate applicability of linguistic theory to practical concerns. For example:

> We need not quarrel over whether good grammatical descriptions are better than bad ones, and much of what is presented here is good. But mere honesty compels us to admit that we do not know how to convert the information in a good description into pedagogically optimal format. The contributions of linguistics have been too substantial in their own right for linguists to continue making undocumented assertions about "the applications of linguistics" to second-language acquistion. We linguists do a disservice both to ourselves and to our colleagues in language departments by deceiving them into believing that we have access to some secret information about how to teach foreign languages. (Saporta 1967, 200)

See also Newmark (1973, 205–6) and Corder (1973b, 18).

3. This frustration has been shared by agencies funding linguistic research, both pure and applied. For example, Kenneth W. Mildenberger, then treasurer and director of programs of the Modern Language Association, complained that:

> projects dealing with the practical applications of linguistics have, during the past decade, received very large sums of money; and the volume of activity has greatly taxed available linguistic manpower. However, confidence in the promise of Applied Linguistics appears to be lessening among language teachers and others. Specifically, linguistic

Additional frustration came from the slow emergence of applications of generativist theory in areas where it might be reasonably expected to make contributions (e.g., language teaching). By the mid 1970s the slow pace of application had contributed to the general air of disillusionment with the theory. However, even granting that application was as slow as the generativists' critics claimed, as I shall argue in section 5.3, the *implications* of the theory were immediate and have been profound. (For discussion of the relevance of the application/implication distinction, see Spolsky 1970; Wilkins 1972; Harris 1973.) Also, for whatever reason, many applied linguists have displayed a curious impatience for applicable results. It often takes a *long* time to successfully apply a new theory, as work in other areas demonstrates. Several decades elapsed between the rediscovery of Mendelian genetics and its application to plant and animal breeding. Certain early nineteenth century developments in number theory by Gauss and his students found no application until quite recently (in cryptography). And some of the most promising developments in modern physics have not yet found a single application. One cannot judge the worth of a theory by its ability to yield immediately applicable results.

Two final sources of frustration have been the frequent changes in the generativists' model and the numerous competing frameworks sharing its basic assumptions. One is tempted to sympathize with Roger Brown when he complains:

> The fact that linguistic theory changes, and does so at a rapid clip, poses real difficulties for the psychologist who wants to use linguistic theory in his own work. What one discipline wants from another—in interdisciplinary work—is always The Word. "Don't tell me your troubles tell me your results," is the borrower's real attitude. It is not a possible attitude for the psycholinguist in 1969. (Brown 1970, ix)

But Brown was writing barely ten years after the theory he wished to apply to his own work was first proposed, and only four years after the first students working in that theory received their Ph.D.s. It may be disconcerting that generativists have not all agreed upon a single framework, but even now, more than two decades since the publication of *Syntactic Structures*, it is hardly surprising that a diversity of opinion exists within grammatical theory. I wonder how many theories after

---

applications to machine translation and programmed language instruction seem to have reached an impasse; and the psycholinguistic research base and the lasting effectiveness of audio-lingualism are under serious challenge. An immense credibility gap is opening rapidly. (1968, 205)

Earlier Mildenberger, as chief of the Language Development Section of the United States Office of Education, had endorsed the view that linguists should "put up or shut up" (1962, 163).

twenty years have had the unanimity among their supporters that many want in linguistics. And the rapid changes in the model are to be both expected and welcomed in a healthy science. For example, physical theory changes so fast that letters to the editors of the *Physical Review* are a major avenue through which new theoretical ideas are transmitted!

I think the problem has been exacerbated because many early publications about generative grammar for nonspecialists invited their readers to conclude that the theory was well worked out in all its fine points. Despite Chomsky's word of caution in the introduction, the incredible detail and overconfident manner of presentation of Paul Roberts's *English Syntax* (1964) surely conveyed an ill-advised certainty of accomplishment to those who relied upon it for their first exposure to transformational grammar. Somewhat analogously, Rosenbaum (1965) based an important pedagogical point on the hypothesis that a rule deleting *'s* in *Does your mother dislike your brother('s) coming home late?* and one deleting *for* in *Mary would hate (for) the boys to come home early* are the same rule. The realization a few years later that virtually all of Roberts's rules had been modified and that virtually no syntacticians equated Rosenbaum's two deletions must have contributed to the general cynicism about the worth of transformational generative grammar that developed in the mid 1970s.

It is important for theoreticians to emphasize to students who have applied interests the tentative nature of many specific theoretical proposals. Typically, such students have minimal training in the sciences and tend to share the layperson's idea that progress in science involves the cumulative addition of new theories to already "proved" ones. Hence they are extremely disconcerted to find that the statements of the rules presented in their introductory syntax and phonology texts have been changed—in some cases drastically. Actually, theoreticians should stress that these texts are only *slightly* out-of-date compared to those in the "hard" sciences, a fact that reflects the immaturity of linguistics as a science. It seems to be a general rule that the more developed the science, the more out-of-date the textbooks—physics students do not move into the twentieth century until their second year of study. Also, it is worth pointing out that another aspect of this immaturity, the lack of theoretical harmony on many important issues, is shared by *all* the cognitive sciences. It takes only a glance at a typical introduction to cognitive psychology, say Reynolds and Flagg (1977), to make one realize that as much theoretical disharmony exists among researchers of vision, memory, perception, and so forth, as among those of language.

5.2.2   Unsuccessful Applications of the Theory

Most of the early attempts to apply grammatical theory, particularly to second-language teaching (where the greatest resources were directed) met with results that were at best ambiguous. As the seventies progressed, the number of papers in the applied journals that purported to use the generativists' work for some practical purpose steadily declined. Lamendella (1969) offered a reason for the failure of the attempted applications: transformational generative grammar was simply "irrelevant" to pedagogy. Such a conclusion led irrevocably to another, more drastic, one: that the theory itself was therefore misconceived.

But misguided applications do not entail a misconceived theory. And the earliest application attempts seem, in retrospect, rather naive. Many apparently were based on the assumption that the structure of a particular theory dictates the structure of the application of that theory. For example:

> Each of the four major models contributes something toward the understanding and generation [*sic*] of the structure of language; each model is reflected in specific types of drill:—
>
> Grammar Model   Grammar Drill
> Traditionalist................. Parsing
> Structuralist.................. Completion/Substitution
> (Immediate Constituent)
> Tagmemicist .... Substitution/Correlational
> Transformationalist .... Conversion, Expansion,
>   and Reduction of Sentences
> (Gefen 1966, 230)

Analogously, Banathy, Trager, and Waddle (1966) and Lado (1968) proposed to teach transformational rules to the second-language learner in the order the generativist posited that they applied in the grammar.

The idea that practice could be made to mirror theory so directly was derived ultimately, I believe, from a view of the nature of theoretical constructs that was popular in the United States until the 1950s. The dominant view among philosophers of science until then was that theoretical constructs are "validated" if and only if they can be given operational definitions. (Note that the constructs of post-Bloomfieldian structural linguistics had just this property—if anybody wanted to know, for example, why the claim had been made that /p/ was a phoneme of English, that person could (in principle) be given a list of the operations that led to that conclusion.) But today, virtually no philosopher of science has this conception of theoretical constructs (see, e.g., Hempel 1965; Lakatos 1970; Suppe 1977). The dominant view today is that it is the theory as a whole that is given an empirical interpretation, not the individual terms and statements that constitute it. Granting this, there is no reason to expect that one should be able to mirror in practice the internal composition of a theory. Thus, the failures of such attempts by applied linguists do not in themselves point to any inherent defect of the generativists' conception of language, but rather were an inevitable result of a faulty conception of the nature of a scientific theory.

The realization in the 1970s that many putative "applications" of the results of the generativists were not applications at all also contributed to the atmosphere of disillusionment with transformational generative grammar. Earlier, it was common to see in the applied journals and anthologies papers that did little more than adopt the technical vocabulary of generative theory in the name of "applying" that theory to some practical end. Literally dozens of papers and books (see, e.g., Ohmann 1964; Gefen 1967; Rutherford 1968; Hunt 1970) spoke of applying "transformations" and "transformational grammar" simply by exploiting the fact that in every language there are classes of sentences that share certain syntactic properties. Many others (Jacobson 1966; Di Pietro 1968) wrote of applying "deep structures" in the classroom, when it is clear they meant no more than that students should understand the meanings of the sentences they learn. Surely it must have occurred to the perceptive reader that one does not need a difficult-to-master linguistic theory to supply the information that sentences are related and have meanings. Besides this obvious intuitive fact, grammars have been written for hundreds of years that catalog in great detail the various types of intrasentential relations. Along the same lines, the tone of Ohmann (1966) actually makes it sound as if the realization that sentences contain understood elements was a great insight of generative grammar, and the tone of Rosenbaum (1965) conveys the same impression for the fact that some sentences are ambiguous. Many must have come away from a reading of these papers with the conviction that the generativists' theory was little more than a set of new names for old concepts, with nothing of substance to contribute. It is difficult to disagree with Robin Lakoff's assessment:

> These authors are not really using transformational grammar; they are using only its hollow shell of formalism; they are not employing rationalism at all, but resorting to new forms of the same old mumbo-jumbo; they have substituted one kind of rote learning for another, and the new kind is harder than the old. . . . Rather than teaching students to reason, they seem to me to be teaching students to use new formulas. (1969b, 130)

5.2.3   The Supposed Indifference of Generativists
to Applied Concerns

Probably the belief that has had the most damaging consequences is that Chomsky and his supporters consider unworthy of investigation anything that is not a grammatical phenomenon in the narrowest sense of the term. For example, M. A. K. Halliday accused Chomsky of desiring "to exclude social context from the study of language" (1974, 183).

George Lakoff, once one of Chomsky's most ardent supporters (see Lakoff 1969), echoed Halliday with the charge that the generativists "set up artificial boundaries and rule out of the study of language such things as human reasoning, context, social interaction, deixis, fuzziness, sarcasm, discourse types, fragments, variation among speakers, etc." (1974, 178). Dell Hymes is of the same opinion, arguing that since "[t]he goal of explanation in linguistics is set [by generativists] as universal properties of the human mind; the present interest and relevance of a sociolinguistic perspective is rejected" (1974, 77).

Why would Halliday, Lakoff, and Hymes—not to mention countless others!—believe such a thing? If they are right in their characterization of Chomsky's attitude, then it certainly seems they have valid grounds for complaint. If the work of the majority of the world's linguists is not "the study of language," then what is it? An undercurrent of hostility to generative grammar arises because many who identify themselves as linguists believe that Chomsky wishes to define them out of the field of linguistics.

This belief is due in part to the assimilation of a remark of Chomsky's that it is common to hear cited out of context: "I am, frankly, rather skeptical about the significance, for the teaching of languages, of such insights and understanding as have been attained in linguistics and psychology" (1966, 52). Many applied linguists, unaware of Chomsky's following sentence, have cited this remark to justify their belief that he considers the problems they are concerned with of no intellectual interest. They furthermore have drawn the natural conclusion that if generativist theory is irrelevant to their work, then that theory must be fundamentally deficient. But consider Chomsky's long-forgotten next sentence: "Surely the teacher of language would do well to keep informed of progress and discussion in these fields, and the efforts of linguists and psychologists to approach the problems of language teaching from a principled point of view are extremely worthwhile, from an intellectual as well as a social point of view" (1966, 52). Certainly Chomsky cannot be accused of maintaining that language teaching lacks intellectual interest or is not dependent on the results of linguistics. I. M. Roca puts Chomsky's comments in historical perspective:

> Chomsky's words must be put in the context of the "technological revolution" in language teaching which followed the linguistic theories of the forties and fifties, engrained, as has been seen, in behaviouristic principles. Unconditional optimism in the then prevailing linguistic theories led to the opinion that the problem of teaching second languages had been solved, and an extensive technological programme ensued. Instances which readily spring to mind are the language laboratory, programmed learning, and the whole paraphernalia of audio-visual aids for classroom use, all of which seemed to have replaced the teacher and done so in such a way as to make the operation

successful. Some of these offshoots still have considerable following, but an atmosphere of caution has replaced the original unreserved optimism, in this as in other fields. Recall, however, that the Chomskyan revolution in linguistics also brought about waves of hope. The danger of a premature technology being hurriedly brought in was probably a real one, and Chomsky warns about its present futility. To infer from this that the language teaching theoretician can safely turn his back on Chomskyan insights, or, even, content himself with keeping a keen but uncommitted eye on the advances of linguistic theory and accompanying philosophical thought is, to my mind, a clear distortion of the facts as well as of Chomsky's intentions. (1979, 183)

It cannot be denied, however, that there is a rational interpretation of some other published statements by Chomsky and gives credence to the accusations by Halliday, Lakoff, and Hymes that he does have a very narrow view of what constitutes "linguistics." For example, Chomsky has more than once defined linguistics as a "branch of cognitive psychology" (1972c, 1). Surely there is no way that all the study of language in its social context can be subsumed under cognitive psychology. Or again, after defining "performance" as "the actual use of language in concrete situations" (1965, 4) he wrote that "the only studies of performance, outside of phonetics . . . , are those carried out as a by-product of work in generative grammar" (1965, 15). Dell Hymes's reaction to this assertion was probably more restrained than that of many:

> However, if (outside phonetics) only by-products of generative grammar qualify as studies of performance, what is to be said of more than two thousand years of rhetoric and poetics, and of investigations of the use of language in social interaction and cultural behavior? If these investigations are not performance, then the equation of performance with use of language has reduced the notion of "use" so much as to exclude most aspects of speaking. If these investigations *do* deal with performance subject-matter, then the term "study" is oddly restricted to just those investigations that arise as generative grammar by-products. (Hymes 1971, 10–11)

Chomsky's statements (and his ambiguous use of the term "performance"—see section 1.5.1) could well be a reflection of his long-standing belief that a (scientific) field of study is defined, essentially, by its axiomatizability. Since only the theory of formal grammar itself and a few areas of performance relating to speech perception have this property at present, it appears that Chomsky is implicitly characterizing many other phenomena as falling outside both competence and performance and therefore, by implication, branding their study as outside linguistics.[4]

4. Chomsky has informed me (personal communication) that "studies of performance" in the quotation above refers only to formalized performance *models*, which indeed are largely, if not entirely, by-products of generative work. He furthermore maintains that he has never suggested, nor does he desire, any limitation on the study of performance.

But it seems inconceivable that Chomsky regards as "nonlinguistics" any investigation of the sociological or humanistic aspects of language. If he does, then what could one make of his own discussion (1970b) of language and human freedom? Even if Chomsky *has* such a view, it is one few generativists share. There have been numerous generativists, "doctrinaire" on all the fundamental theoretical issues, who have made contributions to the understanding of language in its social and cultural setting. To cite only a few examples, consider Keyser's (1969) and Kiparsky's (1977) work on poetics; Banfield's (1973a) study of narrative style; Langendoen's (1970) paper on language in advertising; Newmeyer's (1973, 1978) publications on prescriptive grammar; Saporta's (1977, 1979) publications on language and sexism; Pullum's (1972) paper on Indian scripts; O'Neil's (1972) paper on bidialectalism; Hale's (1973) discussion of linguistics and bilingual education; Jackendoff's work on the structure of music (Lerdahl and Jackendoff 1977); Zwicky's (1976) remarks on feature rhyme in rock and roll music; Aronoff's (1981) paper on automobile names; and so on. It seems to me that only the most uncharitable attitude toward generative grammarians could lead one to conclude that they feel linguists should not address the functioning of language in *all* its aspects.[5]

5.3   Some Implications and Applications of Grammatical Theory

5.3.1   Second Language Learning

As we have seen, the inability of grammatical theory to produce immediate practical results in language teaching was a prime factor in the disillusionment with it that is so prevalent among applied linguists. And, of course, if one wants the theory to dictate a specific classroom teaching technique, there is no question that the theory has not been applied and will *never* be. Does this mean, then, that grammatical theory is irrelevant to pedagogy? Far from it. I hope to demonstrate in this section that the *implications* of the theory of language teaching, both at the most general level and at the level of specifics, have been profound. Furthermore, I will suggest that second language learning research, in turn, has uncovered facts of great potential interest to theoreticians.

To appreciate the dramatic changes in second language teaching practice ushered in by the Chomskyan revolution, one need only reflect that not long ago the following chapter headings from Wilga Rivers's *The Psychologist and the Foreign-Language Teacher* (1964) summed up the

---

5. Which is not to deny that some (I believe a minority) share the "pure" scientists' lack of interest in practical or applicable results. For discussion, see Newmeyer and Emonds (1971).

attitude of the vast majority of language teachers in the English-speaking world: "Foreign-language learning is basically a mechanical process of habit formation," "Habits are strengthened by reinforcement," "Foreign-language habits are formed most effectively by giving the right response, not by making mistakes," and "Language is behavior and . . . behavior can be learned only by inducing the student to behave."[6]

The generativist approach to language was able to provide an *explanation* for the failure of the behaviorist-inspired foreign language teaching methods like the audiolingual method and programmed instruction,[7] and thereby set the stage for a more "active" role for the learner. Spolsky (1970) has discussed in some detail other implications of grammatical theory for second language learning. After characterizing the theory as embodying the following four assumptions, he suggested that at least ten implications for pedagogy (listed below) followed from these assumptions:

I.   Language is essentially creative; thus, the notion of language as habit is not possible.
II.   The best explanation of this aspect of language is to say that the speaker of a language has available a system of rules to be used to produce and understand new sentences.
III.   The rules concerned are both intricate and abstract.
IV.   The underlying intellectual organization required to acquire rules of this type suggests that there are universal properties of grammar.
Implication 1. It is not enough to teach a language learner to respond automatically to predetermined stimuli: language instruction must lead to creative language use in new situations.
Implication 2. Language can be acquired by active listening (listening and doing) even better than by listening and repeating.
Implication 3. Programmed language instruction will have limited results in language teaching.
Implication 4. The teacher or textbook writer will not be able to find a complete grammar of the language he is teaching. He will need to be able to draw on all available materials and to prepare his own.
Implication 5. When you learn a language, you have to learn its semantic system too: accepting word-by-word translation obscures this.
Implication 6. The learning of fundamental syntactic relations and processes will not be accomplished by drill based on analysis of surface structure alone.
Implication 7. A language learner will need to be able to recognize the

---

6. It must be pointed out that in this book Rivers herself was very critical of the behaviorist assumptions she presented.

7. For documentation of the failure of the audiolingual method, see Scherer and Wertheimer (1964), Smith and Berger (1968), and Smith and Baranyi (1968); for documentation of the failure of programmed instruction, see Spolsky (1966) and Ornstein (1968).

phonological distinctions made by speakers of the language and to produce recognizable distinctions. The more he masters the language, the less important phonology will be in this recognition.
Implication 8. Knowledge of the structure of the learner's native language will help the teacher.
Implication 9. Systematic errors (saying *I goed* instead of *I went*) are useful evidence to the teacher that the student is learning major rules.
Implication 10. Presentation of material should encourage formation of rules rather than memorization of items. (Spolsky 1970, 150–52)

It is easy to lose sight of the fact that most of these implications were either points of intense controversy before the generativist revolution in linguistics or else were rejected outright. Today, most are simply taken for granted.

I certainly do not wish to imply that the changed attitudes of language teachers in the 1960s and 1970s were solely (or even principally) a by-product of generativist principles. Equally important were the rise of more "humanistic" approaches to teaching, with emphasis on positive feedback, environments of relaxation, the desirability of expressing oneself creatively, and so forth. Nevertheless, their way was paved in large part by the overthrow of the mechanical and rigid methodology invited by behaviorist ideology.

Just as behaviorism has been disconfirmed by studies of first language acquisition (see section 1.3.2), recent research has led to the conclusion that a full account of second language learning must involve reference to more than the learner's response history and external stimuli received during the learning process. In a review of the literature, Dulay and Burt (1978) show that "cognitive creativity" is every bit as important in second language learning as in first. Input factors such as perceptual salience, frequency of occurrence of a particular construction, the amount of corrective feedback, and the degree of reinforcement correlate very poorly with the learner's progress. More specific evidence for a diminished role for external input factors will be discussed below.

Recent research suggests other ways that external input factors seem to play a diminished role in second language learning. For example, it appears that some of the same principles that shape first language acquisition also shape second. In an important paper, Ervin-Tripp (1974) documents a number of ways second language learners (unconsciously) recapitulate many of the stages passed through by the first language learner. For example, English-speaking children learning French typically interpret French passives as actives, even though they have mastered the English passive. In doing so they appear to be following the strategy of first language learners, who go through a stage in which they interpret their own passives as actives. Likewise, d'Anglejan and Tucker (1975) note that French learners of English go through a stage in which they interpret sentences like *John is easy to see* as *it is easy for John to see*. Significantly, Carol Chomsky (1969) has found that children learning English go through an identical stage. "Interference" can hardly be appealed to for an explanation, since not only is the French "easy-to-please" construction like the English (*Jean est difficil à voir*), but is differentiated from the "eager-to-please" construction by the choice of preposition. D'Anglejan and Tucker note that their subjects

> did *not* revert to the syntactic structure of their native language as a strategy to aid in comprehension. Furthermore, these results suggest that second language learners tend to process the linguistic data of the target language independent of the syntax of their native language. They appear to draw upon their own incipient rule system for English, a finding which lends credence to the hypothesis that second language learning involves a creative construction process at least with respect to the development of comprehension. (1975, 288)

Zobl (1980a) also makes the observation that facts about second language learning correlate in interesting ways with facts about language *change*. For example, the last position in which German speakers give up post–main verb negation in favor of negation with supportive *do* is after intransitive verbs in main clauses. This is also the last position in which English, historically, developed negation with *do*. Likewise, German speakers (as well as Norwegian speakers—see Ravem 1968) learn subject-auxiliary inversion in *wh*-questions after they have mastered it for *yes-no* questions. Again, this correlates with the historical development of English.

One hesitates to label as "applications" the changes in pedagogical practice that result from the adoption of a new theory. After all, generative theory does not dictate—even indirectly—a specific classroom technique. Yet it does help delimit the set of reasonable techniques. For example, I. M. Roca gives several examples of how "concepts such as creativity or generative grammar (with its implication of finite means to infinite ends) brought about by the Chomskyan revolution find a direct and crucial application to language teaching practice" (1979, 178). Roca reports considerable success by stressing to his students the grammatical generalizations underlying the creative linguistic process he wishes to teach. It is important to emphasize that he advocates teaching not the rules themselves (as did would-be appliers of generative grammar in the 1960s), but rather the principles underlying the rules. He relies on the students' knowledge of universal grammar for the correct application of these language-specific principles to the target language.

If Roca's methods have any general validity, then it follows that the ideal teacher and researcher of English as a second language will be knowledgeable in generative grammar. And there is some evidence that this is correct; for example, Larry Selinker (personal communication) reports that the best students he has directed in applied linguistics have had strong backgrounds in linguistic theory.

There is evidence that the results of generativist theorizing have implications for the understanding of second language learning beyond the fairly general learning theoretic implications discussed above. While it is clearly premature to claim to have "confirmed" some specific theoretical proposal on the basis of an observation of second language learning, given the bewildering complexity of the factors involved,[8] a number of papers in the past decade have described phenomena that seem to support some fairly specific generativist notions.

For example, there is evidence that second language learning—even by adults—is constrained by the same abstract universal principles that constrain first language acquisition (for general discussion of the issues involved, see Jenkins 1979). Ritchie (1978a) found that Japanese learners of English were sensitive to Right Roof Constraint violations in English, even though they had not learned the English extraposition rules that the constraint affects. The Right Roof Constraint is stated as in (1) and prevents, for example, (2b) from being derived from (2a):[9]

(1)   *The Right Roof Constraint*
       Surface strings in which an element has been moved to the right out of the sentence in which the element originated are ill formed.

(2)   a. [$_S$that it surprised Mary that John had left] amused Alice
       b. *[$_S$that it surprised Mary] amused Alice that John had left

Japanese speakers learning English readily identified sentences such as (2b) as deviant. The special importance of this result comes from the fact that Japanese itself has no rightward movement rules. In other words, the subjects' sensitivity to the constraint cannot be attributed to "positive transfer" from Japanese but must reflect some deeper internalized principle.

The case for abstract grammatical universals has received its greatest support from the nature of the *errors* made by second language learners. It may prove useful to review the changing views about such errors. The earliest assumption was that they resulted primarily from interference from the native language (see Fries 1945; Lado 1957; Carroll 1968; Wardhaugh 1970). As Carroll put the matter:

8. Not the least of which is the language learner's own motivation. For discussion of some of the attitudinal factors involved, see Gardner and Lambert (1959, 1972), Lambert et al. (1963), and Spolsky (1969).

9. For discussion of the Right Roof Constraint, see Ross (1968) and Grosu (1973). It appears that this constraint is a manifestation of the more general Subjacency principle (Chomsky 1973).

> My major assumption is that we are concerned here with the problems of facilitation and interference that apparently arise whenever an individual who has already learned one linguistic system to a high degree of competence attempts to learn another linguistic system in which his competence is, initially at least, virtually nil. Between any two linguistic systems there may be both similarities and contrasts in proportions that will vary with the languages involved. The hypothesis of applied contrastive linguistics is that wherever there are similarities, learning can be facilitated, and wherever there are contrasts, learning may be retarded or interfered with. In the psychology of learning, facilitation and interference phenomena are considered under the generic concept of transfer—transfer of learning or transfer of training. Facilitation and interference are spoken of as representing positive or negative transfer, respectively. (1968, 115)

The idea that interference should be the crucial factor in causing errors follows automatically, of course, from the position that learning a language is nothing more than acquiring a set of habits. Second language acquisition research, in this view, boils down to doing *contrastive analysis*, that is, examining the properties of the native and target languages for the purpose of predicting the learners' difficulties.

The sufficiency of transfer as an explanation of learners' errors was challenged by many researchers in the early 1970s (see Corder 1971; Nemser 1971; Richards 1971; Selinker 1972). Richards, for example, stressed learning strategies as an important variable:

> Interference from the mother tongue is clearly a major source of difficulty in second language learning, and contrastive analysis has proved valuable in locating areas of interlanguage interference. Many errors however, derive from the strategies employed by the learner in language acquisition, and from the mutual interference of items within the target language. (1971, 214)

Gundel and Tarone (1981) give an example of an hypothesis-testing strategy employed by English-speaking learners of French. Apparently it is common for learners to go through three stages in learning the correct positioning of French object pronouns. In the first stage they place the pronoun directly after the verb, as in (3a); in the second stage they omit the pronoun entirely, as in (3b); in the third stage, exemplified by (3c), they correctly cliticize the pronoun to the front of the verb:

(3)   a. Stage one   *SVpro   *il n'est pas prend le
         b. Stage two   *SV∅   *je n'ai pas voir
         c. Stage three   Spro-V   je l'aime

Stage one might reasonably be attributed to transfer from English, but how does one explain stage two? Gundel and Tarone build a case for a learners' hypothesis-testing strategy that leads them to conclude that

French has zero anaphora in object position, despite the fact that neither English nor French ever allows zero anaphora in that position.

While an error such as (3a) might be attributable to negative transfer, negative transfer would also predict that French learners of English should say things like *I her see*, which apparently they *never* do (see Zobl 1980a). Perhaps this is because all speakers are aware that the unmarked case is to have the same order of subject-verb-object whether the object is fully lexical or pronominal. French speakers learning English would thus be unlikely to place the pronoun in a marked position.

Other sorts of errors point to the correctness of specific generativist proposals about grammars. For example, all generativist frameworks have posited that words have complex entries in the lexicon, consisting (minimally) of a phonological form and an inventory of morphological, syntactic, and semantic properties associated with that form. Adjémian (1981) provides evidence that learners' errors show the correctness of this view of the lexicon—citing examples of typical errors made by English speakers learning French, he illustrates cases of learners erring along one or more of the lexical parameters while producing correct forms along the others.

Literally dozens of publications in the past decade have discussed phenomena that are inexplicable from the point of view of direct transfer but that point to the learners' drawing on their knowledge of the principles of universal grammar. It's worth mentioning a few of these. The unmarked case in language is for the negative element to directly precede the verb. Ravem (1968) notes that Norwegians learning English will say *I not like that*, although transfer from Norwegian would lead to their saying *I like that not*.

Along the same lines, Ioup and Kruse (1977) and Gass (1979) find that subjects from diverse linguistic backgrounds accept (ungrammatical) English relative clauses that have resumptive pronouns marking extraction from an oblique position. For example, even a significant number of subjects whose native language has no resumptive pronouns at all accepted sentences such as (4):

(4)   The bed that the boy put the shoes under it is in the corner.

This fact admits to no explanation based on language transfer, but rather seems related (in a way at present unclear) to the fact that, in the world's languages, resumptive pronouns more commonly occur as objects of prepositions than in other structural positions (see Keenan 1972).

Finally, Dulay and Burt (1974) show for child second language learners of English, and Bailey, Madden, and Krashen (1974) show for adults, that the acquisition of "functors" (inflections, articles, etc.) proceeds in the same order regardless of the properties of functors in the native language and the degree to which they differ from English functors. Dulay and Burt draw explicit nativist conclusions from this:

This similarity of errors [among speakers learning English from a variety of linguistic backgrounds], as well as the specific error types, reflect what we refer to as creative construction, more specifically, the process in which children [learning a second language] gradually reconstruct rules for speech they hear, guided by universal innate mechanisms which cause them to formulate certain types of hypotheses about the language system being acquired, until the mismatch between what they are exposed to and what they produce is resolved. (1974, 37)

General language-independent principles appear to affect the learning of phonology as well as syntax. Broselow (1983) points out that the contrastive analysis hypothesis predicts two possible mispronunciations by Arabic speakers of English saying *this ink: the sink* and *this ?ink*. Both could result from applying the syllable structure assignment rules of Arabic to English. However, only the latter occurs. Broselow suggests that this is a consequence of the principle that universally permits syllabification on the domain of the word, with insertion of a glottal stop before an initial vowel. In another paper (Broselow 1981) she suggests that the pronunciation of English *study* by speakers of Egyptian Arabic as [istadi] instead of the expected [sitadi] supports the universal sonority hierarchy motivated in Selkirk (1983). English clusters beginning with an *s* followed by a stop are exceptional in that they are the only syllable-initial clusters that violate the principle that segments within a syllable tend to be arranged in terms of their sonority, with their most sonorous element— the vowel—in the middle and with segments decreasing in sonority as they approach the margins of the syllable. In initial *s*-stop clusters, a more sonorant fricative precedes a less sonorant stop. The pronunciation of such clusters by Arabic speakers is thus more a reflection of their internalized unconscious knowledge of the hierarchy than of simple interference from their native language.

Eckman (1977) also discusses facts about the learning of phonology that point to internalized abstract principles guiding the learner. For example, it is well known that English speakers learn to devoice final consonants in German more readily than German speakers learn the final voiced/voiceless contrast in English. Why should this be? Contrastive analysis alone is of no special help, since both groups of speakers have something "new" to learn—for English speakers, an extra rule not found in their native language. Eckman suggests that the answer lies in markedness theory. After defining "markedness" as in (5), he proposes a "markedness differential hypothesis" (stated in [6]) that can predict a class of learners' errors:

(5)   *Markedness*
       A phenomenon A in some language is more marked than B if the presence of A in a language implies the presence of B; but the presence of B does not imply the presence of A.

(6)   *Markedness Differential Hypothesis*
       The areas of difficulty that a language learner will have can be
       predicted on the basis of a systematic comparison of the gram-
       mars of the native language, the target language, and the
       markedness relations stated in universal grammar, such that,
       a. Those areas of the target language that differ from the native
          language and are more marked than the native language will
          be difficult.
       b. The relative degree of difficulty of the areas of the target
          language that are more marked than the native language will
          correspond to the relative degree of markedness;
       c. Those areas of the target language that are different from the
          native language but are not more marked than the native
          language will not be difficult.

Since the English final voicing contrast is more marked than the lack of a
contrast in German (a claim Eckman supports with empirical evidence),
it follows that German speakers will have more difficulty than English
speakers in mastering this aspect of the target language. Along the same
lines, Eckman argues that the relative ease with which English speakers
learn initial /ž/ in French follows from the markedness differential
hypothesis as well.

The phenomena alluded to in the preceding paragraphs suggest that
fairly abstract principles help shape the acquisition of syntax and
phonology[10] by second language learners. The precise nature of these
principles and their relation to the principles arrived at by theoreticians
from their own grammatical investigations is, of course, a vital question
for research. We may hope the barriers that have impeded collaboration
between theoretical linguists and those engaged in "applied" research
will break down in the near future and the next decade will see progress in
answering this question.

5.3.2   Natural Language Processing

It is a bit curious that the field that has greater right than any other to
call itself "applied linguistics" is almost never referred to as such, either
by its own practitioners or by those who write applied linguistics texts.
This is the field now generally known as *natural language processing*, in
which the results of linguistics are built into a computer-based system for
the purpose of solving some practical problem in which language plays a
central role. Most linguists are aware of the numerous mechanical translation projects of the 1950s and 1960s and their ultimate failure; fewer are

---

10. Quite a bit of work has also been devoted to the acquisition of pragmatic abilities by
second language learners. For representative papers, see R. Lakoff (1969b), Hatch (1978),
and Larsen-Freeman (1980).

aware that the past few years have seen the flowering of a wide variety of projects involving cooperation between the linguist and the computer specialist not dreamed of twenty years ago. It is estimated that there are now sixty-five natural language processing projects in progress around the world, and the number is increasing steadily (see Kaplan 1981).

Certainly not all natural language processing work involves applying the results of grammatical theory, but it is worth mentioning a few that do. Possibly the most advanced is the ILIAD (Interactive Language Instruction Assistance for the Deaf) system developed at Bolt, Beranek, and Newman, Inc. (see Bates and Wilson 1981). The goal of ILIAD is to aid deaf students in producing and comprehending English sentences. Its linguistic core is a partial transformational grammar of English, along with semantic and pragmatic subprograms. ILIAD currently has six tutorials, each of which address a different grammatical topic and draws upon a different area of the system's capability. The tutorials include tests for the student of sentence well-formedness, subject-verb agreement, question formation, recognition of sentence types, and the proper use of sentences conveying requests. An interesting feature of ILIAD is its ability to handle and analyze *ungrammatical* sentences, especially ones commonly used by deaf people.

Some other projects involving the integration of formal grammars with computer technology include the question-answering system designed at IBM (see Petrick 1981), the data base query system at Stanford (see Kaplan 1980), the analogical reasoning program at the MIT Artificial Intelligence Laboratory (see Winston 1981), as well as less advanced projects at Hewlett-Packard, SRI International, the Xerox Palo Alto Research Center, and the University of Sussex.

5.3.3   Linguistics and Literature

The relevance of generativist theory to understanding the literary process was first raised in Jakobson (1959) and Hill (1961), who objected to Chomsky's characterizing certain sentences in *Syntactic Structures* as ungrammatical on the grounds that such sentences might be found in modern poetry. Chomsky replied that "the question of whether a sequence of words might appear in a poem is entirely beside the point, since it is perfectly plain that deviation from well-formedness is not only tolerable, in prose or poetry, but can even be effectively used as a literary device" (1961, 231). Since then, quite a few researchers have addressed the question of grammatical deviance as it relates to creativity in literature (for a representative sampling see Freeman 1970, 1981).

Since the early 1960s, dozens of publications have drawn on generativist concepts in their treatment of literary *style*—for particularly interesting work, see Thorne (1965, 1969, 1970), Banfield (1973a, 1982), Kuroda (1973), and Schauber and Spolsky (1982). Much of this work does not present what might be counted as evidence for grammatical theory and thus will not be discussed here, but there are a few cases where generativist principles have been shown to be instantiated in creative writing. For example, Austin (1981) shows how understanding the style of Shelley's *Adonais* demands reference to some highly abstract properties of grammars. Austin illustrates that part of the difficulty involved in interpreting this poem comes from Shelley's violation of three linguistic constraints: the Tensed S Condition (see Chomsky 1973), as in (7a); the Up-to-Ambiguity Constraint (see Banfield 1973b), as in (7b); and the principles that lead to the avoidance of center-embedded constructions (see section 1.3.1 above), as in (7c) (excerpts are from Shelley 1965):

(7)   a. "And happier they their happiness who knew."

> (2:390, line 39)

       b. "He died [. . .]
          [. . .] when his country's pride
          The priest, the slave, and the liberticide
          Trampled and mocked with many a loathed rite of
          lust and blood."

> (2:390, lines 29, 31–34)

       c. "The extreme hope, the loveliest and the last,
          The bloom, whose petals nipt before they blew
          Died on the promise of the fruit, is waste."

> (2:390, lines 51–53)

That aspect of literature from which the basic constructs of linguistic theory have received the greatest support is the study of *metrics*, that is, the characterization of the rules that specify the treatment of syllables in verse. A number of general studies have indicated the suitability of the formalism of generative phonology for the description of metrical patterning (see, e.g., Beaver 1968; Freeman 1968; Keyser 1969; Halle 1970; Kiparsky 1973, 1977). As it turns out, the proper characterization of metrical patterns often requires reference to *underlying* phonological representations. With respect to pregenerativist approaches to metrics, Paul Kiparsky has pointed out:

> It was long an unquestioned axiom of metrical theory that the metrically relevant features of a line are phonetic, that is, audible in the recitation intended by the poet (although they might be omitted when recited at a later stage of the language, when a linguistic change had taken place eliminating this feature). As Sturtevant put it, "We may take it for granted that an obligatory feature of versification must in some way be audible" (1924:337). (1972, 174)

The "audibility" requirement, of course, was a corollary of the empiricist conception of language held by many early twentieth century structural linguists. Since this conception ruled out abstract theoretical constructs, it followed that only surface phonetics (or phenomes derivable operationally from surface phonetics) could be relevant to metrical patterning.

Some structuralists, however, realized that the audibility requirement was too rigid. Jakobson (1963) weakened the requirement to that of "potential audibility." In his discussion of the Serbian oral epic, he noted that word boundaries counted as vital structural elements of verse, even though they might not be marked phonetically.

Research in the past two decades has demonstrated that even the "potential audibility" requirement is too strong. Metrical structure cannot be adequately described without reference to abstract nonoperationally derivable constructs provided by a generative phonology. The results of this research are summarized very briefly below (for more detailed general discussion, see Kiparsky 1973; Jakobson and Waugh 1979; and O'Connor 1982):

1. A Latvian rule of vowel apocope, which is obligatory in the spoken language, is optionally disregarded in folksongs in the scanning of a line, so that a word reduced by the apocope from n to $n-1$ syllables can be metrically counted as either n or $n-1$ syllables (Zeps 1963).

2. The phonological representations to which the metrical constraints of the Finnish epic *Kalevala* apply are neither phonetic nor morphophonemic, but are intermediate representations reached after the application of at least three rules but before the application of at least four others (Kiparsky 1968b).

3. The metrical structure of the Rig-Veda can be described adequately only if the rules of versification apply before the synchronic Sanskrit rules of glide formation and Sievers's Law (Kiparsky 1972).

4. Some German poets (e.g., Stefan George) restrict their use of rhyme to words that rhyme only in the underlying phonological representations (Kiparsky 1973).

5. The account of rhyming patterns in Old Norse skaldic verse demands that certain instances of rhyming [ö] be derived from underlying /a/ (Anderson 1973).

6. The metrical structure of Chinese poetry demands an account incorporating the theory of suprasegmental phenomena presented in Liberman and Prince (1977) (Chen 1979).

7. In traditional Turkish verse, the vowels of a rhyme set must be identical (or perhaps nondistinct) on the underlying level (Malone 1982).

5.3.4 Linguistics as the Core of a Science Curriculum

Kenneth Hale has written extensively on the political and ethical problems that arise because the study of American Indian languages is virtually always carried out by whites, whose society is responsible for increasing extinction of those languages, not to mention the culture of their speakers (see, e.g., Hale 1965, 1972, 1973, 1976b, n.d.). Many of Hale's suggestions, which relate to bilingual education and the training of Native Americans as linguists, among other things, do not bear on questions of linguistic theory per se. However, Hale has also suggested that *theoretical* linguistics can contribute directly to the fulfillment of progressive educational goals in Native American communities. Hale writes:

> I am convinced, however, that theoretical linguistics is directly relevant to the search for a perpetual and pedagogically powerful role for local languages in achieving the educational goals of bilingual communities. I base my belief on the following two premises: (1) that linguistics is a science, and (2) that an important purpose in modern education is to prepare students to enter careers which make use of the methods, concepts, and attitudes of scientific inquiry—i.e. to enable them to gain experience in constructing and articulating abstract, testable, explanations for superficially mysterious and contradictory observations. If these premises are accepted, then there is an educationally powerful use to which knowledge of a local language can be put in bilingual communities—specifically, it can serve as the basis of a curriculum for teaching scientific method.
>
> What I am proposing then, is that the study of language should form a part of the science curriculum. Linguistic science has the advantage over other sciences that the data relevant to it are immediately accessible, even to the youngest of students, and it requires a minimum of material equipment. It is possible, using immediately accessible linguistic data, to exercise a student's ability to employ the scientific method in coming to grips with problems which compare in their theoretical complexity and importance with problems in the physical sciences whose study (i.e. empirical testing) can be carried out only with the most sophisticated and costly apparatus. Thus, this approach to science enables students to use their native language in activities which offer enormous intellectual challenge, a most important factor in early education. And most important, this approach makes effective educational use of the intellectual wealth which exists in the community to which the students belong, an essential resource which is all too often allowed to go unused in education systems conforming to the traditional model. (n.d., 2–3)

Hale goes on to discuss ways these ideas might be put into practice. They include teaching children language games that can encourage them to develop a "consciously experimental" attitude toward language, as well as presenting them with specific problems that lead to the reconstruction of abstract linguistic representations.

Hale is careful to point out that his proposals are neutral between competing theories of language. However, the reliance on native speakers' intuitions as data, combined with the orientation that leads the children to construct nonobservable levels of structure, points to a necessity for adopting generativist assumptions for the program's implementation.

5.3.5   Grammatical Theory and Nonstandard Dialects

Linguists hardly need to be told that, grammatically speaking, one language or dialect is as good as another. While Edward Sapir was surely not the first to express the sentiment, it is hard to improve on his eloquent "When it comes to linguistic form, Plato walks with the Macedonian swineherd, Confucius with the head-hunting savage of Assam" (1921, 219).

As we all know, the general public—even the highly literate and politically progressive segment of it—is not convinced. The disastrous educational programs based on the idea that nonstandard dialects, particularly those spoken by blacks, are linguistically inferior to the standard need not be documented here (see Labov 1970b,c for discussion). William Labov and many others have carried the case for the linguistic equality of nonstandard dialects into the popular press, though, judging from current educational practice, their results have fallen far short of what we might desire.

Clearly, one does not need to appeal to a sophisticated linguistic theory to make the point that the Black English Vernacular (BEV) and other nonstandard dialects are "real" languages. Anybody who has passed an introductory course in descriptive linguistics taught in *any* framework knows that such phenomena as the neutralization of vowel contrasts in certain environments, negative concord, and the absence of number agreement are widespread among the world's languages.

However, there do seem to be instances where, in order to adequately make the case that a nonstandard construction is "linguistically normal," "one must know a great deal about many underlying rules of the nonstandard dialect, and also a great deal about the rules of English in general" (Labov 1970c, 13). Labov himself has given quite a few examples where knowledge of "underlying rules" is important. For example, consider the following BEV sentence:

(8)   Didn't nobody see it.

This sentence is the simple negation of *somebody saw it*. One might thereby conclude that a fundamental difference exists between BEV and the standard dialect or, even, given the most uncharitable (i.e., racist) interpretation of BEV, that its speakers confuse the concepts of negating and questioning. As Labov points out, however, if one understands the processes involved in the auxiliary construction in Standard English, one can see easily that the differences between it and BEV are trivial:

These [constructions such as (8)] appear to be question forms used as declaratives, which would be a truly radical difference from standard English. But closer investigation shows that this is merely an extension of the standard rule of literary English which gives us *Never did he see it*, or *Nor did anybody see it*: the negative is placed at the beginning of the sentence along with the first member of the verb phrase, which contains the tense marker. This inversion of the tense marker and the subject shows the same order as in questions, but it does not indicate a question with *Never did he see it* any more than with *Didn't nobody see it*. (1970c, 40)

Another example can be drawn from those sentences in BEV that have no copula, despite the presence of a copula in analogous sentences in Standard English (see Labov 1969):

(9)   a. She the first one started us off.
        b. He fast in everything he do.
        c. But everybody not black.

Labov demonstrates that the differences between BEV and Standard English in this respect are trivial: "We find that the following general principle holds without exception: wherever SE can contract, NNE [=BEV] can delete *is* and *are*, and vice versa; wherever SE cannot contract, NNE cannot delete *is* and *are*, and vice versa" (1969, 722). Labov then proceeds to present a set of formal rules characterizing the differences between the two dialects. Now, while Labov's descriptive generalization does not appeal to generativist principles (though, of course, his rules do), one can clinch the case for the linguistic sophistication of BEV by alluding to those cases in Standard English where expected contraction is blocked. As was mentioned above in section 3.5.2, the conditions blocking contraction are complex and highly abstract. It is worth pointing out that exactly the same conditions block deletion in BEV. Just as (10a–b) are ungrammatical in Standard English, (11a–b) are ungrammatical in BEV:

(10)   a. *I wonder how much wine there's in the bottle.
        b. *That's the way it's in real life.
(11)   a. *I wonder how much wine there in the bottle.
        b. *That's the way it in real life.

An example of a rather different sort has been discussed by Edward Klima (in unpublished work). Klima calls attention to the nonstandard dialects in which (12a–c) are grammatical, but not (13a–c):

(12)   a. He left.
        b. I left.
        c. Him and me left.

(13)   a. *Him left.
       b. *Me left.
       c. *He and I left.

Klima suggests that even most linguists would regard Standard English as more "regular" than this dialect, in that the principles of case assignment in the nonstandard appear to require an extra statement to account for both the nominative and the objective case manifested by pronominal subjects. Surely prescriptive grammarians would delight in calling attention to (12) and (13) as a means of reinforcing the idea that nonstandard dialects are "illogical."

Klima, however, argues that it is the *standard* dialect that is more "irregular" in this regard. He states the rule for nominative case assignment in the nonstandard as follows:

(14)   Assign nominative case to a pronoun only if it is immediately dominated by S.

As can be seen by examining the phrase markers below, case is correctly assigned in (12a–c):

(15)

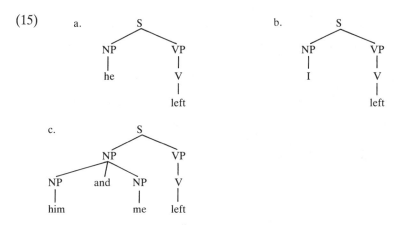

Rule (14) generalizes to correctly assign objective case in the following two sentences; in neither sentence is the pronoun immediately dominated by S:

(16)   a. It's me.
       b. John is taller than me.

Standard speakers, most of whom use (16) in their colloquial speech, but not (12c), have therefore a rather complex rule of case assignment. Klima's example is thus a good one to cite in defense of "the logic of nonstandard English" (Labov 1970b).

Emonds (1983) carries Klima's findings a step further. For reasons too complex to elaborate here, Emonds concludes that the prestige usage of the nominative pronoun in *he and I left* cannot be accounted for by a rule of linguistic competence. In his view, the "prestige usage is not a grammatical construct, but an extragrammatical deviation imposed . . . *exclusively* through paralinguistic cultural mechanisms of the dominant socio-economic class: exclusive and higher education, standard reference handbooks for business and journalism, paid or unpaid secretarial help, ghost writers, etc."

Not all prestige dialect forms are linguistically unnatural of course. For example, the negative concord rule responsible for *I don't have any questions* (as opposed to equally natural—in the technical sense—but nonprestigious *I don't have no questions*) violates no principles of linguistic competence. Several sociolinguistic factors indicate to Emonds that the prestige subject pronouns usage has a status distinct from that of the prestige ban on double negatives:

(a) College and business writing handbooks, of the type consulted by secretaries, technical and ghost writers, journalists, copy-editors, etc., typically include large sections on subject pronouns, but dismiss negative concord as presenting no difficulties.

(b) These handbooks, as well as casual observation of "educated speakers," testify to widespread "overcorrection" in pronoun usage and zealously combat it, while "overcorrection" in negative concord usage seems barely to exist.

(c) The handbooks resort to the "avoid the construction" strategy only with subject pronouns, but no such strategy is ever suggested with negative concord.

(d) Middle class children brought up without significant working class contact acquire consistent middle class negative concord long before they exhibit prestige subject pronoun usage.

Emonds argues for the elimination of all English prestige usages, such as that exemplified by the subject pronoun example, which can be shown to conform to no natural language dialect. Such a move he sees as a step in breaking down social class divisions in the English-speaking world.

5.4 Conclusion

The true applications of grammatical theory to date have been modest, but they are not insignificant. It would certainly be premature (if not presumptuous) to dwell at length on *potential* applications. However, it does not seem unreasonable to speculate briefly on some possibilities. As an example, it seems likely that as the interface between the grammar and the mechanisms involved in language processing becomes better understood, theoretical linguistics will at last be in a position to contribute to speech therapy. Or improved understanding of the interaction of grammatical and conversational principles in discourse might aid the already extensive work in progress that attempts to apply linguistics to questions that arise in the law. Or, again, as theories of the lexicon become more highly articulated, the practice of lexicography might well benefit. All these possibilities strike me as quite reasonable. But whatever the future may hold, there is no question that generativist theory has already demonstrated that it has implications for, and applications to, a number of important language-related problems, from second language learning to natural language processing to the unequal social status of speakers of nonstandard dialects.

References

Adjémian, Christian, 1981. The transfer of lexical properties. Paper presented at the Conference on Language Transfer in Language Learning, Ann Arbor, Mich.

Akers, Glenn. 1980. Admissibility conditions on final consonant clusters in the Jamaican continuum. In Muysken (1980), 1–24.

———. 1981. *Phonological variation in the Jamaican continuum.* Ann Arbor, Mich.: Karoma.

Akmajian, Adrian, Richard Demers, and Robert Harnish. 1979. *Linguistics: An introduction to language and communication.* Cambridge: MIT Press.

Akmajian, Adrian, and Frank Heny. 1975. *An introduction to the principles of transformational syntax.* Cambridge: MIT Press.

Alatis, James, ed. 1968. *Report of the Nineteenth Annual Round Table Meeting on Linguistics and Language Studies.* Washington, D.C.: Georgetown University Press.

———, ed. 1970. *Georgetown University Round Table on Languages and Linguistics 1969.* Washington, D.C.: Georgetown University Press.

Allen, J. P. B. 1978. New developments in curriculum: The notional and the structural syllabus. Paper read at the TEAL conference, Vancouver, B.C., March 1978.

Allwood, Jens. 1976. The complex NP constraint as a nonuniversal rule. *University of Massachusetts Occasional Papers in Linguistics*, vol. 2.

Anderson, John. 1976. *Language, memory and thought.* Hillsdale, N.J.: Erlbaum.

Anderson, John, and G. Bower. 1973. *Human associative memory.* Washington, D.C.: Winston.

Anderson, Stephen. 1973. *u*-umlaut and skaldic verse. In Anderson and Kiparsky (1973), 3–13.

———. 1981. Why phonology isn't natural. *Linguistic Inquiry* 12:493–540.

Anderson, Stephen, and Paul Kiparsky, eds. 1973. *A festschrift for Morris Halle.* New York: Holt, Rinehart and Winston.

Anshen, Frank. 1975. Varied objections to variable rules. In Fasold and Shuy (1975), 1–10.

Applegate, Joseph. 1961. Phonological rules of a subdialect of English. *Word* 17:186–93.

Arbini, Ronald. 1969. Tag-questions and tag-imperatives in English. *Journal of Linguistics* 5:205–14.

Armagost, James. 1974. Declarative tag sentences and threatening tag sentences. Ph.D. diss., University of Washington.

Aronoff, Mark. 1976. *Word formation in generative grammar*. Cambridge: MIT Press.

———. 1981. Automobile semantics. *Linguistic Inquiry* 12:329–48.

Austin, J. L. 1962. *How to do things with words*. Oxford: Oxford University Press.

Austin, Timothy. 1981. Constraints on syntactic rules and the style of Shelley's "Adonais": An exercise in stylistic criticism. In Freeman (1981), 138–65.

Bach, Emmon, and Robert Harms, eds. 1968. *Universals in linguistic theory*. New York: Holt, Rinehart and Winston.

Bailey, Charles-James. 1973a. *Variation and linguistic theory*. Arlington, Va.: Center for Applied Linguistics.

———. 1973b. Variation resulting from different rule orderings in English phonology. In Bailey and Shuy (1973). 211–52.

Bailey, Charles-James, and Roger Shuy, eds. 1973. *New ways of analyzing variation in English*. Washington, D.C.: Georgetown University Press.

Bailey, Nathalie, C. Madden, and S. Krashen. 1974. Is there a "natural sequence" in adult second language learning? *Language Learning* 24:235–43.

Baker, C. L. 1979. Syntactic theory and the projection problem. *Linguistic Inquiry* 10:533–82.

Baker, C. L., and John McCarthy, eds. 1981. *The logical problem of language acquisition*. Cambridge: MIT Press.

Baltin, Mark. 1977. Quantifier negative interaction. In Fasold and Shuy (1977), 30–36.

———. 1982. A landing site theory of movement rules. *Linguistic Inquiry* 13:1–38.

Banathy, Bela, Edith Trager, and Carl Waddle. 1966. The use of contrastive data in foreign language course development. In Valdman (1966), 35–56.

Banfield, Ann. 1973a. Narrative style and the grammar of direct and indirect speech. *Foundations of Language* 10:1–40.

———. 1973b. Stylistic transformations in *Paradise Lost*. Ph.D. diss., University of Wisconsin.

———. 1982. *Unspeakable sentences*. London: Routledge and Kegan Paul.

Baron, Naomi. 1981. *Speech, writing, and sign*. Bloomington: Indiana University Press.

Bates, Elizabeth. 1976. *Language and context: The acquisition of pragmatics*. New York: Academic Press.

Bates, Madeline, and Kirk Wilson. 1981. *Interactive language instruction for the deaf: final report*. Report no. 4771. Cambridge, Mass.: Bolt, Beranek, and Newman.

Bazell, C. E., J. C. Catford, M. A. K. Halliday, and R. H. Robins, eds. 1966. *In memory of J. R. Firth*. London: Longmans.

Beaver, Joseph. 1968. A grammar of prosody. *College English* 29:310–21. Reprinted in Freeman (1970), 427–47.

Beilin, Harry. 1975. *Studies in the cognitive basis of language development*. New York: Academic Press.

Bellugi, Ursula. 1967. The acquisition of the system of negation in children's speech. Ph.D. Diss., Harvard University.

———. 1971. Simplification in children's language. In *Language acquisition: Models and methods*, ed. R. Huxley and E. Ingram, 95–119. New York: Academic Press.

Berwick, Robert, and Amy Weinberg. 1983. The role of grammars in models of language use. *Cognition*, vol. 13. In press.

Bever, Thomas. 1970. The cognitive basis for linguistic structures. In Hayes (1970), 277–360.

———. 1974. The ascent of the specious; or, There's a lot we don't know about mirrors. In Cohen (1974), 173–200.

———. 1975. Functional explanations require independently motivated functional theories. In Grossman, San, and Vance (1975), 580–609.

Bever, Thomas, Jerrold Katz, and D. Terence Langendoen, eds. 1976. *An integrated theory of linguistic ability*. New York: Crowell.

Bickerton, Derek. 1971. Inherent variability and variable rules. *Foundations of Language* 7: 457–92.

———. 1973a. Quantitative versus dynamic paradigms: The case of Montreal *que*. In Bailey and Shuy (1973), 22–43.

———. 1973b. The structure of polylectal grammars. In *Sociolinguistics*, ed. R. Shuy, pp. 17–42. Washington, D.C.: Georgetown University Press.

———. 1973c. The nature of a creole continuum. *Language* 49:640–69.

———. 1975. *The dynamics of a creole system*. Cambridge: Cambridge University Press.

———. 1981. *Roots of language*. Ann Arbor, Mich.: Karoma.

———. 1982. Learning without experience the Creole way. In Obler and Menn (1982), 15–29.

Bierwisch, Manfred, and Karl Heidolph, eds. 1970. *Progress in linguistics*. The Hague: Mouton.

Black, Maria, and Shulamuth Chiat. 1981. Psycholinguistics without "psychological reality." *Linguistics* 19:37–62.

Blank, Marion, Myron Gessner, and Anita Esposito. 1979. Language without communication: A case study. *Journal of Child Language* 6:329–52.

Bloom, Lois. 1970. *Language development: Form and function in emerging grammars*. Cambridge: MIT Press.

Blumstein, Sheila. 1973. *A phonological investigation of aphasic speech*. The Hague: Mouton.

———. 1981. Neurological disorders: Language-brain relationships. In *Handbook of clinical neuropsychology*, ed. S. Fiskov and T. Boll. New York: John Wiley.

———. 1982. Language dissolution in aphasia: Evidence for linguistic theory. In Obler and Menn (1982), 203–15.

Bolinger, Dwight. 1968. Judgments of grammaticality. *Lingua* 21:34–40.

———. 1971. Semantic overloading: A restudy of the verb *remind*. *Language* 47:522–47.

———. 1975. Meaning and form: Some fallacies of asemantic grammar. In Koerner (1975), 3–36.

———. 1977a. *Meaning and form*. London: Longmans.

———. 1977b. Another glance at main clause phenomena. *Language* 53:511–19.

Bowen, J. Donald, and R. P. Stockwell. 1968. Foreword to Rutherford (1968), vii–viii.

Bowerman, Melissa. 1973a. *Early syntactic development: A cross-linguistic study with special reference to Finnish*. London: Cambridge University Press.

———. 1973b. Structural relations in children's utterances: Syntactic or semantic? In *Cognitive development and the acquisition of language*, ed. T. Moore, pp. 197–214. New York: Academic Press.

Bowers, John. 1970. A note on "remind." *Linguistic Inquiry* 1:559–60.

Bradley, Diane, Merrill Garrett, and Edgar Zurif. 1980. Syntactic deficits in Broca's aphasia. In Caplan (1980), 269–86.

Braine, Martin. 1963. The ontogeny of English phrase structure: The first phase. *Language* 39:1–13.

———. 1971. On two models of the internalization of grammars. In *The ontogenesis of grammars*, ed. D. Slobin. New York: Academic Press.

Brame, Michael. 1978. *Base generated syntax*. Seattle: Noit Amrofer Press.

Bransford, J. D., and J. J. Franks. 1971. The abstraction of linguistic ideas. *Cognitive Psychology* 2:331–50.

Bresnan, Joan. 1972. Theory of complementation in English syntax. Ph.D. diss., Massachusetts Institute of Technology.

———. 1978a. A realistic transformational grammar. In Halle, Bresnan, and Miller (1978), 1–59.

———. 1978b. *Contraction and the transformational cycle in English*. Bloomington: Indiana University Linguistics Club.

Broselow, Ellen. 1981. Non-obvious transfer: On predicting epenthesis errors. Paper presented at the Conference on Language Transfer in Language Learning, Ann Arbor, Mich.

———. 1983. An investigation of transfer in second language phonology. *IRAL*, vol. 21. In press.

Brown, Roger. 1970. *Psycholinguistics*. New York: Free Press.

———. 1973. *A first language: the early stages*. Cambridge: Harvard University Press.

———. 1977. Introduction to Snow and Ferguson (1977), 1–27.

Brown, Roger, and Camille Hanlon. 1970. Derivational complexity and the order of acquisition in child speech. In Hayes (1970), 11–54.

Bruner, Jerome. 1974. From communication to language: A psychological perspective. *Cognition* 3:255–87.

———. 1975. The ontogenesis of speech acts. *Journal of Child Language* 2:1–20.

Burling, Robbins. 1972. Review of J. Fishman, *Sociolinguistics*. *Language* 48:233–36.

Canale, Michael, and Merrill Swain. 1980. Theoretical bases of communicative approaches to second language teaching and testing. *Applied Linguistics* 1:1–47.

Candlin, Christopher N., Jonathan H. Leather, and Clive J. Bruton. 1976. Doctors in casualty: Applying communicative competence to components of specialist course design. *IRAL* 14:245–72.

Caplan, David, ed. 1980. *Biological studies of mental processes.* Cambridge: MIT Press.

———. 1981a. Prospects for neurolinguistic theory. *Cognition* 10:59–64.

———. 1981b. Comments on J. A. Fodor, "The modularity of mind." Paper delivered at the Conference on the Foundations of Cognitive Science, University of Western Ontario, October 1981.

Caramazza, Alfonso, and Edgar Zurif. 1976. Dissociation of algorithmic and heuristic processes in language comprehension: Evidence from aphasia. *Brain and Language* 3:572–82.

Carden, Guy. 1970. A note on conflicting idiolects. *Linguistic Inquiry* 1:281–90.

———. 1973a. *English quantifiers: Logical structure and linguistic variation.* Tokyo: Taishukan.

———. 1973b. Dialect variation and abstract syntax. In *Some new directions in linguistics*, ed. R. Shuy, 1–34. Washington, D.C.: Georgetown University Press.

———. 1973c. Disambiguation, favored readings, and variable rules. In Bailey and Shuy (1973), 171–82.

———. 1976. Syntactic and semantic data: Replication results. *Language in Society* 5:99–104.

Carden, Guy, and Thomas Dieterich. 1978. Testing the value of introspective judgments as evidence for linguistic theory. Unpublished paper, Yale University.

———. 1981. Introspection, observation, and experiment: An example where experiment pays off. In *PSA 1980, Volume 2*, ed. P. D. Asquith and R. N. Giere. East Lansing, Mich.: Philosophy of Science Association.

Carlson, Greg, and Michael Tanenhaus. 1982. Some preliminaries to psycholinguistics. *CLS* 18:48–60.

Carnap, Rudolf. 1956. The methodological character of theoretical concepts. In *Minnesota Studies in the Philosophy of Science*, 1:38–76. Minneapolis: University of Minnesota Press.

Carroll, John B. 1968. Contrastive linguistics and interference theory. In Alatis (1968), 113–22.

Carroll, John M. 1981. Modularity and naturalness in cognitive science. IBM Research Report # 39482.

Cedergren, Henrietta, and David Sankoff. 1974. Variable rules: Performance as a statistical reflection of competence. *Language* 50:333–55.

Cena, R. M. 1977. *An experimental explication of the notion "psychologically real phonological generalization."* Bloomington: Indiana University Linguistics Club.

Chen, Matthew. 1979. Metrical structure: Evidence from Chinese poetry. *Linguistic Inquiry* 10:371–420.

Chomsky, Carol. 1969. *The acquisition of syntax in children from five to ten.* Cambridge: MIT Press.

Chomsky, Noam. 1957. *Syntactic structures.* The Hague: Mouton.

———. 1959. Review of B. F. Skinner, *Verbal behavior. Language* 35:26–57.

———. 1961. Some methodological remarks on generative grammar. *Word* 17:219–39.

———. 1964. *Current issues in linguistic theory*. The Hague: Mouton.

———. 1965. *Aspects of the theory of syntax*. Cambridge: MIT Press.

———. 1966. Linguistic theory. In *Northeast Conference on the Teaching of Foreign Languages, working committee reports*, pp. 43–49. Reprinted in Lester (1970), 51–60.

———. 1970a. Remarks on nominalization. In Jacobs and Rosenbaum (1970), 184–221. Reprinted in Chomsky (1972b), 11–61.

———. 1970b. Language and freedom. *Abraxis* 1:9–24.

———. 1971. Deep structure, surface structure, and semantic interpretation. In Steinberg and Jakobovits (1971), 183–216. Reprinted in Chomsky (1972b), 62–119.

———. 1972a. Some empirical issues in the theory of transformational grammar. In Peters (1972), 63–130. Reprinted in Chomsky (1972b), 120–202.

———. 1972b. *Studies on semantics in generative grammar*. The Hague: Mouton.

———. 1972c. *Language and mind*, enlarged ed. New York: Harcourt Brace Jovanovich.

———. 1973. Conditions on transformations. In Anderson and Kiparsky (1973), 232–86. Reprinted in Chomsky (1977a), 81–162.

———. 1975a. Questions of form and interpretation. *Linguistic Analysis* 1:75–109. Reprinted in Chomsky (1977a), 25–62.

———. 1975b. *Reflections on language*. New York: Pantheon.

———. 1976. Conditions on rules of grammar. *Linguistic Analysis* 2:303–51.

———. 1977a. *Essays on form and interpretation*. New York: North-Holland.

———. 1977b. On *wh*-movement. In Culicover, Wasow, and Akmajian (1977), 71–132.

———. 1980. *Rules and representations*. New York: Columbia University Press.

———. 1981. *Lectures on government and binding*. Dordrecht: Foris.

Chomsky, Noam, and Morris Halle. 1968. *The sound pattern of English*. New York: Harper and Row.

Chomsky, Noam, and Howard Lasnik. 1977. Filters and control. *Linguistic Inquiry* 8:425–504.

———. 1978. A note on contraction. *Linguistic Inquiry* 9:268–74.

Chomsky, Noam, and George Miller. 1963. Introduction to the formal analysis of natural languages. In *Handbook of mathematical psychology*, ed. P. Luce, R. Bush, and E. Galanter, 2:269–322. New York: Wiley.

Churma, Donald. 1979. Arguments from external evidence in phonology. Ph.D. diss., Ohio State University.

Clark, Herbert, and Eve Clark. 1977. *Psychology and language*. New York: Harcourt, Brace, Jovanovich.

Clark, Herbert, and Susan Haviland. 1974. Psychological processes as linguistic explanation. In Cohen (1974), 91–124.

Clyne, Paul, William Hanks, and Carol Hofbauer, eds. 1979. *The elements: A parasession on linguistic units and levels*. Chicago: Chicago Linguistic Society.

Cohen, David, ed. 1974. *Explaining linguistic phenomena*. Washington, D.C.: Hemisphere.

Cohen, David, and Jessica Wirth, eds. 1975. *Testing linguistic hypotheses*. Washington, D.C.: Hemisphere.

Cole, Peter, ed. 1978. *Syntax and semantics*. Vol. 9. New York: Academic Press.
Cole, Peter, and Jerry Morgan, eds. 1975. *Syntax and semantics*. Vol. 3. New York: Academic Press.
Conant, James B. 1951. *Science and common sense*. New Haven: Yale University Press.
Condon, William, and Louis Sander. 1974. Neonate movement is synchronized with adult speech: interactional participation and language acquisition. *Science* 183:99–101.
Cooper, William, and John R. Ross. 1975. World order. In Grossman, San, and Vance (1975), 63–111.
Cooper, William, and Edward Walker, eds. 1979. *Sentence processing*. Hillsdale, N.J.: Erlbaum.
Corder, S. Pit. 1971. Idiosyncratic dialects and error analysis. *IRAL* 9:147–60.
———. 1973a. *Introducing applied linguistics*. Harmondsworth: Penguin.
———. 1973b. Linguistic theory and applied linguistics. In Corder and Roulet (1973), 11–20.
Corder, S. Pit, and E. Roulet, eds. 1973. *Theoretical linguistic models in applied linguistics*. Brussels: AIMAV.
Corum, Claudia, T. Cedric Smith-Stark, and Ann Weiser, eds. 1973. *You take the high node and I'll take the low node*. Chicago: Chicago Linguistic Society.
Creider, Chet. 1979. On the explanation of transformations. In Givón (1979a), 3–22.
Culicover, Peter. 1973. On the coherence of syntactic descriptions. *Journal of Linguistics* 9:35–51.
———. 1976. *Syntax*. New York: Academic Press.
Culicover, Peter, Thomas Wasow, and Adrian Akmajian, eds. 1977. *Formal syntax*. New York: Academic Press.
Culler, Jonathan. 1975. *Structuralist poetics*. Ithaca: Cornell University Press.
Curtiss, Susan. 1977. *Genie: A psycholinguistic study of a modern-day "wild child."* New York: Academic Press.
———. 1982. Developmental dissociations of language and cognition. In Obler and Menn (1982), 285–312.
d'Anglejan, Alison, and C. Richard Tucker. 1975. The acquisition of complex English structures by adult learners. *Language Learning* 25:281–96.
Davidson, Donald, and Gilbert Harmon, eds. 1972. *Semantics of natural language*. Dordrecht: Reidel.
Dennis, Maureen. 1980a. Capacity and strategy for syntactic comprehension after left or right hemidecortication. *Brain and Language* 10:287–317.
———. 1980b. Language acquisition in a single hemisphere: Semantic organization. In Caplan (1980), 159–85.
Dennis, Maureen, and Bruno Kohn. 1975. Comprehension of syntax in infantile hemiplegics after cerebral hemidecortication: Left-hemisphere superiority. *Brain and Language* 2:477–82.
Dennis, Maureen, and Harry Whitaker. 1976. Language acquisition following hemidecortication: Linguistic superiority of the left over the right hemisphere. *Brain and Language* 3:404–33.
Derbyshire, Desmond. 1979. *Hixkaryana*. Amsterdam: North-Holland.
Derwing, Bruce. 1973. *Transformational grammar as a theory of language acquisition*. Cambridge: Cambridge University Press.

De Villiers, Jill. 1980. The process of rule learning in child speech: A new look. In Nelson (1980), 1–44.

Dijk, Teun van. 1972. *Some aspects of text grammars*. The Hague: Mouton.

———. 1977. *Text and context*. London: Longmans.

Dik, Simon. 1980. Seventeen sentences: Basic principles and application of functional grammar. In Moravcsik and Wirth (1980), 45–76.

Dingwall, William Orr, ed. 1971. *A survey of linguistic science*. College Park: Linguistics Program, University of Maryland.

Dinneen, Francis P., ed. 1974. *Georgetown University Round Table on Languages and Linguistics 1974*. Washington, D.C.: Georgetown University Press.

Dinnsen, Daniel. 1980. Phonological rules and phonetic explanation. *Journal of Linguistics* 16:171–91.

Di Pietro, Robert. 1968. Contrastive analysis and the notions of deep and surface grammar. In Alatis (1968), 65–82.

Diver, William, ed. 1980. *Columbia University working papers in linguistics*, vol. 5.

Donegan, Patricia, and David Stampe. 1979. The study of natural phonology. In *Current approaches to phonological theory*, ed. D. Dinnsen, 126–73. Bloomington: Indiana University Press.

Dore, John. 1974. A pragmatic description of early language development. *Journal of Psycholinguistic Research* 3:343–50.

Doron, Edit. 1981. On formal models of code-switching. Unpublished manuscript, University of Texas.

Dresher, B. Elan. 1981. Abstractness and explanation in phonology. In Hornstein and Lightfoot (1981), 76–115.

Dresher, B. Elan, and Norbert Hornstein. 1976. On some supposed contributions of artificial intelligence to the scientific study of language. *Cognition* 4:321–98.

Dressler, Wolfgang. 1979. External evidence for an abstract analysis of the German velar nasal. *Wiener Linguistische Gazette* 19:3–28.

Dulay, Heidi, and Marina Burt. 1974. Natural sequences in child second language acquisition. *Language Learning* 24:37–53.

———. 1978. Some remarks on creativity in language acquisition. In Ritchie (1978b), 65–90.

Ebeling, C. L. 1960. *Linguistic units*. The Hague: Mouton.

Eckman, Fred. 1977. Markedness and the contrastive analysis hypothesis. *Language Learning* 27:315–30.

Emonds, Joseph. 1970. *Root and structure-preserving transformations*. Bloomington: Indiana University Linguistics Club.

———. 1976. *A transformational approach to English syntax*. New York: Academic Press.

———. 1983. *Adjacency in grammar: The theory of language-particular rules*. New York: Academic Press, forthcoming.

Edwards, Derek. 1973. Sensory-motor intelligence and semantic relations in early child grammar. *Cognition* 2:395–434.

Elliott, Dale, Stanley Legum, and Sandra Thompson. 1969. Syntactic variation as linguistic data. *CLS* 5:52–59.

Erteschik-Shir, Nomi. 1979. Discourse constraints on dative movement. In Givón (1979a), 441–68.

Ervin-Tripp, Susan. 1974. Is second language learning like the first? *TESOL Quarterly* 8:111–28.

Fasold, Ralph. 1978. Language variation and linguistic competence. In Sankoff (1978), 85–96.

Fasold, Ralph, and Roger Shuy, eds. 1975. *Analyzing variation in language*. Washington, D.C.: Georgetown University Press.

———. eds. 1977. *Studies in language variation*. Washington, D.C.: Georgetown University Press.

Fay, David, and Anne Cutler. 1977. Malapropisms and the structure of the mental lexicon. *Linguistic Inquiry* 8:505–20.

Feldman, Heidi, Susan Goldin-Meadow, and Lila Gleitman. 1978. Beyond Herodotus: The creation of language by linguistically deprived deaf children. In *Action, gesture, and symbol*, ed. A. Lock, 351–414. New York: Academic Press.

Ferguson, Charles. 1982. Simplified registers and linguistic theory. In Obler and Menn (1982), 49–66.

Fillmore, Charles. 1979. On fluency. In *Individual differences in language ability and language behavior*, ed. C. Fillmore, D. Kempler, and W. Wang. New York: Academic Press.

Fillmore, Charles, and D. Terence Langendoen, eds. 1971. *Studies in linguistic semantics*. New York: Holt, Rinehart and Winston.

Fischer, Susan. 1971. The acquisition of the verb-particle and dative constructions. Ph.D. diss., Massachusetts Institute of Technology.

Fodor, Janet Dean. 1978. Parsing strategies and constraints on transformations. *Linguistic Inquiry* 9:427–74.

———. 1979. Superstrategy. In Cooper and Walker (1979), 249–80.

Fodor, Jerry A. 1982. *The modularity of mind*. Cambridge: MIT Press.

Fodor, Jerry A., Thomas Bever, and M. F. Garrett. 1974. *The psychology of language*. New York: McGraw-Hill.

Fodor, Jerry A., and Merrill Garrett. 1966. Some reflections on competence and performance. In *Psycholinguistic papers*, ed. J. Lyons and R. J. Wales, 135–54. Edinburgh: Edinburgh University Press.

———. 1967. Some syntactic determinants of sentential complexity. *Perception and Psychophysics* 2:289–96.

Fodor, Jerry A., and Jerrold Katz, eds. 1964. *The structure of language: Readings in the philosophy of language*. Englewood Cliffs, N.J.: Prentice-Hall.

Forster, K. I. 1979. Levels of processing and the structure of the language processor. In Cooper and Walker (1979), 27–86.

Fraser, Bruce. 1972. Optional rules in grammar. In Shuy (1972), 1–16.

———. 1977. Pragmatics: On conversational competence. In *Linguistic theory: What can it say about reading?* ed. R. Shuy, 110–22. Newark, Del.: International Reading Association.

Freeman, Donald. 1968. On the primes of metrical style. *Language and Style* 1:63–101. Reprinted in Freeman (1970), 448–91.

———, ed. 1970. *Linguistics and literary style*. New York: Holt.

———, ed. 1981. *Essays in modern stylistics*. London: Methuen.

Fries, Charles C. 1945. *Teaching and learning English as a foreign language*. Ann Arbor: University of Michigan Press.

Fromkin, Victoria. 1971. The nonanomalous nature of anomalous utterances. *Language* 47:27–52. Reprinted in Fromkin (1973), 215–42.

———, ed. 1973. *Speech errors as linguistic evidence.* The Hague: Mouton.

———. 1975. When does a test test a hypothesis; or, What counts as evidence? In Cohen and Wirth (1975), 43–64.

———, ed. 1980. *Errors in linguistic performance.* New York: Academic Press.

Fry, D. B. 1973. The linguistic evidence of speech errors. In Fromkin (1973), 157–63.

García, Erica. 1975. *The role of theory in linguistic analysis.* Amsterdam: North-Holland.

———. 1979. Discourse without syntax. In Givón (1979a), 23–50.

Gardner, H., and G. Denes. 1973. Connotative judgments by aphasic patients on a pictorial adaptation of the semantic differential. *Cortex* 9:183–96.

Gardner, Robert, and Wallace Lambert. 1959. Motivational variables in second-language acquisition. *Canadian Journal of Psychology* 13:266–72.

———. 1972. *Attitudes and motivation in second-language learning.* Rowley, Mass.: Newbury House.

Garner, Robert. 1971. Presupposition. In Fillmore and Langendoen (1971), 23–42.

Garnica, Olga. 1977. Some prosodic and paralinguistic features of speech to young children. In Snow and Ferguson (1977), 63–88.

Gass, Susan. 1979. Language transfer and universal grammatical relations. *Language Learning* 29:327–44.

Gazdar, Gerald. 1977. *Pragmatics: Implicature, presupposition, and logical form.* Bloomington: Indiana University Linguistics Club.

———. 1981. Phrase-structure grammar. In *The nature of syntactic representation,* ed. P. Jacobson and G. Pullum, 131–86. Dordrecht: Reidel.

Gefen, Raphael. 1966. Theoretical prerequisites for second-language teaching. *IRAL* 4:227–43.

———. 1967. "Sentence patterns" in the light of language theories and classroom needs. *IRAL* 5:185–92.

Givón, Talmy, ed. 1979a. *Syntax and semantics.* Vol. 12. New York: Academic Press.

———. 1979b. *On understanding grammar.* New York: Academic Press.

Glass, Andrea, Michael Gazzaniga, and David Premack. 1973. Artificial language training in global aphasics. *Neuropsychologia* 11:95–103.

Gleason, J. B., H. Goodglass, E. Green, N. Ackerman, and M. R. Hyde. 1975. The retrieval of syntax in Broca's aphasia. *Brain and Language* 2:451–71.

Gleitman, Lila. 1981. Maturational determinants of language growth. *Cognition* 10:103–14.

Gleitman, Lila, and Eric Wanner. 1982. Language acquisition: State of the art. In *Language acquisition: State of the art,* ed. E. Wanner and L. Gleitman. Cambridge: Cambridge University Press.

Goodglass, H., J. Gleason, N. A. Bernholtz, and M. R. Hyde. 1972. Some linguistic structures in the speech of a Broca's aphasic. *Cortex* 8:191–212.

Goodluck, Helen, and Lawrence Solan, eds. 1978. *Papers in the structure and development of child language.* University of Massachusetts Occasional Papers in Linguistics, vol. 4. Amherst: University of Massachusetts.

Gordon, David, and George Lakoff. 1971. Conversational postulates. *CLS* 7:63–84. Reprinted in Cole and Morgan (1975), 83–106.

Green, Georgia. 1974. *Semantics and syntactic regularity*. Bloomington: Indiana University Press.

———. 1981. Pragmatics and syntactic description. *Studies in the Linguistic Sciences* 11:27–38.

———. 1982. Linguistics and the pragmatics of language use. In *Neurolinguistics and cognition*;, ed. R. Buhr. New York: Academic Press.

Greenbaum, Sidney, and Randolph Quirk. 1970. *Elicitation experiments in English*. London: Longmans.

Greenberg, Joseph, Charles Ferguson, and Edith Moravcsik, eds. 1978. *Universals of human language*. Stanford: Stanford University Press.

Greene, Judith. 1972. *Psycholinguistics*. Harmondsworth: Penguin.

Grice, H. P. 1975. Logic and conversation. In Cole and Morgan (1975), 41–58.

Grimshaw, Jane. 1979. Complement selection and the lexicon. *Linguistic Inquiry* 10:279–326.

Grinder, John, and Paul Postal. 1971. Missing antecedents. *Linguistic Inquiry* 2:269–312.

Gross, Maurice. 1979. On the failure of generative grammar. *Language* 55:859–85.

Grossman, Robin, L. J. San, and Timothy Vance, eds. 1975. *Papers from the parasession on functionalism*. Chicago: Chicago Linguistic Society.

Grosu, Alexander. 1972. The strategic content of island constraints. *Ohio State University Working Papers in Linguistics*, no. 13.

———. 1973. On the status of the so-called right roof constraint. *Language* 49:294–311.

———. 1981. *Approaches to island phenomena*. Amsterdam: North-Holland.

Gumperz, John. 1972. The communicative competence of bilinguals: Some hypotheses and suggestions for research. *Language in Society* 1:143–54.

Gundel, Jeanette, and Elaine Tarone. 1981. Lexical transfer and the acquisition of pronominal anaphora. Paper presented at the Conference on Language Transfer in Language Learning. Ann Arbor, Mich.

Hagège, Claude. 1976. *La grammaire générative: Réflexions critiques*. Paris: Presses Universitaires de France.

Hale, Kenneth. 1965. On the use of informants in field work. *Canadian Journal of Linguistics* 10:108–19.

———. 1972. Some questions about anthropological linguistics. In *Reinventing anthropology*, ed. D. Hymes, 382–97. New York: Pantheon.

———. 1973. The role of American Indian linguistics in bilingual education. In *Bilingualism in the Southwest*, ed. P. R. Turner, 203–25. Tucson: University of Arizona Press.

———. 1976a. Linguistic autonomy and the linguistics of Carl Voegelin. *Anthropological Linguistics* 18:120–28.

———. 1976b. Theoretical linguistics and American Indian communities. In *American Indian languages and American linguistics*, ed. W. Chafe, 35–50. Lisse: Peter de Ridder Press.

———. 1981. *On the position of Walbiri in a typology of the base*. Bloomington: Indiana University Linguistics Club.

————. n.d. Linguistics and local languages in a science curriculum for bilingual bicultural programs. Unpublished manuscript, Massachusetts Institute of Technology.

Hale, Kenneth, La Verne Jeanne, and Paul Platero. 1977. Three cases of over-generation. In Culicover, Wasow, and Akmajian (1977), 379–416.

Halle, Morris. 1962. Phonology in generative grammar. *Word* 18:54–72. Reprinted in Fodor and Katz (1964), 334–52.

————. 1970. On meter and prosody. In Bierwisch and Heidolph (1970), 64–80.

————. 1973. Prolegomena to a theory of word formation. *Linguistic Inquiry* 4:3–16.

Halle, Morris, Joan Bresnan, and George Miller, eds. 1978. *Linguistic theory and psychological reality.* Cambridge: MIT Press.

Halliday, M. A. K. 1974. The context of linguistics. In Dinneen (1974), 179–97.

Harnish, Robert. 1976. The argument from *lurk*. In Bever, Katz, and Langedoen (1976), 261–70.

Harré, Rom. 1970. *The principles of scientific thinking.* Chicago: University of Chicago Press.

Harris, James W. 1973. Linguistics and language teaching: Applications versus implications. In Jankowsky (1973), 11–18.

Harris, Zellig. 1951. *Methods in structural linguistics.* Chicago: University of Chicago Press.

————. 1957. Co-occurrence and transformation in linguistic structure. *Language* 33:283–340.

Hasegawa, Nobuko. 1979. Casual speech vs. fast speech. *CLS* 15:126–37.

Hatch, Evelyn. 1978. Discourse analysis, speech acts, and second language acquisition. In Ritchie (1978b), 137–56.

Hayes, John, ed. 1970. *Cognition and the development of language.* New York: Wiley.

Hempel, Carl. 1965. Empiricist criteria of cognitive significance: Problems and changes. In *Aspects of scientific explanation,* ed. C. Hempel, pp. 101–22. New York: Free Press.

Heringer, James. 1970. Research on quantifier-negative idiolects. *CLS* 6:287–96.

Hill, Archibald. 1958. *Introduction to linguistic structures.* New York: Harcourt, Brace and World.

————. 1961. Grammaticality. *Word* 17:1–10.

Hiż, Henry. 1967. Methodological aspects of the theory of syntax. *Journal of Philosophy* 64:67–74.

Hockett, Charles. 1948a. Biophysics, linguistics, and the unity of science. *American Scientist* 36:558–72.

————. 1948b. A note on structure. *IJAL* 14:269–71.

————. 1955. *A manual of phonology.* Baltimore: Waverly Press.

Hooper, Joan. 1976. *An introduction to natural generative phonology.* New York: Academic Press.

Horn, Laurence. 1972. *On the semantic properties of logical operators in English.* Bloomington: Indiana University Linguistics Club.

————. 1978. Remarks on neg-raising. In Cole (1978), 129–220.

Hornstein, Norbert, and David Lightfoot, eds. 1981. *Explanation in linguistics.* London: Longmans.

Huddleston, Rodney. 1970. Two approaches to the analysis of tags. *Journal of Linguistics* 6:215–22.

Hughes, Jennifer. 1975. Acquisition of non-vocal "language" by aphasic children. *Cognition* 3:41–55.

Hunt, Kellogg W. 1970. How little sentences grow into big ones. In Lester (1970), 170–86.

Hust, Joel, and Michael Brame. 1976. Jackendoff on interpretive semantics. *Linguistic Analysis* 2:243–78.

Hymes, Dell. 1971. Competence and performance in linguistic theory. In *Language acquisition: Models and methods*, ed. R. Huxley and E. Ingram, 3–24. New York: Academic Press.

———. 1974. *Foundations in sociolinguistics*. Philadelphia: University of Pennsylvania Press.

Ioup, Georgette, and Anna Kruse. 1977. Interference versus structural complexity in second language acquisition. In *Teaching and learning English as a second language: Trends in research and practice,* ed. H. D. Brown, C. Yorio, and R. Crymes, 159–71. Washington, D.C.: Teachers of English to Speakers of Other Languages.

Jackendoff, Ray. 1972. *Semantic interpretation in generative grammar*. Cambridge: MIT Press.

Jacobs, Roderick, and Peter Rosenbaum, eds. 1970. *Readings in English transformational grammar*. Waltham, Mass.: Ginn.

Jacobson, Rudolfo. 1966. The role of deep structure in language teaching. *Language Learning* 16:153–60.

Jaeggli, Osvaldo. 1980. Remarks on *to* contraction. *Linguistic Inquiry* 11:239–45.

Jakobson, Roman. 1959. Boas' view of grammatical meaning. *American Anthropologist* 61:139–45.

———. 1963. On the so-called vowel-alliteration in Germanic verse. *Zeitschrift für Phonetik* 16:85–92.

Jakobson, Roman, and Linda Waugh. 1979. *The sound shape of language*. Bloomington: Indiana University Press.

Jankowsky, Kurt, ed. 1973. *Georgetown University Round Table on Languages and Linguistics 1973*. Washington, D.C.: Georgetown University Press.

Jenkins, Lyle. 1979. Generative grammar and second language learning. *Wiener Linguistische Gazette* 20:43–62.

Joos, Martin, ed. 1957. *Readings in linguistics*. Washington, D.C.: American Council of Learned Societies.

Joshi, Aravind. 1983. Processing of sentences with intra-sentential code-switching. In *Syntactic theory and how people parse sentences*, ed. L. Karttunen, D. Dowty, and A. Zwicky. Cambridge: Cambridge University Press.

Kaisse, Ellen. 1981. Appositive relatives and the cliticization of *who*. *CLS* 17:108–15.

———. 1982. Sentential clitics and Wackernagel's law. In *Proceedings of the First West Coast Conference on Formal Linguistics*, pp. 1–14. Stanford, Calif.: Stanford University Department of Linguistics.

———. 1983a. The syntax of auxiliary reduction in English. *Language* 59:93–122.

———. 1983b. *Clitics and connected speech*. New York: Academic Press, forthcoming.

Kaplan, S. Jerrold. 1980. Appropriate responses to inappropriate questions. In *Elements of discourse understanding*, ed. A. Joshi, I. Sag, and B. Webber, 127–44. Cambridge: Cambridge University Press.

———, ed. 1981. *Natural language processing work in progress. SIGART*, special issue.

Karttunen, Lauri. 1974. Presupposition and linguistic context. *Theoretical Linguistics* 1:182–94.

Katz, Jerrold. 1964. Mentalism in linguistics. *Language* 40:124–37.

———. 1973. On defining "presupposition." *Linguistic Inquiry* 4:256–60.

Katz, Jerrold, and Jerry Fodor. 1963. The structure of a semantic theory. *Language* 39:170–210. Reprinted in Fodor and Katz (1964), 479–518.

Katz, Jerrold, and Paul Postal. 1964. *An integrated theory of linguistic descriptions*. Cambridge: MIT Press.

Kay, Paul, and Chad McDaniel. 1979. On the logic of variable rules. *Language in Society* 8:151–87.

Kean, Mary-Louise. 1975. The theory of markedness in generative grammar. Ph.D. diss., Massachusetts Institute of Technology.

———. 1977. The linguistic interpretation of aphasic syndromes: Agrammatism in Broca's aphasia, an example. *Cognition* 5:9–46.

———. 1981a. Explanation in neurolinguistics. In Hornstein and Lightfoot (1981), 174–208.

———. 1981b. On a theory of markedness: Some general considerations and a case in point. In *Theory of markedness in generative grammar*, ed. A. Belletti, L. Brandi, and L. Rizzi. Pisa: Scuola Normale Superiore.

Keenan, Edward. 1971. Two kinds of presupposition in natural language. In Fillmore and Langendoen (1971), 45–54.

———. 1972. The logical status of deep structures. Paper presented at the Eleventh International Congress of Linguists, Bologna, Italy.

Keenan, Elinor Ochs, and Bambi Schieffelin. 1976. Topic as a discourse notion: A study of topic in the conversations of children and adults. In Li (1976), 335–84.

Kempson, Ruth. 1975. *Presupposition and the delimitation of semantics*. Cambridge: Cambridge University Press.

Kempson, Ruth, and Annabel Cormack. 1981. Ambiguity and quantification. *Linguistics and Philosophy* 4:259–309.

Keyser, S. J. 1963. Review of H. Kurath and R. McDavid, *The pronunciation of English in the Atlantic states. Language* 39:303–16.

———. 1969. The linguistic basis of English prosody. In Reibel and Schane (1969), 379–94.

Kim, W. C. 1976. The theory of anaphora in Korean syntax. Ph.D. diss. Massachusetts Institute of Technology.

Kimball, John. 1970. 'Remind' Remains. *Linguistic Inquiry* 1:511–24.

———. 1973. Seven principles of surface structure parsing in natural language. *Cognition* 2:15–47.

King, Harold. 1970. On blocking the rules for contraction in English. *Linguistic Inquiry* 1:134–36.

Kiparsky, Paul. 1968a. Linguistic universals and linguistic change. In Bach and Harms (1968), 170–202.

———. 1968b. Metrics and morphophonemics in the Kalevala. In *Studies pre-*

sented to Roman Jakobson by his students, ed. C. Gribble. Cambridge: Slavica. Reprinted in Freeman (1970), 165–81.

———. 1972. Metrics and morphophonemics in the Rigveda. In *Contributions to generative phonology*, ed. M. Brame, 171–200. Austin: University of Texas Press.

———. 1973. The role of linguistics in a theory of poetry. *Daedalus* 102:231–45. Reprinted in Freeman (1981), 9–23.

———. 1975. What are phonological theories about? In Cohen and Wirth (1975), 187–210.

———. 1977. The rhythmic structure of English verse. *Linguistic Inquiry* 8:189–248.

———. 1979. Pāṇini as a variationist. Cambridge: MIT Press.

Klavans, Judith. 1980. Some problems in a theory of clitics. Doctoral diss., University College London.

Klima, Edward. 1964a. Negation in English. In Fodor and Katz (1964), 246–323.

———. 1964b. Relatedness between grammatical systems. *Language* 40:1–20.

Koerner, E. F. K., ed. 1975. *The transformational-generative paradigm and modern linguistics*. Amsterdam: John Benjamins.

Kosslyn, Stephen, and S. Schwartz. 1977. A simulation of visual imagery. *Cognitive Science* 1:265–96.

Koster, Jan. 1978. *Locality principles in syntax*. Dordrecht: Foris.

Koutsoudas, Andreas, Gerald Sanders, and Craig Noll. 1974. On the application of phonological rules. *Language* 50:1–28.

Kuno, Susumu. 1972. Functional sentence perspective: A case study from Japanese and English. *Linguistic Inquiry* 3:269–320.

———. 1973. *The structure of the Japanese language*. Cambridge: MIT Press.

———. 1975. Conditions for verb phrase deletion. *Foundations of Language* 13:161–75.

———. 1976. Gapping: A functional analysis. *Linguistic Inquiry* 7:300–318.

———. 1978. Generative discourse analysis in America. In *Current trends in textlinguistics*, ed. W. Dressler, 275–94. New York: Walter de Gruyter.

———. 1980. Functional syntax. In Moravcsik and Wirth (1980), 117–36.

Kuroda, S. -Y. 1973. Where epistemology, style, and grammar meet: A case study from Japanese. In Anderson and Kiparsky (1973), 377–91.

Labov, William. 1969. Contraction, deletion, and inherent variability of the English copula. *Language* 45:715–62.

———. 1970a. The study of language in its social context. *Studium Generale* 23:30–87. Reprinted in Labov (1972b), 183–259.

———. 1970b. The logic of nonstandard English. In Alatis (1970), 1–44. Reprinted in Labov (1972c), 201–40.

———. 1970c. *The study of nonstandard English*. Champaign, Ill.: National Council of Teachers of English.

———. 1971. Methodology. In Dingwall (1971), 412–97.

———. 1972a. Some principles of linguistic methodology. *Language in Society* 1:97–120.

———. 1972b. *Sociolinguistic patterns*. Philadelphia: University of Pennsylvania Press.

———. 1972c. *Language in the inner city*. Philadelphia: University of Pennsylvania Press.

————. 1973. The place of linguistic research in American society. In *Themes in linguistics: The 1970's*, ed. E. Hamp, 97–129. The Hague: Mouton.

————. 1975. *What is a linguistic fact?* Lisse: Peter de Ridder Press.

Labov, William, P. Cohen, C. Robins, and J. Lewis. 1968. *A study of the non-standard English of Negro and Puerto Rican speakers in New York City.* Cooperative Research Project #3288. New York: Columbia University.

Lado, Robert. 1957. *Linguistics across cultures.* Ann Arbor: University of Michigan Press.

————. 1968. Contrastive linguistics in a mentalistic theory of language learning. In Alatis (1968), 123–35.

Lakatos, Imre. 1970. Falsification and the methodology of scientific research programmes. In *Criticism and the growth of knowledge*, ed. I. Lakatos and A. Musgrave, 91–196. Cambridge: Cambridge University Press.

Lakoff, George. 1969. Empiricism without facts. *Foundations of Language* 5:118–27.

————. 1970. Global rules. *Language* 46: 627–39.

————. 1971. On generative semantics. In Steinberg and Jakobovits (1971), 232–96.

————. 1974. Interview. In Parret (1974), 151–78.

Lakoff, George, and Henry Thompson. 1975. Introducing cognitive grammar. *BLS* 1:295–313.

Lakoff, Robin, 1968. *Abstract syntax and Latin complementation.* Cambridge: MIT Press.

————. 1969a. A syntactic argument for negative transportation. *CLS* 5:140–47.

————. 1969b. Transformational grammar and language teaching. *Language Learning* 19:117–40. Reprinted in Lester (1973), 284–310.

————. 1971. Passive resistance. *CLS* 7:149–62.

Lambert, Wallace, R. C. Gardner, H. C. Barik, and K. Tunstall. 1963. Attitudinal and cognitive aspects of intensive study of a second language. *Journal of Abnormal and Social Psychology* 66: 358–69.

Lamendella, John. 1969. On the irrelevance of transformational grammar to second language pedagogy. *Language Learning* 19:255–70.

Landesmann, Charles. 1972. *Discourse and its presuppositions.* New Haven: Yale University Press.

Langacker, Ronald. 1969. On pronominalization and the chain of command. In Reibel and Schane (1969), 160–86.

Langendoen, D. Terence. 1970. A study of the linguistic practices of the Federal Trade Commission. Paper read at winter meeting of the Linguistic Society of America.

Langendoen, D. Terence, and Thomas Bever. 1973. Can a not unhappy person be called a not sad one? In Anderson and Kiparsky (1973), 392–409.

Langer, Susanne. 1942. *Philosophy in a new key.* Cambridge: Harvard University Press.

Larsen-Freeman, Diane, ed. 1980. *Discourse analysis in second language research.* Rowley, Mass.: Newbury House.

Lees, Robert B. 1957. Review of Noam Chomsky, *Syntactic structures. Language* 33:375–408.

Lenneberg, Eric. 1967. *Biological foundations of language.* New York: Wiley.
––––––. 1973. The neurology of language. *Daedalus* 102:115-33.
Lerdahl, Fred, and Ray Jackendoff. 1977. Toward a formal theory of tonal music. *Journal of Music Theory* 21:111–171
Lester, Mark, ed. 1970 (second edition 1973). *Readings in applied transformational grammar.* New York: Holt.
Li, Charles, ed. 1976. *Subject and topic.* New York: Academic Press.
Liberman, Alvin. 1974. The specialization of the language hemisphere. In *The neurosciences: Third study program,* ed. F. Schmitt and F. Worden. Cambridge: MIT Press.
Liberman, Mark, and Allen Prince. 1977. On stress and linguistic rhythm. *Linguistic Inquiry* 8:249–336.
Lightfoot, David. 1979a. *Principles of diachronic syntax.* Cambridge: Cambridge University Press.
––––––. 1979b. Review of C. Li, *Mechanisms of syntactic change. Language* 55:381–95.
––––––. 1981. Review of G. Sampson, *Liberty and language. Journal of Linguistics* 17:160–74.
Lust, Barbara, and Yu Chin Chien. 1983. The structure of coordination in first language acquisition of Mandarin Chinese: Evidence for a universal. Unpublished manuscript, Cornell University.
Lust, Barbara, K. Loveland, and R. Kornet. 1980. The development of anaphora in first language: Syntactic and pragmatic constraints. *Linguistic Analysis* 6: 359–92.
McCawley, James. 1979. Remarks on Cena's vowel shift experiment. In Clyne, Hanks, and Hofbauer (1979), 110–18.
McNeill, David. 1966. Developmental psycholinguistics. In Smith and Miller (1966), 15–84.
––––––. 1971. The capacity for the ontogenesis of grammar. In *The Ontogenesis of grammar,* ed. D. Slobin, 17–40. New York: Academic Press.
McTear, Michael. 1978. Review of C. Snow and C. Ferguson, eds., *Talking to children. Journal of Child Language* 5:521–30.
Makkai, Adam, Valerie Makkai, and Luigi Heilmann, eds. 1977. *Linguistics at the crossroads.* Lake Bluff, Ill.: Jupiter Press.
Maling, Joan, and Annie Zaenen. 1978. The nonuniversality of a surface filter. *Linguistic Inquiry* 9:475–98.
Malone, Joseph. 1982. Generative phonology and Turkish rhyme. *Linguistic Inquiry* 13:550–53.
Maratsos, Michael, and Mary Anne Chalkley. 1980. The internal language of children's syntax: The ontogenesis and representation of syntactic categories. In Nelson (1980), 127–214.
Marcus, Mitchell. 1980. *A theory of syntactic recognition for natural language.* Cambridge: MIT Press.
Marin, Oscar, Eleanor Saffran, and Myrna Schwartz. 1976. Dissociations of language in aphasia: Implications for normal functions. *Annals of the New York Academy of Sciences* 280:868–84.
Martinet, André. 1964. *Elements of general linguistics.* London: Faber and Faber.

Matthews, G. Hubert. 1964. *Hidatsa syntax*. The Hague: Mouton.

Mattingly, Ignatius. 1972. Speech cues and sign stimuli. *American Scientist* 60:327–37.

Mayer, Judith, Ann Erreich, and Virginia Valian. 1978. Transformations, basic operations, and language acquisition. *Cognition* 6:1–13.

Menn, Lise. 1979. Towards a psychology of phonology: Child phonology as a first step. In *Metatheory III: Applications of linguistic theory in the human sciences*. East Lansing: Department of Linguistics, Michigan State University.

———. 1982. Child language as a source of constraints for linguistic theory. In Obler and Menn (1982), 247–59.

Menyuk, Paula. 1963. Syntactic structures in the language of children. *Child Development* 34:407–22.

Mildenberger, Kenneth. 1962. The National Defense Education Act and linguistics. In *Report of the Eleventh Roundtable Meeting on Linguistics and Language Studies*, ed. B. Choseed, 157–64. Washington, D.C.: Georgetown University Press.

———. 1968. Confusing signposts: The relevance of applied linguistics. In Alatis (1968), 205–14.

Miller, George, E. Galanter, and K. Pribram. 1960. *Plans and the structure of behavior*. New York: Holt, Rinehart and Winston.

Miller, Wick, and S. Ervin-Tripp. 1964. The development of grammar in child language. In *The acquisition of language*, ed. U. Bellugi and R. Brown, 9–35. Monograph of the Society for Research in Child Development 29.

Moravcsik, Edith, and Jessica Wirth, eds. 1980: *Syntax and semantics*. Vol. 13. New York: Academic Press.

Morgan, Jerry. 1977. Conversational postulates revisited. *Language* 53:277–84.

Moulton, Janice, and George Robinson. 1981. *The organization of language*. Cambridge: Cambridge University Press.

Muysken, Pieter, ed. 1980. *Generative studies on Creole languages*. Dordrecht: Foris.

Muysken, Pieter, Anne-Marie di Sciullo, and Rajendra Singh. 1982. Code-mixing and government. Unpublished manuscript, University of Montreal.

Napoli, Donna Jo, and Marina Nespor. 1979. The syntax of word-initial consonant gemination in Italian. *Language* 55:812–41.

Naro, Anthony. 1980. Review of D. Sankoff, ed., *Linguistic variation. Language* 56:158–70.

Nelson, Keith, ed. 1980. Children's language. vol. 2. New York: Gardner Press.

Nemser, William. 1971. Approximative systems of foreign language learners. *IRAL* 9:115–24. Reprinted in Richards (1974), 55–63.

Newell, Allen, and Herbert Simon. 1973. *Human problem solving*. Englewood Cliffs, N.J.: Prentice-Hall.

Newmark, Leonard. 1973. Grammatical theory and the teaching of English as a foreign language. In Lester (1973), 202–10.

Newmeyer, Frederick. 1971. The derivation of the English action nominalization. *CLS* 6:408–15.

———. 1973. Aspects of prescriptivism. *CLS* 9:475–81.

———. 1978. Linguistic theory and linguistic practice. In *Approaches to language: Anthropological issues*, ed. W. McCormack and S. Wurm, 581–94. The Hague: Mouton.

———. 1980a. *Linguistic theory in America.* New York: Academic Press.

———. 1980b. A reply to James McCawley's review of *Linguistic Theory in America. Linguistics* 18:931–37.

———. 1982a. Review of Talmy Givón, *On understanding grammar. Journal of Linguistic Research* 2:1–11.

———. 1982b. On the applicability of transformational generative grammar. *Applied Linguistics* 3:98–120.

Newmeyer, Frederick, and Joseph Emonds. 1971. The linguist in American society. *CLS* 7:285–306.

Newport, Elissa, Henry Gleitman, and Lila Gleitman. 1977. Mother, I'd rather do it myself: Some effects and non-effects of maternal speech style. In Snow and Ferguson (1977), 109–49.

Ney, James. 1975. The decade of private knowledge. *Historiographia Linguistica* 2:143–56.

Nickel, Gerhard. 1971. Variables in a hierarchy of difficulty. *Working Papers in Linguistics* 3:185–94.

Obler, Loraine, and Lise Menn, eds. 1982. *Exceptional language and linguistics.* New York: Academic Press.

Ochs, Elinor, and Bambi Schieffelin. 1979. *Developmental pragmatics.* New York: Academic Press.

O'Connor, M. 1982. "Unanswerable the knack of tongues": The linguistic study of verse. In Obler and Menn (1982), 143–68.

Oehrle, Richard. 1976. The grammatical status of the English dative alternation. Ph.D. diss., Massachusetts Institute of Technology.

Ohmann, Richard. 1964. Generative grammars and the concept of literary style. *Word* 20:423–39. Reprinted in Lester (1970), 117–36, and Freeman (1970), 258–78.

———. 1966. Literature as sentences. *College English* 27:261–67. Reprinted in Lester (1970), 137–48.

Oller, John. 1977. On the relation between syntax, semantics, and pragmatics. In Makkai, Makkai, and Heilmann (1977), 42–54.

O'Neil, Wayne. 1972. The politics of bidialectalism. *College English* 33:433–38.

Ornstein, Jacob. 1968. Programmed instruction and educational technology in the language field: Boon or failure? *Modern Language Journal* 52:401–10.

Otero, Carlos. 1972. Acceptable ungrammatical sentences in Spanish. *Linguistic Inquiry* 3:233–42.

Parret, Herman. 1974. *Discussing language.* The Hague: Mouton.

Partee, Barbara. 1972. Opacity, coreference, and pronouns. In Davidson and Harmon (1972), 415–41.

Peizer, David, and David Olmsted. 1969. Modules of grammar acquisition. *Language* 45:60–96.

Perlmutter, David. 1968. Deep and surface structure constraints in syntax. Ph.D. diss., Massachusetts Institute of Technology.

178   References

———. 1971. *Deep and surface structure constraints in syntax.* New York: Holt, Rinehart and Winston.

Perren, G. E., and J. L. M. Trim, eds. 1971. *Applications of linguistics.* Cambridge: Cambridge University Press.

Peters, Stanley, ed. 1972. *Goals of linguistic theory.* Englewood Cliffs, N.J.: Prentice-Hall.

Petöfi, János. 1973. Towards an empirically motivated theory of verbal texts. In *Studies in text grammar,* ed. J. Petöfi and H. Reiser. Dordrecht: Reidel.

Petrick, S. R. 1981. Field testing the transformational question answering (TQA) system. *Proceedings of the Nineteenth Annual Meeting of the ACL,* June 1981, pp. 35–36.

Pfaff, Carol. 1979. Constraints on language mixing. *Language* 55:291–318.

Piaget, Jean. 1970. *Structuralism.* New York: Basic Books.

Pike, Kenneth. 1977. Recent developments in tagmemics. In Makkai, Makkai, and Heilmann (1977), 155–66.

Pinker, Steven. 1979. Formal models of language learning. *Cognition* 7:217–83.

Poplak, Shana. 1980. Sometimes I'll start a sentence in English y termino en español: Toward a typology of code-switching. *Linguistics* 18:581–618.

Postal, Paul. 1969. On so-called "pronouns" in English. In Reibel and Schane (1969), 201–24.

———. 1970. On the surface verb "Remind." *Linguistic Inquiry* 1:37–120.

———. 1971. *Cross-over phenomena.* New York: Holt, Rinehart and Winston.

Postal, Paul, and Geoffrey Pullum. 1978. Traces and the description of English complementizer contraction. *Linguistic Inquiry* 9:1–30.

Premack, David. 1971. Language in chimpanzees? *Science* 172:808–22.

Prince, Ellen. 1978. A comparison of *wh*-clefts and *it*-clefts in discourse. *Language* 54:883–906.

Pullum, Geoffrey. 1972. Indian scripts and the teacher of English. *English Language Teaching* 25:278–84.

———. 1979a. Review of Greenberg, Ferguson, and Moravcsik, eds., *Universals of human language. Linguistics* 17:925–44.

———. 1979b. *Rule interaction and the organization of a grammar.* New York: Garland.

———. 1981. Languages with object before subject: A comment and a catalog. *Linguistics* 19:147–56.

Pullum, Geoffrey, and Paul Postal. 1979. On an inadequate defense of "trace theory." *Linguistic Inquiry* 10:689–706.

Putnam, Hilary. 1967. The "innateness hypothesis" and explanatory models in linguistics. *Synthese* 17:12–23.

Ravem, Roar. 1968. Language acquisition in a second language environment. *IRAL* 6:175–85. Reprinted in Richards (1974), 124–33.

Reibel, David, and Sanford Schane, eds. 1969. *Modern studies in English.* Englewood Cliffs, N.J.: Prentice-Hall.

Reinhart, Tanya. 1981. Definite NP anaphora and c-command domains. *Linguistic Inquiry* 12:605–36.

———. 1982. *Pragmatics and linguistics: An analysis of sentence topics.* Bloomington: Indiana University Linguistics Club.

Reynolds, Allan, and Paul Flagg. 1977. *Cognitive psychology*. Cambridge, Mass.: Winthrop.

Richards, Jack. 1971. A noncontrastive approach to error analysis. *English Language Teaching* 25:204–19. Reprinted in Richards (1974), 172–88.

———, ed. 1974. *Error analysis*. London: Longmans.

Ringen, Catharine. 1972. On arguments for rule ordering. *Foundations of Language* 8:266–73.

Ringen, Jon. 1975. Linguistic facts: A study of the empirical scientific status of transformational generative grammars. In Cohen and Wirth (1975), 1–42.

Ritchie, William. 1978a. The right roof constraint in an adult-acquired language. In Ritchie (1978b), 33–64.

———, ed. 1978b. *Second language acquisition research*. New York: Academic Press.

Rivers, Wilga. 1964. *The psychologist and the foreign-language teacher*. Chicago: University of Chicago Press.

Rizzi, Luigi. 1978. Violations of the *wh*-island constraint in Italian and the subjacency condition. In *Montreal Working Papers in Linguistics*, vol. 11, ed. C. Dubisson, D. Lightfoot, and Y. Morin. Montreal: University of Montreal, Department of Linguistics.

Roberts, Paul. 1964. *English syntax*. New York: Harcourt Brace and World.

Roca, I. M. 1979. Language learning and the Chomskyan revolution. *Studia Anglica Posnaniensia* 10:141–209.

Roeper, Thomas. 1982. Review of Halle, Bresnan, and Miller, eds., *Linguistic theory and psychological reality*. *Language* 52:467–70.

Rosch, Eleanor. 1973. On the internal structure of perceptual and semantic categories. In *Cognitive development and the acquisition of language*, ed. T. E. Moore. New York: Academic Press.

Rosenbaum, Peter. 1965. On the role of linguistics in the teaching of English. *Harvard Educational Review* 35:332–48.

———. 1969. Phrase structure principles of English complex sentence formation. In Reibel and Schane (1969), 316–30.

———. 1970. A principle governing deletion in English sentential complementation. In Jacobs and Rosenbaum (1970), 20–29.

Ross, John R. 1968. *Constraints on variables in syntax*. Bloomington: Indiana University Linguistics Club.

———. 1969a. On the cyclic nature of English pronominalization. In *To honor Roman Jakobson*, 1669–82. The Hague: Mouton. Reprinted in Reibel and Schane (1969), 187–200.

———. 1969b. A proposed rule of tree pruning. In Reibel and Schane (1969), 289–97.

———. 1970. On declarative sentences. In Jacobs and Rosenbaum (1970), 222–72.

———. 1973. The penthouse principle and the order of constituents. In Corum, Smith-Stark, and Weiser (1973), 397–422.

Rutherford, William E. 1968. *Modern English*. New York: Harcourt, Brace, and World.

Sadock, Jerrold. 1974. *Toward a linguistic theory of speech acts*. New York: Academic Press.

Sampson, Geoffrey. 1978. Linguistic universals as evidence for empiricism. *Journal of Linguistics* 14:183–206.

Sankoff, David, ed. 1978. *Linguistic variation: Models and methods*. New York: Academic Press.

Sankoff, David, and Henrietta Cedergren. 1976. The dimensionality of grammatical variation. *Language* 52:163–78.

Sankoff, David, and William Labov. 1979. On the uses of variable rules. *Language in Society* 8:189–222.

Sankoff, David, and Shana Poplak. 1980. *A formal grammar for code-switching*. Working Papers in the Center for Puerto Rican Studies, no. 8. New York: City College of New York.

Sankoff, Gillian. 1973. Above and beyond phonology in variable rules. In Bailey and Shuy (1973), 44–61.

Sankoff, Gillian, and Penelope Brown. 1976. The origins of syntax in discourse. *Language* 52:631–66.

Sapir, Edward. 1921. *Language*. New York: Harcourt, Brace, and World.

———. 1925. Sound patterns in language. *Language* 1:37–51.

Saporta, Sol. 1965. Ordered rules, dialect differences, and historical processes. *Language* 41:218–24.

———. 1967. Review of R. Stockwell and J. Bowen, *The sounds of English and Spanish*. *Hispania* (March), 200.

———. 1977. The sexism of language and the language of sexism. In *Linguistic Studies Offered to Joseph Greenberg*, ed. A. Juilland, 179–82. Saratoga, Calif.: Anma Libri.

———. 1979. Sexist language and the competence/performance distinction. In *Festschrift for Oswald Szemerenyi on the occasion of his sixty-fifth birthday*, ed. B. Brogyanyi. Amsterdam: John Benjamins.

Saussure, Ferdinand de. 1966. *Course in general linguistics*. New York: McGraw-Hill. (Translation of *Cours de linguistique générale*. Paris: Payot, 1916.)

Schank, Roger. 1972. Contextual dependency: A theory of natural language understanding. *Cognitive psychology* 3:552–631.

Schauber, Ellen, and Elaine Spolsky. 1982. *The competence of the experienced reader*. Bloomington: Indiana University Press.

Scherer, George, and Michael Wertheimer. 1964. *A psycholinguistic experiment in foreign-language learning*. New York: McGraw-Hill.

Schlesinger, I. M. 1971. Production of utterances and language acquisition. In *The ontogenesis of grammar*, ed. D. Slobin. New York: Academic Press.

———. 1974. Relational concepts underlying language. In *Language perspectives: Acquisition, retardation, and intervention*, ed. R. L. Schiefelbusch and L. L. Lloyd, 129–51. Baltimore: University Park Press.

Schnitzer, Marc. 1974. Aphasiological evidence for five linguistic hypotheses. *Language* 50:300–315.

Searle, John. 1975. Indirect speech acts. In Cole and Morgan (1975), 59–82.

Selinker, Larry. 1972. Interlanguage. *IRAL* 10: 201–31.

Selkirk, Elizabeth. 1972. The phrase phonology of English and French. Ph.D. diss., Massachusetts Institute of Technology.

———. 1983. *Phonology and syntax: The relation between sound and structure*. Cambridge: MIT Press, forthcoming.

Shattuck-Hufnagel, Stefanie. 1982. Three kinds of speech error evidence for the role of grammatical elements in processing. In Obler and Menn (1982), 133–42.

Shelley, Percy B. 1965. *The complete works of Shelley*. Ed. R. Ingpen and W. Peck. New York: Gordian Press.

Sherzer, Joel. 1970. Talking backwards in Cuna: The sociological reality of phonological descriptions. *Southwestern Journal of Anthropology* 26:343–53.

———. 1976. Play languages: Implication for (socio) linguistics. In *Speech play,* ed. B. Kirshenblatt-Gimblett, 19–36. Philadelphia: University of Pennsylvania Press.

Shih, Mary, Guy Carden, and Linda Lane. 1979. Unobtrusive data collection: An evaluation of the appropriate-response methodology. Unpublished paper, Yale University.

Shipley, Elizabeth, Carlota Smith, and Lila Gleitman. 1969. A study in the acquisition of language. *Language* 45:322–42.

Shuy, Roger, and C.-J. Bailey, eds. 1973. *Toward tomorrow's linguistics.* Washington, D.C.: Georgetown University Press.

Simon, Herbert. 1962. The architecture of complexity. *Proceedings of the American Philosophical Society* 106:467–82.

Skinner, B. F. 1957. *Verbal behavior.* New York: Appleton-Century-Crofts.

Slobin, Daniel. 1966a. The acquisition of Russian as a native language. In Smith and Miller (1966), 129–48.

———. 1966b. Grammatical transformations and sentence comprehension in childhood and adulthood. *Journal of Verbal Learning and Verbal Behavior* 5:219–27.

———. 1972. Children and language: They learn the same way all around the world. *Psychology Today* 6:71–82.

Smith, Carlota. 1964. Determiners and relative clauses in a generative grammar of English. *Language* 40: 37–52. Reprinted in Reibel and Schane (1969), 247–63.

Smith, Frank, and George Miller. 1966. *The genesis of language.* Cambridge: MIT Press.

Smith, Neilson. 1981. Consistency, markedness, and language change: On the notion "Consistent Language." *Journal of Linguistics* 17:39–54.

Smith, Philip, and Helmut Baranyi. 1968. A comparison study of the effectiveness of the traditional and audiolingual approaches to foreign language instruction utilizing laboratory equipment. Final report, USOE project 7-0133.

Smith, Philip, and Emanuel Berger. 1968. An assessment of three foreign language teaching strategies utilizing three language laboratory systems. Final report, USOE project 5-0683.

Snow, Catherine, and Charles Ferguson, eds. 1977. *Talking to children: Language input and acquisition.* Cambridge: Cambridge University Press.

Solan, Lawrence. 1978. The acquisition of tough movement. In Goodluck and Solan (1978), 127–44.

———. 1981. Acquisition of structural restrictions on anaphora. In Tavakolian (1981), 59–73.

Spencer, N. J. 1973. Differences between linguists and nonlinguists in intuitions of grammaticality-acceptability. *Journal of Psycholinguistic Research* 2:83–98.
Spolsky, Bernard. 1966. A psycholinguistic critique of programmed foreign language instruction. *IRAL* 4:119–29.
———. 1969. Attitudinal aspects of second language learning. *Language Learning* 29:271–83.
———. 1970. Linguistics and language pedagogy—Applications or implications? In Alatis (1970), 143–55. Reprinted in Lester (1973), 269–83.
———. 1978. *Educational linguistics: An introduction*. Rowley, Mass.: Newbury House.
Stampe, David. 1973. A dissertation on natural phonology. Ph.D. diss., University of Chicago.
Stankiewicz, Edward. 1972. *A Baudouin de Courtenay anthology*. Bloomington: Indiana University Press.
Stark, Jacqueline. 1974. Aphasiological evidence for the abstract analysis of the German velar nasal [ŋ]. *Wiener Linguistische Gazette* 7:21–37.
Steinberg, Danny, and Leon Jakobovits, eds. 1971. *Semantics: An interdisciplinary reader*. Cambridge: Cambridge University Press.
Steinberg, Danny, and Robert Krohn. 1975. The psychological validity of Chomsky and Halle's vowel shift rule. In Koerner (1975), 233–62.
Stokes, William. 1974. All of the work on quantifier-negation isn't convincing. *CLS* 10:692–700.
Sturtevant, Edward. 1924. The doctrine of the caesura, a philological ghost. *American Journal of Philology* 45:329–50.
Suppe, Frederick, ed. 1977. *The structure of scientific theories*. Urbana: University of Illinois Press.
Swintramont, A. 1973. Some aspects of underlying syllable structure in Thai: Evidence from khamphuan—a Thai word game. *Studies in the Linguistic Sciences* 3 no. 1:121–42.
Tanenhaus, Michael, J. M. Leiman, and M. S. Seidenberg. 1979. Evidence for multiple stages in the processing of ambiguous words in syntactic contexts. *Journal of Verbal Learning and Verbal Behavior* 18:427–41.
Tavakolian, Susan, ed. 1981. *Language acquisition and linguistic theory*. Cambridge: MIT Press.
Thomas, Owen. 1965. *Transformational grammar and the teacher of English*. New York: Holt, Rinehart and Winston.
Thorne, James. 1965. Stylistics and generative grammars. *Journal of Linguistics* 1:49–59. Reprinted in Freeman (1970), 182–96.
———. 1969. Poetry, stylistics, and imaginary grammars. *Journal of Linguistics* 5:147–49.
———. 1970. Generative grammar and stylistic analysis. In *New horizons in linguistics,* ed. J. Lyons, 185–97. Harmondsworth: Penguin. Reprinted in Freeman (1981), 42–52.
Tissot, R., F. Lhermitte, and B. Ducarne. 1963. Etat intellectuel des aphasiques. *L'encéphale* 52:285–320.
Twaddell, W. Freeman. 1935. On defining the phoneme. *Language Monograph,* no. 16. Reprinted in Joos (1957), 55–80.

Tyler, Lorraine, and William Marslen-Wilson. 1977. The on-line effects of semantic context on syntactic processing. *Journal of Verbal Learning and Verbal Behavior* 16:683–92.

Vachek, Josef. 1964. *A Prague school reader in linguistics*. Bloomington: Indiana University Press.

Valdman, Albert, ed. 1966. *Trends in language teaching*. New York: McGraw-Hill.

Valian, Virginia. 1979. The wherefores and therefores of competence-performance distinction. In Cooper and Walker (1979), 1–26.

Van Lancker, Diana. 1980. Cerebral lateralization of pitch cues in the linguistic signal. *Papers in Linguistics* 13:201–77.

Van Valin, Robert. 1981. Review of T. Givón, *On understanding grammar*. *Lingua* 54:47–85.

Van Valin, Robert, and William Foley. 1980. Role and reference grammar. In Moravcsik and Wirth (1980), 329–52.

Vennemann, Theo. 1973. Phonological concreteness in natural generative grammar. In Shuy and Bailey (1973), 202–19.

Vihman, Marilyn. 1982. Formulas in first and second language acquisition. In Obler and Menn (1982), 261–84.

Wackernagel, Jacob. 1892. Über ein Gesetz der Indogermanischen Wortstellung. *Indogermanische Forschungen* 1:333–436.

Wardhaugh, Ronald. 1970. The contrastive analysis hypothesis. *TESOL Quarterly* 4:123–30.

Waryas, Carol Lynn, and Kathleen Stremel-Campbell. 1978. Grammatical training for the language-delayed child. In *Language intervention strategies*, ed. R. Schiefelbusch, 145–92. Baltimore: University Park Press.

Watt, William. 1970. On two hypotheses concerning psycholinguistics. In Hayes (1970), 137–220.

———. 1974. Mentalism in linguistics II. *Glossa* 8:1–39.

Weigl, Egon, and Manfred Bierwisch. 1970. Neuropsychology and linguistics: Topics of common research. *Foundations of Language* 6:1–18.

Weinreich, Uriel, William Labov, and Marvin Herzog. 1968. Empirical foundations for a theory of language change. In *Directions for historical linguistics*, ed. W. Lehmann and Y. Malkiel, 95–188. Austin: University of Texas Press.

Wexler, Kenneth, and Peter Culicover, 1980. *Formal principles of language acquisition*. Cambridge: MIT Press.

Whitaker, Haiganoosh, and Harry Whitaker, eds. 1976–79. *Studies in neurolinguistics*. Vols. 1–4. New York: Academic Press.

———. 1978. Language disorders. In *A survey of applied linguistics*, ed. R. Wardhaugh and H. D. Brown, 250–74. Ann Arbor: University of Michigan Press.

Whitaker, Harry. 1971. *On the representation of language in the human brain*. Edmonton, Alberta: Linguistic Research.

———. 1972. Unsolicited nominalizations by aphasics: The plausibility of the lexicalist hypothesis. *Linguistics* 78:62–71.

White, Lydia. 1980. *Grammatical theory and language acquisition*. Bloomington: Indiana University Linguistics Club.

———. 1981. The responsibility of grammatical theory to acquisitional data. In Hornstein and Lightfoot (1981), 241–71.

White, Ronald. 1974. Communicative competence, registers, and second language teaching. *IRAL* 12:127–41.

Widdowson, H. G. 1971. The teaching of rhetoric to students of science and technology. In *Science and technology in second language.* London: Centre for Information on Language Teaching and Research.

Wilkins, D. A. 1972. *Linguistics in language teaching.* Cambridge: MIT Press.

Wilkinson, Louise, Elfrieda Hiebert, and Karen Rembold. 1981. Parents' and peers' communication to toddlers. *Journal of Speech and Hearing Research* 24:383–88.

Williams, Edwin. 1975. Small clauses in English. In *Syntax and semantics, vol. 4,* ed. J. Kimball, 249–74. New York: Academic Press.

Wilson, Deirdre. 1975. *Presupposition and non-truth conditional semantics.* London: Academic Press.

Winner, E., and H. Gardner. 1977. Sensitivity to metaphor in organic patients. *Brain* 100:719–27.

Winston, Patrick. 1981. Learning new rules from precedents and exercises. *AIM* 632, May 1981.

Wolf, Meyer. 1970. A note on the surface verb "Remind." *Linguistic Inquiry* 1:561.

Wolfram, Walt. 1978. Contrastive linguistics and social lectology. *Language Learning* 28:1–28.

Woolford, Ellen. 1981. A formal model of bilingual code-switching. Paper presented to the PILEI Symposium, Cornell University.

Zangwill, O. L. 1964. Intelligence in aphasia. In *Disorders of language*, ed. A. V. S. de Reuck and M. O'Connor. London: Churchill.

Zeps, Valdis. 1963. The meter of the so-called trochaic Latvian folksongs. *Internal Journal of Slavic Linguistics and Poetics* 7:123-28.

Zipf, George. 1935. *The psycho-biology of language.* Boston: Houghton Mifflin.

Zobl, Helmut. 1980a. The formal and developmental selectivity of L1 influence on L2 acquisition. *Language learning* 30:43–58.

———. 1980b. Developmental and transfer errors. *TESOL Quarterly* 14:469–82.

Zurif, Edgar. 1980. Language mechanisms: A neurophysiological perspective. Paper presented at the University of Washington, Seattle.

Zurif, Edgar, and Sheila Blumstein. 1978. Language and the brain. In Halle, Bresnan, and Miller (1978), 229–46.

Zurif, Edgar, and Alfonso Caramazza. 1976. Psycholinguistic structures in aphasia: Studies in syntax and semantics. In Whitaker and Whitaker (1976), 1:261–92.

Zwicky, Arnold. 1972. On casual speech. *CLS* 8:607–15.

———. 1976. Well, this rock and roll has got to stop. Junior's head is hard as a rock. *CLS* 12:676–97.

———. 1982. Classical malapropisms and the creation of a mental lexicon. In Obler and Menn (1982), 115–32.

———. 1983. Stranded *to* and phonological phrasing in English. *Linguistics* 20:3–58.

Zwicky, Arnold, and Geoffrey Pullum. 1983. Cliticization versus inflection: English *n't. Language,* vol. 59. In press.

Name Index

Subject Index

Abkhaz, 19
Acceptability, 50–53
Admissibility conditions, 81–82
American Association for Applied Linguistics, 132
American Indian languages, 151–52
Anaphora, 33–34
  first language acquisition and, 17–18
Aphasia, 24–27
Applied linguistics, 130–57
  contrasted with other applied sciences, 132–33
  generativist contributions to, 140–57
Arabic, 147
Audiolingual method, 141
Australian languages, 70
Autonomy of grammar, 2–27
  creole continua and, 82–83
  discourse-based alternatives to, 96–97, 105–11
  first language acquisition evidence for, 11–23
  grammatical evidence for, 5–11
  neurological evidence for, 23–27
  opposition to, 4–5
  psychological reality of, 45–46
  variable rules and, 78–79
Auxiliary in English, 79, 153–54

Baby talk, 22–23
Bambara, 102
Behaviorism, 4, 130, 142

Bilingual code switching, 94–95
Black English
  differences from Standard English, 87, 153–55
  variable rules and, 77–78, 80
Brain and language. *See* Neurolinguistics

Case inflection, 7–8, 87–88, 155
Casual speech, 83–86
Categories. *See* Syntactic categories
C-command and language acquisition, 17–18
Center-embedded constructions, 29–30, 124, 150
Center for Applied Linguistics, 132
Child language. *See* First language acquisition
Chinese, 17, 151
Classical Greek, 8
Clitics, 102–3
Code switching. *See* Bilingual code switching
Communication-based approaches. *See* Discourse-based grammar
Communicative competence, 37–38
Communicative function, 96, 100–101, 113, 118, 120–23
  constraints and, 104–10
  morphology and, 7–8, 114
  phonology and, 5–7, 114
  structure-dependence and, 103 (*see also* Discourse-based grammar)